NANCY TAYLOR

D1312175

NANCY TAYLOR

Roddy Llewellyn's

ELEGANCE & ECCENTRICITY

Roddy Llewellyn's
ELEGANCE & ECCENTRICITY

Edited By Robert Holt

WARD LOCK

AUTHOR'S ACKNOWLEDGEMENTS

The several mentors who helped me with the research on this book include Norman Hudson, editor/publisher of the *Historic House Directory*; Lord de Saumarez; Patrick Moore Esq; Susan Campbell; Hugh Palmer, the photographer; my editor, Denis Ingram; and my word processor which, despite the fact that it gave me several minor heart attacks, was nonetheless baptized with the book.

Finally, my very special thanks go to Robert Holt for his invaluable help and inspiration.

half title:
Hidcote Gardens — the view through the gazebo to the long walk.
title page:
Castle Howard — an 18th century palace designed by John Vanbrugh and his first major achievement.
page 7:
Rievaulx — the half-mile long, grass-covered terrace.
page 9:
Stowe — the Palladian Bridge.
page 25:
Nymans Garden – the stone dovecote

© Roderic Llewellyn, 1989

First published in Great Britain in 1989
by Ward Lock Limited, Artillery House, Artillery Row,
London SW1P 1RT, a Cassell Company.

All Rights Reserved. No part of this publication may be reproduced, stored in a retrieval system, or transmitted, in any form or by any means, electronic, mechanical, photocopying, recording, or otherwise, without the prior permission of the Copyright owners.

House editor Denis Ingram
Text set in Baskerville No. 2 by Litho Link Limited,
Welshpool, Powys, Wales.
Printed and bound in Italy.

British Library Cataloguing in Publication Data

Llewellyn, Roddy
Elegance and eccentricity : ornamental and architectural features of historic British gardens.
1. Garden features : ornaments
I. Title
717

ISBN 0-7063-6746-4

for
NATASHA

CONTENTS

5. PATTERNS FOR PLEASURE · 117

Steps · Terrace · Balustrade
Parterre/Knot garden · Potager/Herb garden · Mount
Bosket · Quincunx · Sunken garden · Exedra
Plant sculpture · Hedge · Maze/Labyrinth · Topiary
Espalier · Cordon · Fan · Pleach · Plashing
Tunnel · Trelliswork/Treillage · Pergola
Arbour · Seat · Aviary · Trompe l'oeil · Ha-ha
Bowling green/Croquet lawn · Path · Patte d'oie
Rond-point/Rondel
Amphitheatre · Allée/Avenue/Vista

PART III
GLOSSARY · 161

PREFACE

The features of a garden prove the most enduringly memorable after a leisurely visit and, with some gardens, it is these features which can prove all-absorbing. Who has not marvelled at the cascade at Chatsworth or been entranced by Stourhead's lake and buildings? Who has not stood in awe above the water parterre at Blenheim, gazing across the lake to the vista beyond and its columnar eyestopper?

But on viewing so many of these features, and reading the guidebooks, you must have found yourself questioning the origin of their names, or the very reason for their existence.

Take, for example, the National Trust's newly restored landscape garden at Claremont. The first item you see as you step through the entrance is a kiosk. As we understand the word today, it acts as a small shop yet it corresponds well with the original Persian meaning of the word. Then, on the island in the lake is a temple — or is it a summerhouse, or even a pavilion? Overlooking the lake is a grass amphitheatre, now a great rarity in British gardens. But why? High above that is a bowling green, but not a bowling green as we understand the term today. And glowering

down its length is a gigantic stone structure with the appearance of an isolated castellated keep. It is, assuredly, a folly, for it was certainly built with no defensive purpose in mind. Some references, however, call it a belvedere.

There are two ways to attempt to answer these and many other questions. The first would have been to produce a dry-as-dust alphabetically listed treatise. The second would be to lead you on a voyage of discovery in words and pictures to show how certain of the features can be used to great effect in modern gardens.

The latter course has been chosen in this book, in the hope that further visits to the wealth of great gardens with which Great Britain is bestowed may be even more enjoyable experiences. Very many of your questions will be answered. Some, for it is the very nature of man to continually modify and misuse his language, will remain, perhaps encouraging you to further research and an even greater love and understanding of one of our country's most resplendent heritages.

R.H.

PART I

HISTORICAL SURVEY

Man's interest in the cultivation of plants, or 'gardening', is almost as old as civilization itself and the influences which have effected the features of our gardens are astonishingly diverse.

EARLY CIVILIZATION

Plants were first cultivated when man progressed from a hunter/gatherer to living in settled communities, but for our purposes the most appropriate point of departure is between 3000 and 2000 B.C. when two great civilizations, the Sumerians in the river valleys of the Tigris and the Euphrates and the Egyptians in the valley of the Nile, were in the ascendant. As they were both parts of the world where the sun played a significant role, their gardens were designed, first and foremost, as shady, cool oases where water was of great significance.

The gardens of the Sumerians contained sophisticated irrigation channels — the forerunners of our canals and rills — with a central water tank or basin from which radiated four channels in the shape of a cross. This cross symbolized the four rivers of heaven which are mentioned in the second chapter of *Genesis* — 'And a river went out of Eden to water the garden, and from thence it was parted, and became into four heads.' It was this same cosmic cross, with its religious significance long predating Christian times, which dictated the formal layout of these early gardens and has had a considerable influence on garden design ever since.

Apart from adopting this Sumerian concept the Egyptians, in their continued search for shade, are recorded as building the first arbours and pavilions, both of which had vines and roses trained over them.

When the Assyrians conquered the Sumerians in about 1275 B.C. they established hunting parks where large areas of land were walled in and planted up with trees in orderly rows — the first recorded avenues. These parks were stocked with wild animals which were hunted from horseback — not so far removed from our 'drive-round' safari parks, where the sounds of shots have, thankfully, been replaced by clicks.

It would also seem that the Assyrians were the first to build terraced gardens and they are believed to have been the influence behind the most famous of all these, 'The Hanging Gardens of Babylon', one of the Seven Wonders of the Ancient World.

On conquering the Assyrians in 540 B.C., the Persians took over their hunting parks and it is to them that we can attribute fairly accurately the first garden houses, which were built as resting and eating places within the park. By further rounds of conquest the original Sumerian influence was carried by the Arabs all the way to Spain where similar cross-shaped formal pools were built from the eighth century A.D.

At an even later date the Mogul emperors carried this same influence eastwards, and their most famous creation, the Taj Mahal, was fronted by the familiar cross-shaped water feature. The Moguls will always be remembered for their imaginative use of water. The icy waters from the Himalayas were directed into various features including canals, pools and cascades. Jets played around marble pavilions and behind the cascades candles in niches lit up the water by night.

CHINA

We should direct our minds even further eastwards – to China. Although legend tells us that the 'informal' Chinese gardens developed as early as 2000 B.C., and it is possible that the first gardens in that country may have been made as early as the fourth millenium B.C., their earliest recorded gardens were during the Ch'in dynasty (221–206 B.C.).

The ancient Chinese believed that mountains, rocks, seas, rivers and the sky all possessed spirits and their gardens were designed to achieve spiritual calm. The layout of the true Chinese garden has no rigid rules but it always had two significant elements, mountain and water, symbolized by small hillocks and pools. Intricate paths meandered from one vantage point to another over water-spanning bridges, around rocks, up hills and down dales. Some of these small hills were built of eroded rocks and contained grottoes which were designed to provide cool shade in summer, although it is difficult to assess whether it was the Chinese or the Greeks who conceived of the idea first, if it did not, indeed, predate them both.

Elements of chinoiserie began to appear in British garden design during the latter half of the 17th century and extended throughout the

18th century landscape garden movement, even though totally China-influenced gardens were few, if any. The Japanese developed Chinese concepts even further.

JAPAN

It is difficult for a Westerner to understand the full significance of the layout of Japanese gardens by just looking at them, for they became far more intricate than their Chinese prototypes, being based on a mixture of traditionalism, superstition and Zen Buddhism. Carefully raked expanses of gravels which represented 'seas' became a hallmark of the Japanese style as it tended towards greater formality, but both Chinese and Japanese gardens shared the one basic theme — that they were in close harmony with nature and designed for quiet meditation.

It was as late as 1853, when the visit of Commander Perry's naval squadron to Japan opened the country to the West, before all things Japanese became fashionable, and it was during the last two decades of the 19th century

that the Japanese garden style flourished in Britain.

GREEKS AND ROMANS

We must now go back in time to ancient Greece where we find Homer describing Alcinous' garden in *The Odyssey*, but this was more practical than ornamental in concept. Although the Greeks do not appear to have been great gardeners, we owe to them the concepts of topiary, decorative statuary and the nymphaeum, the latter being a natural grotto and a sacred place where offerings were made to the nymphs.

The Romans took up all of these concepts and expanded upon them greatly. Their gardens became more and more lavish and the hills outside Rome were soon covered with grand country villas. The architects of ancient

Above: *The Hanging Gardens of Babylon — justifiably named one of the Seven Wonders of the World. The hanging gardens were held up by vast arches built upon arches so the plants seemed to be suspended in the air.*

Rome were experts in proportion and style and the gardens they built were beyond anything dreamed up by the Greeks. Ornamental pools with fountains, fine statuary and furniture, temples to the gods, and arbours smothered in roses and grapes (presumably an idea borrowed from the Egyptians), were just some of the ingredients which made up an extremely comfortable, not to say luxurious, lifestyle. Their houses also had enclosed courtyards with geometrically shaped beds of herbs and other plants, pools, canals, statues and fountains, direct descendants of the Sumerian originals. Shade and flowing water still played an important role.

THE ITALIAN RENAISSANCE

On the collapse of the Roman Empire, everything was swept away in an orgy of destruction and neglect, which we have come to know as the Dark Ages. Now, therefore, we have to make the great leap forward about 1000 years to when the Italian Renaissance rose like a glistening jewel from the dust and decay of ancient Rome during the 15th century.

Using the Roman concepts as their prototypes, astounding gardens began to spring up again on Roman hill slopes, under the aegis of powerful families such as the renowned Medicis; basic elements were flowing water, terracing, statuary and formality, the last originating with the 'knot', a development from the patterned garden patches of Italian monasteries.

TUDORS

It was during the first half of the 16th century that the British garden was born. The Tudor Age saw a society changing for the better as it emerged from the more unsettled Middle Ages. The necessity for living in fortified communities became gradually less acute and people moved from dwellings clustered around fortified castles to the countryside. At the same time Henry VIII broke from Catholicism and dissolved the monasteries, handing many of them over to his nobles who suddenly found themselves the

Right: *Hatfield House — the low box maze, set in gravel in the format of a knot maze, and the knot garden. On the left is the Old Palace seen from the south.*

owners of the walled gardens which had been used by the monks to grow food.

Many of the great houses of the time spread their gardens beyond their fortifications in the knowledge that they would be safe from marauding gangs and armies. Hampton Court, given by Cardinal Wolsey to Henry VIII, in an attempt to save himself, could be called the prototype of the British garden. These early Tudor gardens were walled and compartmentalized, each section having little or nothing in common with the next. Within this disunited patchwork the growing of fruit and vegetables for food was still of the greatest importance, even the pools being used for a convenient supply of fresh fish; but very soon Italian influences spread via Holland, bringing with them the knot, topiary, mazes and formal circular pools.

The fashion established by Henry VIII, both at Hampton Court and the now non-existent Palace of Nonsuch, near Ewell in Surrey, was followed by the eminent families of the day and during the reign of his daughter Elizabeth I. The Cecils at Hatfield House and the Boleyns at Hever Castle (where Henry courted young Anne, his future Queen) planted mazes and potagers and laid out knots, while Sir Francis Carew, at Beddington in Surrey, laid out extensive gardens planted with innumerable fruit trees and built what is believed to have been the first orangery in Britain.

Other popular garden features of the Tudor era were grass seats, often enclosed by an arbour, covered walkways by the house to protect the ladies from the sun, banqueting houses and mounts. These latter, originally built as defensive look-out posts, were designed to give views over gardens which had no natural contours (the equivalent, therefore, of the Italian terraces), and particularly so that the layout of knots could be best admired.

ANDRÉ LE NÔTRE (1613-1700)

It was in Stuart times that garden building really took off in Britain. It is said that gardens multiplied tenfold during the reign of Charles II, many influences still coming direct from Italy or via Holland. But it was to France that Britain looked most of all, and to the Palace of Versailles in particular. Versailles and its surrounding garden and park were built for Louis XIV, the 'Sun King', who ruled from 1643 to 1715 and therefore had a great deal of time in which to develop and extend his influence. The key figure for us is André le Nôtre.

Although there is no evidence that le Nôtre actually set foot upon our shores, there is no doubt that he and his pupils influenced British garden design to a very significant extent during the latter half of the 17th century and the early part of the 18th.

Le Nôtre's father had been head gardener at the Palace of the Tuileries, a post to which he himself succeeded in 1637. Yet we might not have remembered him today had it not been for Louis XIV's hatred of Paris and his desire to move the court from the Tuileries to Versailles.

His first major commission was to design the gardens of the Château of Vaux-le-Vicomte for Louis' Superintendent of Finances, Nicolas Fouquet, and these can be seen today restored to his original designs. There we are able to admire, in a relatively small space, the features for which he became famous with Versailles: the sweeping vista developed from Italian Renaissance gardens but laid out with French logic, together with the widespread use of formal water and woodland. There is even an example of that rarest of features today, a rectangular bosket backing onto the parterre to the east of the Château.

When completed in 1661, both the house and garden were considered to be the most magnificent in the whole of France. Fouquet, hopeful of succeeding Cardinal Mazarin as Prime Minister, invited Louis to a luxurious feast to show off his property to the King. As a result Louis arranged for his captain of musketeers, none other than d'Artagnan, to arrest Fouquet, who was later tried for misappropriating State funds. He never returned to Vaux and spent the rest of his life in prison.

Louis, however, recognized a good thing when he saw it and commissioned the three geniuses behind Vaux — the other two being the architect Louis le Vau and the painter Charles le Brun — to transform Louis XIII's modest hunting lodge at Versailles into the magnificent palace we see today. There, on the most staggering scale imaginable, le Nôtre developed his work at the Tuileries and Vaux

Right: *The Château of Villandry — the formal 16th century gardens reconstructed by Dr. Carvallo.*

into what many consider to be the greatest garden in the world.

It is not, like Vaux, precisely as le Nôtre conceived it. The woods have been completely replanted, the boskets are no more and the huge orangery, said to be able to house 2000 orange trees together with 1000 oleanders, pomegranates and palms, is a replacement by Mansart of le Vau's smaller original. Yet le Nôtre would still recognize with pride the great majority of it: the parterres, the Royal Avenue, the Grand Canal and the wide allées crossing at formal pools with their fountain centrepieces. Handing down his influence through his pupils, all these features were adopted for the burgeoning English gardens of the time, if never on quite such a grand scale, though sadly only to be swept away during the following century.

JOHN EVELYN (1620-1706)

This was also the age of our first major writer on gardening, John Evelyn, and our first nurserymen, among whom the most famous were George London and Henry Wise.

Although he owned two gardens of his own it is for his writings that we remember Evelyn. One of the great specialities of le Nôtre and his school was the planting of boskets and woods.

Above: *Versailles — the Salle des Antiques as designed in 1688, showing boskets to either side controlled by treillage fencing.*
Right: *Blenheim Palace — the East parterre designed by Achille Duchêne for the ninth Duke of Marlborough.*

It was surely not a complete coincidence that Evelyn published *Sylva, or a Dissertation of Forest Trees* in 1664, which remained the standard work on the subject for over a century. It would seem that his interest originally stemmed from worries about the shortage of timber for use in the construction of naval ships and he urged that trees should be planted everywhere. (Things don't change!) It was also Evelyn who promoted the yew as the best subject for topiary.

The problem for many landowners during the 17th century was a shortage of trees suitable for topiary.

GEORGE LONDON (c.1640-1714)

In what must surely have been an early example of seeing and grabbing a marketing opportunity, George London (a pupil of John Rose, the Royal gardener at St. James' Park) established with several partners a nursery just down the road at Brompton in 1681. Having learnt much of his trade in Holland he had absorbed their love for plant sculpture.

In 1687, by which time his other partners had gone their various ways, he took into partnership Henry Wise and together they were Royal gardeners to Queen Anne, their outstanding work being at Chatsworth and Blenheim, very much under the influence of le Nôtre. It is to London and Wise in particular that the astonishing growth of plant sculpture and topiary at this time is generally attributed.

JOHN VANBRUGH (1664-1726) AND CHARLES BRIDGEMAN (c.1680-1738)

At one and the same time possibly the most famous of all our architects of garden buildings, John Vanbrugh, was rising to prominence and our landscape was about to be glorified by his great temples.

While Vanbrugh was designing many of the buildings at Stowe the head gardener there was Charles Bridgeman, now a somewhat shadowy figure, possibly because so many of his works were 'improved' by later generations. His single greatest claim to fame was that he is accredited with the invention of the ha-ha, the one garden feature of which even non-gardeners would seem to be aware! It is said that he did not understand its full potential since he did not dig a ditch on its far side and equalize the

level of the land on both sides of the ha-ha; but those which Vanbrugh designed for Castle Howard and Duncombe Park, presumably having got the idea from Bridgeman, were ha-has in their entirety.

Amongst Bridgeman's credits, besides Stowe, were Blenheim, where he worked with London and Wise, Chiswick House, Hampton Court, Hyde Park, Kensington Palace, St. James' Park and Windsor Castle. The reconstructed amphitheatre at Claremont is his outstanding extant creation.

Clearly Bridgeman was not an inconsiderable figure, yet those who followed close on his heels seemed to have overshadowed him completely.

WILLIAM KENT (1685-1748)

The first of these was William Kent. Inspired by the writings of Alexander Pope and the paintings of Poussin and Claude Gelée of Lorraine, he journeyed to Italy in 1719 where he was lucky enough to meet Lord Burlington who became his patron. It is to him that the birth of the English landscape movement — in many people's eyes the only genuinely British contribution to garden design — must assuredly be credited. It was Kent who created the vast romantic landscape of Stowe with its vistas, lakes and ornamental buildings designed by both himself and Vanbrugh. Amongst his other creations, those at Rousham and Claremont, where he 'deformalized' Bridgeman's lake, still exist to give us an idea of his genius.

Yet to most people he pales into insignificance when compared with the man who took over responsibility for Stowe on his death in 1748.

LANCELOT 'CAPABILITY' BROWN (1716-1783)

This son of a Northumberland farmer would appear to have been the first Englishman on whom the title 'landscape gardener' was bestowed. Lancelot Brown joined the staff at

Left: *Blenheim Palace — the water parterre on the west front, another creation of Achille Duchêne in the early 20th century.*

Stowe in 1740 where he was responsible for the kitchen garden. Having proved himself an efficient administrator of both building and gardening schemes, he was Kent's natural successor, and the great landscaped gardens in which he was fortunate enough to develop his trade must have been an astonishing inspiration. Whilst in Lord Cobham's employ he was allowed free rein to advise his employer's friends and neighbours about their gardens and as a result he began to make a name for himself. While at Stowe, he worked on Warwick Castle and Croome Court; then, in 1751, he left and moved to London.

For the next 30 years or so the business-minded Brown, who had in the meantime earned himself the nickname of 'Capability', ruled the British landscape movement. Although he created many beautiful parks and gardens he was also directly responsible for annihilating many examples of outstanding earlier work which would have been fascinating for this and future generations to have seen if they had survived. His widespread destruction of the previously fashionable garden features such as terraces, banqueting houses, mounts, walled and knot gardens, great parterres, etc., made him a marked man in the eyes of many people and even today some people call him a vandal. But then it is our generation which has been lucky enough to inherit his canvasses showing how he intended his works should look in their prime. His list of credits is quite astonishing, one book listing no less than 102 parks and gardens which he is said to have significantly redesigned between 1751 and 1783.

The 18th century was perhaps the most exciting time in which to be a landscape gardener. You could dam rivers, or divert them, reposition hills, or do anything you wished to alter the terrain, and all with a limitless workforce. In today's overpopulated world you can't move a muscle without having to ask permission from some tiresome bureaucrat without a modicum of taste.

But on to jollier things. It was at this time that follies blossomed everywhere. Anyone who was anyone had to have a tower, sham castle or druid's henge. One man in particular, Sanderson Millar, specialized in designing 'ruined castles' for those unfortunates who did not happen to have an authentic model within or outside of their grounds.

HUMPHRY REPTON (1752-1818)

Brown was followed by the last of the great names of the landscape garden movement, Humphry Repton, who, in the self-same book which gives Brown 102 credits, merits 111 between the years 1788 and 1818, although it is said that his influence extended to about 1000 country residences in all.

Unlike Brown, who was born to a family of very modest means, Repton's father was a prosperous Collector of Taxes at Bury St. Edmunds and later Norwich. He is said to have had all the social graces when young and spent much of his early married life studying the 'gentlemanly sciences' of nature, gardening and botany. Settling down near Romford with his large and growing family, he financed a business which failed, losing most of his money. Then one night he awoke and decided that he was perfectly suited to be 'Capability' Brown's successor!

With the ultimate in confidence, the very next morning he wrote to all his influential contacts informing them that he had set up in business as a landscape gardener. He was a man of charm and intelligence, widely read, with a knowledge of mathematics and the theory of design as well as gardening-related subjects. Brown's son, an M.P., allowed him access to his father's papers.

As if it was his destiny Repton was immediately successful, initially following close in Brown's footsteps yet quickly verging away from them to a significant extent. Where Brown had been concerned with the construction of a landscape to be viewed from the house, Repton saw the garden and house as one, reintroducing the terrace to enrich the foreground and give the house a base on which to stand. He is famous for his 'before and after' drawings known as *Red Books* which gave precise details of his recommendations for each garden which he planned; and later in his life he tended towards smaller, 'picturesque' garden buildings, such as cottages, rather than the majestic ones favoured by Brown.

It is said that when Repton died in 1818 the British landscape gardening movement died with him and some cynics equate the Battle of Waterloo with the end of everything that was good in British gardening. There was, certainly, a brief hiatus until Queen Victoria came to the throne.

JOHN CLAUDIUS LOUDON (1783-1843)

Yet one man, John Claudius Loudon fills that gap admirably, together with his wife Jane, who was his principal collaborator (and the first woman to enter our story significantly if we exclude Sarah, Duchess of Marlborough, whose sole claim to gardening fame was the ordering of the destruction of much of Wise's beautiful creation at Blenheim). Loudon was the founder of *The Gardener's Magazine*, and was a prolific writer on many subjects; his *Encyclopaedia of Gardening* appeared in 1822; and his eight-volume *Arboretum et Fruticatum Brittanicum* was published in 1838, this latter covering all the known trees and shrubs of Britain, together with their uses, in astonishing detail. In 1829 it was said of him that, 'Whoever wishes for a complete view of English gardening as at present practised will find no works better calculated for his satisfaction than those of Mr. Loudon'.

Yet, rather than being an original thinker, Loudon was a socially conscious cataloguer of facts. His publications appeared in the right place at the right time, listed everything achieved in garden design almost indiscriminately, and were a fund of ideas on which to be drawn.

VICTORIAN GARDENS

The Industrial Revolution of the early 19th century saw dramatic social changes with the

Above: *Blickling Hall – the Victorian formal garden with its grand-piano shaped yew hedges.*

emergence of the middle class. Landscape gardens no longer remained the prerogative of the *vieux riche*, for now all the houses which sprang up on the outskirts of the major cities had sizeable gardens and the burgeoning industrialists vied with the nobility in terms of expendable wealth. Unfortunately, taste and new wealth do not necessarily go hand in hand. The lack of the former, intermingled with a degree of *folie de grandeur*, resulted in the juxtaposition of styles from different periods, often out of character with the architecture of the houses. At the same time Victorian gardens reverted to formality, which appealed to the neat and orderly minds of the time. They were often planted with 'controllable' conifers, and their lawns were dotted with fussy beds crammed with brightly coloured flowers. Given the appellations 'parterres' and 'Italian gardens', they were usually neither in the traditional, nor beautiful, sense of the words.

Yet it would be unreasonable to write off everything Victorian out of hand. It was also the age of the great plant collectors who were ranging throughout the world to find and introduce new, and ever more exotic, specimens. Rhododendrons poured into the country and beautiful wild gardens, such as those at Leonardslee and Wakehurst Place, were planted with them, usually sited in sheltered valleys through which streams flowed.

The more tender plants, however, required much more protection if they were to grow and flourish and, to house these, conservatories mushroomed prestigiously everywhere, their inspiration being Sir Joseph Paxton's two great creations at Chatsworth and the Crystal Palace. Habitats were stripped of rare orchids or exotic succulents to fill them, and ferneries and camellia houses also became 'the rage'. On a much smaller scale, such oddities as moss and root houses found favour.

Collectors did not always want only plants however. When gardening design ideas were not handed on from one country to another through conquest, actual artifacts such as statues and fountains were frequently looted from their countries of origin. This was certainly true during the 18th and 19th centuries, and even as late as the turn of this

Right: *Hever Castle — A small selection of William Waldorf Astor's vast collection of 'extra luggage' from Italy.*

century. Most of the great gardens in Britain contain such contraband.

One of the last men to stuff his enormously capacious spongebag with beautiful and ancient objects was William Waldorf Astor, later the first Viscount Astor. They were especially used to ornament the gardens at Hever Castle in Kent which he had bought in 1903, and later largely rebuilt. He had previously been American Minister (now called Ambassador) to Rome between 1882 and 1885, giving him plenty of time in which to collect together his various bits and pieces — and it is quite some collection! The Italian garden at Hever is stuffed to the gills with sarcophagi, broken columns, urns from Pompeii, busts, plinths, vases, cisterns, fonts, amphorae and jars, no doubt leaving many a noble Italian turning in his grave with envy.

Other garden ornaments have found their final resting place in a very roundabout fashion. The 4.5m (15ft) high Waterloo Vase which today sits in the gardens of Buckingham Palace started off its chequered career in Milan on the orders of Napoleon. It then came to England unfinished and was decorated for George IV and later given to the National Gallery by William IV. Because of its great and unwieldy size it proved difficult to keep on permanent display, so it was offered back to the Royal Family, in the person of Edward VII, in 1906.

Towards the end of the Victorian era the formal rose garden with its elegant pergolas came into vogue and a new movement arose which was to transform British garden style yet again. In 1883 William Robinson, the arch-advocate of the 'wild' garden, published *The English Flower Garden,* following on from the weekly journal *The Garden* which he edited. One of the contributors to the latter was Gertrude Jekyll (pronounced 'Jeekull').

GERTRUDE JEKYLL (1843-1932)

Surely the epitome of the highly educated, if somewhat formidable, Victorian gentlewoman, Gertrude Jekyll was proficient in several languages, music and drawing and initially worked hard to become a painter. She had the good fortune to meet Ruskin and William Morris early in her life, and turned her attention to the Arts and Crafts Movement, designing such things as embroidery, jewellery and silver plate, but her short sightedness made it increasingly difficult for her to work so delicately and she turned her explosive energies to gardening. In the 1880s she bought herself a 15-acre plot of land at Munstead Wood in Surrey and set about designing herself a garden which breathed life and informality at a time when all things formal were still the fashion.

This remarkable woman is said to have, almost single-handedly, been responsible for the invention of the herbaceous border and, once they had seen the beauty of her creation, she was given commissions by many of her friends to design gardens for them. In 1889, when he was 20 and she 46, Gertrude Jekyll met the up and coming architect Edwin Lutyens, and for the next 25 years or more they designed houses and gardens together in professional symbiosis, her greatest gifts to him being her sureness of taste and understanding of what his clients, amongst whom she moved socially, would want. Her ghost lives on in a great many 20th century gardens.

As an aside, you may have noticed that I have so far used the terms 'gardener', 'architect' and 'landscape gardener', but never 'landscape architect'. The first Englishman to call himself the latter was the Lancastrian Thomas Mawson, who was the first President of the Institute of Landscape Architects. It was said of him that he would have put Henry Wise in charge of Hampton Court rather than Sir Christopher Wren! In 1908 he 'won' a great debate over Lutyens at the Architectural Association about which of their professions should have overall responsibility. He won because he was by far the more accomplished speaker.

PRESENT AND FUTURE

For those who believe that 20th-century Britain is a desert of garden design, and remarkably there are some, I need only point you to Lawrence Johnston's Hidcote or Vita Sackville-West's Sissinghurst. And as we approach the next century post-Jekyll names such as Page, Peto, Russell-Smith, Hobhouse, Verey, Coates, Challis, Chatto, Lloyd and Jellicoe, to mention but a few, have all had much to contribute. If I were to select one of these alone it must be Sir Geoffrey Jellicoe, for the extraordinary diversity of features he includes within his garden designs, while blending them into an organic whole, and the manner in which he draws inspiration from so many parts of the world and other art forms, thus continuing a tradition which is as old as British gardening itself.

Yet at the same time this is an age of conservation and reconstruction, with such remarkable achievements as the recent work to restore Claremont to its former glory and the beauty of the parterre at Oxburgh Hall, and there is great cause for optimism.

Ideas for style and ornamentation are no longer carried from one country to another by conquest but by the gentler means of exhibition and word of mouth. May this peace last, that peace of mind to be found in a garden away from the ever increasing pressures of this materialistic world.

PART II

GARDEN FEATURES

ELEGANCE AND ECCENTRICITY

ENTRANCE GATE/GATEHOUSE
SUMMER HOUSE/SHADED HOUSE
TEMPLE
PAVILION
BANQUETING HOUSE
TEA HOUSE
PAGODA
GAZEBO/BELVEDERE
KIOSK
LOGGIA
MAUSOLEUM
FOLLY/CONCEIT
DOVECOTE/COLUMBARIUM/
PIGEON HOUSE
ICE HOUSE
HERMITAGE
TREE HOUSE · ROOT HOUSE · MOSS HOUSE
GROTTO
ORANGERY
STOVE HOUSE
CONSERVATORY
FERNERY

Left: *Lanhydrock — the castellated 17th century gatehouse viewed across the formal garden. Note the obelisk finials atop the balustrade.*

The variety of garden buildings is astonishing. Ranging, as they do, from the simplest of summer houses, which can be only one step removed from a shaded seat, to the vast Temple of the Four Winds and the Mausoleum at Castle Howard, there must be at least one to suit every taste.

It will become obvious, as you read the various sections of this chapter, that many are known by more than one title, and a great number could be considered as follies and thus be lumped together in a rather untidy and unhelpful *mêlée*.

Some garden buildings were built for a specific reason which went out of fashion. Banqueting houses, for example, were all the rage in Tudor and Stuart times but very few have been built since then. Where they have survived, they have often become known under another name. Those at Montacute, for instance, are now usually referred to as pavilions or gazeboes. On the other hand, a so-called 'banqueting house' at Rievaulx is actually nothing of the kind, but rather a temple in which it has become the practice to hold banquets.

Probably the most difficult to define are . summer house, pavilion, gazebo, and kiosk. Many buildings seem to have originated as simple summer houses, but as time has passed they have been endowed with more illustrious titles.

ENTRANCE GATE/ GATEHOUSE

It was during the Tudor and Jacobean eras that Britain saw the appearance of gateways. Early examples consisted of simple, square piers built in either stone or brick and often surmounted by a stone finial. The gates of that early period were of wood, strapped and bolted with iron.

Several imposing gatehouses of the Tudor period can still be admired today. One built in 1550-51 at Charlecote has a central two-storey structure topped by a pierced balustrade and supported by twin octagonal three-storey towers. The large room, with its bow-fronted window over the arch of the gate, is said to have been used as a dormitory for the household

servants. A smaller one at Hardwick Hall only housed a porter's lodge. The lion gates at Hampton Court are as grand as you'll get, but the pillars and lions are so massive that unfortunately they dwarf the magnificent iron gates between them.

A particularly impressive example of a Tudor fortified gatehouse can be seen at St. Osyth's Priory, near Clacton, Essex. With its elaborate flint decoration, it makes an imposing entrance to the Priory gardens. Dated somewhat later are the twin lozenge-shaped lodges with pyramid roofs which support the gate leading into the walled forecourt at Cranborne Manor, Dorset. These were designed by William Arnold, who it is thought also designed Montacute House.

By the middle of the 17th century gatehouses were tending towards the very ornate, an example being at Lanhydrock where the castellated two-storey gatehouse has surmounting finials matching those on the walls.

Above: Syon House — Robert Adam's gate screen surmounted by the Percy lion as depicted in 1884.

A less imposing, but equally fascinating, example from the late 17th century is the Fish Gate at Kinross, with its light wrought-iron clair-voyée gate. It is known as the Fish Gate because of the carved stone basket set directly above the gate, containing examples of the seven varieties of fish to be found in Loch Leven.

John Vanbrugh designed many of our most imposing gates. Among his creations is the massive East Gate at Blenheim which gives the impression of being a triumphal arch. It is decorated with stone urns by Grinling Gibbons and statues, also thought to be from his workshop, plus lions' heads, wreaths and laurels added by William Chambers. Its size is dictated by the presence above the gateway of the giant cistern on which a large part of the palace once depended for its water supply. The gates themselves, made by Bramah, and which bear the Marlborough Arms, weigh no less than 17 tons. They were shown at the Great Exhibition of 1851.

At Castle Howard he built the extraordinary Pyramid Gate in the centre of a castellated wall with a gigantic pyramid sitting directly over the gates. Also at Castle Howard is Hawksmoor's fanciful Carrmire Gate, a rubble-built arch decorated with pyramids, towers and turrets.

Grand gateways are seldom built today, and we seem to have reverted to the simple Tudor and Jacobean style of the simple stone pier. But what could be nicer?

⌇⌇⌇

SUMMER HOUSE/ SHADED HOUSE

This is one of those occasions when the problem of confused and higgledy-piggledy nomenclature arises. We know that many words have changed in time from their original meaning (for example the origin of the word 'pergola' was actually *pergula*, the Latin for a shed), but coupled with that architects and gardeners have in the past borrowed styles and fashions from other eras and cultures and juggled them around to suit their own fancy. A summer house has taken on a number of styles which stretch the dictionary definition of it as 'a structure in the garden for sitting in'.

We can all of us give birth to our own conceit

(p. 51) and build ourselves a summer house, perhaps with the attractive and ornate designs of gazeboes (p. 39) and belvederes (p. 40) in mind. Personally I don't like most of the mass-produced, 'off-the-peg' structures you see at garden centres. To me a summer house conjures up a roofed building, informal and private, possibly with the electricity laid on but definitely not the telephone. It is a place to sit in for reading or writing over a cup of tea. It must be comfortable with cane chairs and faded cushions. A musty smell with the occasional cobweb and dead butterfly on the floor, a brick fireplace full of charred wood, cracked panes, rusty locks and peeling paint are all part and parcel of a summer house for me.

It is thought that the words 'summer house' evolved from a 'shaded house' which was at one time positioned at the end of the 'long walk' as somewhere cool and refreshing to sit in on a hot day. Before the 18th century they were usually built in the style of the main house, but

Above: *Bodnant — the Pin Mill at the end of the canal, as positioned by the second Lord Aberconway in 1938.*

during the mid-18th century — an era for romanticism — they were built in a variety of Quixotic styles. Their interiors were often elaborately decorated with shell mosaics.

The fashion for summer houses again changed during the Victorian era when they were more often than not built in a rustic style.

Perhaps the best known summer house in Britain is the Pin Mill at Bodnant. Built in 1740 at Woodchester in Gloucestershire, it was bought by the second Lord Aberconway and moved to its present site at the end of the canal in 1938. It gets its name from the fact that at one time it was used for pin manufacture.

Other charming, if far more simple, examples of summer houses can be seen at Ascott, Buckinghamshire, (this one being approached by a gravel walk with herbaceous borders fronting a wall to one side, a hedge to the other), and at Clevedon Court, Somerset, where no fewer than three are positioned around the gardens.

An unusual little shaded house is the 'Bear's Hut' at Killerton, Devon, close by the Ice House, which gets its name from a famous pet of the Acland family.

In contrast to the above the average modern summer house is sadly lacking in charm. It is about time we saw some designers come up with something more exciting than wooden boxes with slanting roofs . . .

Above: *Killerton — view across the parkland to the Bear's Hut. A thatched, shaded summerhouse, its name stems from a famous family pet of the Acland family.*

ↃↄↄↄↄↃ

TEMPLE

Temples were originally built as places of worship. During the 18th and 19th centuries in Britain they were adopted in the parks and gardens of most of the great houses with no practical purpose in mind other than to enhance the landscape. They might therefore be called follies. Many still exist, and what extravagant and splendid edifices they are. At Studley Royal in Yorkshire the Temple of Piety was erected at the edge of a lake, mirrored in the water. The Temple of Apollo at Stourhead in Wiltshire created a romantic focal point, set high on a hill above the lake. You can catch glimpses of it from different angles as you skirt the edge of the water. They were always positioned very carefully in this way, and sometimes used to terminate a vista.

Temples varied enormously in design from Japanese to Roman Doric, from neo-Grecian to Gothic. A classic design commonly used was the 'rotunda', a good example being at Kew. Temples were very much the cup of tea for all the great landscape architects such as Kent, Brown, Vanbrugh and Repton.

Stowe is a temple among temples. Coincidentally, the family who was responsible for creating the garden was called Temple, their motto being *Templa quam delecta* ('How delightful are the temples'). The park was enclosed by Sir Peter Temple, the grandson of John Temple who first bought the property during the 1590s. In 1697, Sir Peter's grandson, Richard, later to become Lord Cobham, succeeded to the property and it was he who, over the next 50 years, laid out the park and organized the building of its many temples. The original garden design was the responsibility of Charles Bridgeman, the temple designs being the work of Kent, Vanbrugh and Gibbs. At Stowe today, you can see the Temple of Venus, the Temple of Ancient Virtue, the Temple of Concord and Victory (copied from the Maison Carrée at Nîmes), the ruined Temple of Modern Virtues, the Queen's Temple and the so-called Temple of British Worthies.

Most spectacular of all, however, is surely the Temple of the Four Winds at Castle Howard. This great Palladian-style building was the last work of Vanbrugh, who competed with Nicholas Hawksmoor, the designer of the

Top: *Castle Howard — Vanbrugh's Temple of the Four Winds with the cupola of Hawksmoor's mausoleum beyond the trees.*
Above: *Shugborough — The Temple of the Winds as depicted c.1770.*
Left: *Stourhead — The Temple of Apollo, designed by Flitcroft in 1765, mirrored in the waters of the lake.*

Mausoleum, for the contract to design it. Its interior is decorated by Hawksmoor's interpretation of Vanbrugh's designs.

In *The Art of Landscape Gardening*, Humphry Repton tells how he remodelled a temple: 'Both the form and the colour of a small house in Langley Park rendered it an object unworthy of its situation; yet, from peculiar circumstances, it was not deemed advisable either to remove it or to hide it by plantations. I therefore recommended a Doric portico to cover the front; and thus a building formerly unsightly, because out of character with the park, became its brightest ornament, doing honour to the taste and feelings of the noble proprietor, who preserved the house for having been a favourite retreat of his mother, and which, thus ornamented, may be considered as a temple sacred to filial piety'.

PAVILION

When we use the word 'pavilion' most of us immediately think of a sort of hut used by cricketers, the most internationally famous one being at Lord's. It is a difficult word to define as it seems to have changed its meaning over the years. A dictionary definition of pavilion is: 'A tent, especially a large or luxurious one; an ornamental or showy building for pleasure purposes; a tent-like covering; a projecting section of a building with a tent-like roof and much decorated; an ornamental building often turreted or domed'.

The word 'tent' crops up so often, it seems safe to assume that a pavilion was originally a tent-like structure. At school we read about Cleopatra's pavilion of 'Cloth of Gold Tissue' and of the magnificent pavilions put up on the occasion of Henry VIII's 'Field of the Cloth of Gold'. This is the sort of structure I have always set in my own mind's eye, with wimpled ladies and heavily armoured gents in the same picture.

Pavilions are known to have been used in England since the 14th century and it is thought that they originated in Spain. In many

Right: *Wrest Park — the Palladian pavilion by Batty Langley at the south end of the lake, known as the Archer pavilion.*

Mahal built by Shah Jahan in the 17th century for his favourite wife, Mumtaz Mahal, has four large pavilions positioned on its roof.

All these 'pavilions' vary so much in style and shape, and are built in so many different materials, that it is no longer possible to be precise as to what exactly a pavilion should be. After all, the famous Brighton Pavilion gives us yet another dimension.

If I were asked to design a pavilion I would revert to the original concept of a tent-like structure, possibly of Moorish influence and painted canvas with the occasional embellishment of a golden pineapple here and a plume of feathers there. Anyway certainly a temporary building more suited to warmer climates than Britain, wimples optional.

❧

BANQUETING HOUSE

The word 'banquet' derives from the French word *banc*, meaning bench, suggesting that it was a building where presumably one sat down to eat. Was it so very rare in those days to sit down to enjoy one's food? If that was the case, it must have caused havoc with the digestion. Anyway, banqueting houses were first built in Tudor times and were used for the consumption of sweets and confectionery — a rare delicacy in those days. Thus light refreshment was often accompanied by music and other entertainment, and how civilized it all sounds — Mars bars and Madonna!

At first they were built as temporary structures, just as marquees are erected for special occasions today. But towards the end of the reign of Henry VIII, they started to be erected as permanent structures. The King himself had one at Nonsuch in Surrey, and chose an elaborate octagonal wooden design.

It appears that banqueting houses lost fashion during the reign of Charles I, and sadly since that time have remained obsolete. Many were destroyed during the great 'natural landscape age' of the 18th century and were replaced by more strategically positioned temples and other more magnificent eye-catching features which dotted the landscape.

old Spanish gardens a central pavilion or 'glorietta' was a common feature, its purpose being to provide shade and a place from which to view the rest of the garden. There exists a good example at Tafalla in Navarre. But there appear to be many different types of pavilion.

The tea house in the Japanese garden at Tully, County Kildare in Eire, laid out by the Japanese gardener Eida in 1906, is described as a pavilion. Then there are the twin Boycott pavilions at Stowe in Buckinghamshire which were designed by James Gibbs around 1728 and later altered by Giovanni Battista Borra before 1763. These originally had pyramidal roofs, before Borra replaced them with domed ones, topped by belvederes. There are also Italianate pavilions at Mereworth Castle in Kent and a bathing pavilion at Kelvedon Hall, Essex. There are even small pavilions in the small garden in the Forbidden City in Peking. The most famous building in the world, the Taj

Above: Stowe — the Oxford Bridge with one of the twin Boycott pavilions, originally designed by James Gibbs in about 1728. Note the belvedere which, with the domed roof, was the later work of Borra before 1763.

Fronting onto the Thames at Hampton Court, set in an angle of the walls of the Sunken Garden, is one of the few surviving banqueting houses, an imposing rectangular

structure with tall chimneys. Also, at the corners of the walled garden at Montacute, are what we now generally refer to as the twin pavilions, presumably because of their curved roofs, but these are believed to have been built originally as banqueting houses, again of the Tudor period.

❧

TEA HOUSE

An interesting point about the concept of this feature is that it would appear to have originated in Japan and been taken up by the Chinese, most ideas having flowed in the opposite direction.

The tea house, as a garden feature, originated in Japan where tea-drinking gatherings have for a very long time been popular entertainments among the upper classes. Contests used to be held to see who was able to identify the greatest numbers of different kinds of tea. It was during the 16th century that the famous tea-master Sen-no-Rikyu developed the prototype for tea house design.

The tea garden usually included a sparsely decorated, adjoining 'waiting shed' where the guests sat until invited into the tea house itself. Once inside they washed in a basin before the ceremony took place.

At Heale House in Wiltshire there is a recently renovated tea house which contains eight sitting mats, otherwise known as an 'eight Tatami', and has been positioned over a small stream. In all respects it is a classical structure, made entirely of wood and with sliding rice-paper shutters which, when opened, reveal a delightful view of a 'Nikko' bridge spanning the stream framed by a mature *Magnolia soulangiana*. It is indeed a serene spot; and this tea house is so meticulously built that there are no visible signs of conventional fixings. All woodwork is left unpainted to show the grain.

I was once invited to a Japanese Tea Ceremony in the West Indies of all places, as the guest of an American lady. Unfortunately,

Above: *Hampton Court Palace — the sunken pool garden with the William III banqueting house overlooking the River Thames in the background. This garden was originally laid out as a knot garden.*

I've never been any good at sitting cross-legged on the floor, and the tea tasted rather nasty which did nothing to comfort my poor cramped limbs. I strongly suggest to those of you wishing to take part in some future tea ceremony to take with you a camping stool (or cushion) and a tea bag of your own choice.

Although tea houses do, generally, have Oriental connotations, it is not essential that this be so. As a westernized interpretation of a Japanese tea house, we can refer to one of the pair of gazeboes at Hidcote. As you approach them from the house the one on the left is, unarguably, a gazebo, for it commands a pleasant view down one of the garden's many walks. However, the one on the right is laid out as a kitchen, presumably for the preparation of tea for those using the gazebo opposite.

Above: *Heale House — the Japanese tea house made entirely of wood with sliding rice-paper shutters.*
Right: *Cliveden – the small pagoda summer house in the Japanese-style water garden.*
Far right: *Alton Towers — the replica of a To Ho Pagoda of Canton built for the 15th Earl of Shrewsbury.*

PAGODA

The word 'pagoda' comes from the Portuguese *pagode*. Originally, pagodas were sacred Indian towers. The Chinese admired them and used their design as ornamental buildings for housing relics of Buddha, and only later on was it the turn of the Japanese to begin building them.

In Britain our most famous pagoda is at Kew — indeed it is one of the hallmarks of the place. It was built by Sir William Chambers in 1761–62. It is octagonal in design, 50m (163 ft) high and ten storeys high. It is typical in design with its tapering multi-storeyed shape and projecting roofs and it was the first major copy of an authentic Chinese building to be built in Britain.

Unfortunately we boast very few pagodas on our shores, but there exist a few more, including the one at Alton Towers designed as a fountain, and yet another feature *extraordinaire* in the gardens laid out by the 15th Earl of Shrewsbury between 1815 and 1827. This pagoda has only three storeys although, according to J. C. Loudon, it was originally designed to have six. Indeed, once this has been pointed out, it does look a little foreshortened. It is built in the centre of a pool into which spills the 21 m (70 ft) high jet of water which gushes from the top. Bells hang from each of the up-curving angles of the octagonal roofs.

In the Japanese gardens at Compton Acres, high above a pond, stands a small granite pagoda. Its scale and position have been carefully thought out as, looking at it from far away, it appears to be the genuine article.

GAZEBO/BELVEDERE

GAZEBO

A gazebo was rarely built for any specific purpose other than to act as an ornamental building; and with very little practical use, except that it was a comfortable place from which to admire a view. You might therefore call a gazebo a folly (like so many other features mentioned in this book).

The origin of the word 'gazebo' is not known for certain and is thought to be a derivation of 'gaze about'. This being the case, as my trusty dictionary also suggests, the word 'gazebo' is synonymous with 'belvedere', which comes from the Italian 'bel' meaning beautiful, and 'vedere', to see.

If indeed it is the case that these two words evolved separately in two different European countries, both describing exactly the same thing, then it is probable that the gazebo is a descendant of the Tudor mount (see p. 126) This is confirmed by the fact that the word is strictly defined as a small structure that overlooks the walls of an enclosed garden. The walls of Packwood House host no less than four such gazeboes, the most outstanding being that built during the reign of Charles II at the north-east angle of the Carolean garden; with its elegant pointed roof, it commands prospects to the south and west. The Tudor octagonal 'garden house' at Melford Hall, Suffolk, although ante-dating the word 'gazebo' (the word appearing in the English language about 1675) is another outstanding example.

A gazebo can be built in any style, formal or informal, but you will have to find another name for it if it does not command a view. I only mention this as I have often visited 'gazeboes' which do not afford even a vestige of a vista. I know it is tempting to have ideas above one's station, but in such cases we should all probably stick to the description 'summer house'.

Left: *Hidcote — one of the gazeboes seen from its twin. Through it can be seen the allée which pierces the heart of the garden. In 1905, when Lawrence Johnston began his work at Hidcote, he drew upon the concept of a series of 'rooms', each one of which was to be simply crammed full of horticultural delights.*

BELVEDERE

The Italian Renaissance era must have been an extraordinarily exciting one, when Rome once more rose in glory from the ruins of mediaeval dereliction. In 1503 Pope Julius commissioned the architect Donato Bramante to re-landscape the Villa Belvedere in Rome to house his collection of classical statuary. Linked to the Pontifical Palace, it was renamed Cortile del Belvedere once it was completed. This is surely the prince among belvederes.

In Britain an outstanding example of this concept of a belvedere is to be seen at Claremont. It was the first building created in the grounds for the Duke of Newcastle after he bought the property in 1711. Designed by Vanbrugh, it stands atop the Mount from which the '-mont' in Claremont is derived. With its angular turrets rising above a two-storey central block and stepped castellations, it is a robust and dramatic creation. It was, apparently, originally equipped with a table for hazard (a gambling game with dice) and a butler's closet.

Finally, with the exception of the one at Claremont, a belvedere is normally thought of as a viewpoint built on a house, whereas a gazebo is a separate structure sometimes attached to a garden wall, but anyway positioned away from the house itself. Few gazeboes or belvederes are built these days, as unspoilt views are becoming increasingly rare in the over-populated world we live in and sites with such panoramas command enormous prices.

I think if I were to design a gazebo as a garden feature I would probably copy the architects of yesteryear and adopt an octagonal gothic shape, with ogival windows, and surround it by rustic poles supporting the roof. If I were to design a new house for myself I would design a turret above roof level so long as there was beautiful countryside beyond, and call it the 'belvedere' at the risk of sounding a little pretentious, perhaps.

✳

KIOSK

The word 'kiosk' comes from the Turkish kiūsk meaning 'pavilion', in turn derived from the Persian kūskh meaning 'palace'.

The fashion for kiosks as a landscape feature developed during the 18th century when they were built as places of shelter. (Tours of some of the larger gardens took many hours.) The unpredictable British weather was, I suppose, responsible for their coming into being.

Kiosks were normally built in a near eastern style but also in rustic and Gothic as well. To all intents and purposes they could be described as small pavilions (see p. 32).

A relatively recent addition to the Indian-inspired garden at Sezincote, designed by Cyril Kleinwort, is an elegant little kiosk which stands near the tennis court. With its hexagonal shape, a pillared portico filling two-thirds of the hexagon, the other one-third being a tiny summer house, it is an ideal example of the genre. Another is the first structure you meet after passing through the entrance into Claremont Landscape Garden. Presumably originally designed as a resting point set halfway around the tour of the garden, it is now used for dispensing refreshments to the weary — thus becoming a 'kiosk' in one of the modern senses of the word.

The old red cast-iron telephone kiosks, which many of us remember with affection, were removed during the mid-'80s only to be replaced by horrid little open shelters of little character in comparison. The old-style kiosks have become collectable, especially in America where they now adorn many a pool-side. Perhaps British Telecom has unwittingly given birth to a kiosk renaissance?

Above: *A typical eastern-influenced kiosk.*
Right: *Claremont Landscape Garden — the belvedere built by Vanbrugh for the Duke of Newcastle in 1715. This view shows the belvedere, as seen looking up the bowling green.*

LOGGIA

In its original Italian usage, a loggia is an open-sided room attached to a house which 'laid it open to the north and was contrived for the gathering of cool air'. It could be said, therefore, that a loggia is not necessarily an essential addition to an English house. However, it has also come to be used to describe a gallery or arcade with one or more sides open to the air which is set apart from, not attached to, the house and is used either as a viewpoint or focal point.

It is the latter which is more often seen as a distinctive feature of gardens today, with the one at Schönbrunn Palace, Vienna, being probably the most impressive of all. Called the 'Gloriette', it is a gigantic structure of 11 arches which stands on the hilltop facing the Palace, almost as if set in confrontation. It was built in 1775 in celebration of the Austrian victory over Frederick the Great of Prussia at the battle of Kolin in 1757, during the Seven Years War. It would appear that after 18 years the Austrians had carefully forgotten that Frederick went on to defeat them twice that year and that the war had finally established Prussia as a great military power! One wonders if the writer of one guide-book, who states that the 'Gloriette' now 'serves no practical purpose whatsoever' was being intentionally sardonic.

To turn to less grandiose concepts, most loggias in British gardens retain a considerable Italianate influence. At Hever Castle there is one designed by Frank Pearson for William Waldorf Astor in the early 20th century, from which one can absorb the tranquillity of the lake. At Wilton House a pleasant three-arched loggia, designed by William Chambers (he of the Pagoda at Kew), is built on a raised dais and looks down across the early 19th century formal Italian-style garden.

Loggias of both kinds are still built today (and very probably often called by different names) though mainly in warm climates as somewhere cool to sit. Although we used to have one in Wales which my father built, it was seldom if ever used for somewhere to sit but it did become a very handy place for storing garden furniture at night or during wet spells. It is important that a loggia is built in sympathy with the architecture of the house. A modern house would get away with brick pillars and tiled roof both matching those of the house. Older children love to sleep out in a loggia *à l'air frais* during the summer; they can always come indoors if it proves too damp and chilly.

MAUSOLEUM

The word 'mausoleum' is derived from the name of Mausolus, King of Caria. His tomb at Helicarnassus, erected in the fourth century B.C. by his Queen, Artemisia, is one of the Seven Wonders of the Ancient World.

Whether or not we would consider them to be suitable decorative features for gardens, there was a fashion for structures of some grandiloquence in the 18th century, and the one at Castle Howard is the outstanding example. Designed by Hawksmoor in 1728–9, for the Third Earl of Carlisle, it took from 1731 to 1742 to build and Hawksmoor died before it was completed. Without doubt, it is an impressive Grecian-style edifice in a remarkable setting — Laurence Whistler described it as 'the noblest invention of them all'.

It also suits well the lowering skies under which it can so often be seen, but whether it is a thing of beauty is surely a matter of opinion. It is believed that the combination of Vanbrugh's lake and bridge, together with his Temple of the Four Winds and the round Mausoleum, was inspired by the romantic landscape paintings of Claude Lorraine.

Bonomi's pyramidal mausoleum at Blickling Hall, Norfolk, which was designed as the burial place for the Earls of Buckingham, is a fascinating example of architecture that is out of the ordinary.

Above right: *Hever Castle – one of Frank Pearson's original drawings for the loggia which he designed for William Waldorf Astor in 1908.*
Right: *Blickling Hall — the Pyramid Mausoleum designed by Joseph Bonomi in 1796-7 as a burial place for the Earls of Buckingham.*
Overleaf: *Castle Howard — the Mausoleum designed by Nicholas Hawksmoor in 1728-9 for the Third Earl of Carlisle. It took twelve years to build and Hawksmoor died before it was completed.*

∾

FOLLY/CONCEIT

FOLLY

A dictionary definition of 'folly', is 'a popular name for any costly structure considered to have shown folly in the builder'. Barbara Jones's standard work on the subject, *Follies and Grottoes*, includes under follies many of the buildings I have chosen to cover under separate sections, such as pagodas, belvederes, hermitages, moss and root houses, even the Pyramid and Carrmire Gates at Castle Howard.

Follies, as you might guess, come in all sorts of shapes and sizes including columns, towers, pyramids, chapels, arches, false facades, etc. They have often been built to look semi-dilapidated, to give them 'instant age', and were thus, as Barbara Jones describes, 'set into the landscape to give the visitor an interesting objective, or a restful pause or a thrill of alarm'.

They were carefully positioned on the top of a far hill, for example, as the site for an occasional picnic. Indeed this pastime didn't always prove popular, as we can deduce from a letter written on 3rd September, 1750, 'Mrs Lyttleton will like to dine at the house better than at the Castle, and my stomach prefers hott (*sic*) meat to cold, though not my taste; so, if you please, we will dine at the foot of the hill . . .'

Landscape architects such as Vanbrugh, Hawksmoor and Kent were among the most ardent of early folly builders, often being inspired by romantic poetry and paintings, just as they were in other aspects of their designs. William Kent, in particular, was greatly influenced by his visit to Italy, and his romantic landscape at Stowe clearly reflects this.

Most follies in Britain were built during the 18th and early 19th centuries. This was a time of feverish rebuilding, when a great many Jacobean and Elizabethan facades were being torn down in favour of the new Palladian and Baroque styles. Vast fortunes were spent on altering houses and their contents but money was a good deal thinner on the ground when it came to landscaping the gardens and park. As a result, follies were built using only the cheapest materials available and that, combined with using an unskilled labour force, meant that many of these structures have since collapsed.

Because so many follies were built some

Left: *Chelsea Flower Show 1987. A modern interpretation of a very cleverly constructed 'instant' folly.*
Above: *Goldney Hall — representative of the very many folly towers built in the 18th and 19th centuries. This one was built in the grounds now owned by Bristol University by Thomas Goldney, a Bristol merchant, at the same time as his famous grotto.*

distance from the house itself, they were not easily protected from vandals. The more precious temples, therefore, were built closer to the house where vigilant estate workers could keep an eye on them.

Many, also, became dilapidated without the help of human hand, as in many cases their novelty appeal soon started to wane, and they have since become overgrown, unseen and forgotten.

Let's take a look at some follies which can be seen today or which were described in contemporary documentation. One of the earliest existing follies is at Rushton in Northamptonshire. There, Sir Thomas Tresham built a 'stone bonnet for a very large bee', as a lodge, between 1593 and 1595. Equally extraordinary, if a much later creation, is the Stone Pineapple at Dunmore Castle, Stirlingshire. It is about 12 m (40 ft) high and stands on a terrace with a room beneath it. Its first 3 m (10 ft) are circular with ogival windows, then the basal leaves curve out up to 1.2 m (4 ft) in length, the body of the pineapple rising from them and being surmounted by a 'top-knot' of further leaves. It is surely one of the oddest follies of all. But there is another in Scotland to compete with it. At Lanrick Castle in Perthshire is an 18 m (60 ft) high stone 'tree'. For its first 9 m (30 ft) it is a tree trunk, but this suddenly comes to an end with a ring of jagged teeth and 4.5 m (15 ft) high stone pillars support a circular platform with another 4.5 m (15 ft) high column standing in its centre. It could well have been the creation of a pre-Surrealist and has a positively sinister ambience.

SHAM CASTLES

These were particularly popular subjects as follies. At Cirencester Park in Gloucestershire one was built, from designs by Pope, for the first Earl Bathurst in 1721, and was later enlarged in 1732. It is mentioned in a contemporary letter from a Mrs Delany that Lord Bathurst had, '. . . greatly improved the house in the wood, which you may remember was but a cottage. It is now a venerable castle and has been taken by an antiquarian as one of King Arthur's!' To this day it is still called variously Arthur's or Alfred's hall.

Two other particularly good sham castles are at Rockingham in Roscommon. One stands on an island in the lake, its tall tower reflected in the water. The other is hidden in the woods

3.2 km (2 miles) from the house. Yet it is a 23 m sq (75 sq ft) castellated fort, on each corner of which is a tower, each being different in style and height.

TOWERS

The most popular folly subjects of all were towers. Of the many still to be admired I would choose to mention just two, for the stories behind them. The first is May's Folly, Hadlow, Kent. In 1830 Walter Barton May built himself a gigantic Gothic mansion and in 1840 added to it a 52 m (170 ft) high brick tower. Octagonal, divided into several tiers and crowned by a slender turret, it is now all that survives, the mansion having been an early example of 'jerry-building'. There are three conflicting reasons mooted as to why Mr. May built the tower. The first is that he wanted to see the sea, but forgot the Downs. The second, that his wife deserted him and he built it to remind her of him whenever she visited Kent. The third is that a prophecy foretold that the house would go out of his family if he was not buried above ground, so he wanted his coffin to be left atop it. It is not there, but in a mausoleum — above ground!

The other tower is Lord Berners' folly at Faringdon in Oxfordshire. It was built as late as 1935 by the 14th Lord Berners, a noted eccentric who wrote witty and irreverent music much beloved by Sir Thomas Beecham. It is a 42.5 m (140 ft) high brick structure, on top of which is a belvedere room surmounted by an octagonal castellated tower. It is said that Admiral Clifton Brown, who lived reasonably close by, objected to it being built on the grounds that it would spoil his view. When it was pointed out that he would only be able to see it with the aid of a telescope he declared that, being an Admiral, it was his custom to admire his view through a telescope! The Admiral lost. The tower was built.

RUINS

Strictly speaking, these cannot be called follies in the true sense of the word; however, ruins often had the qualities of age and apparent uselessness which meant that, as follies became

Right: *Stowe — the Gothic Temple designed by James Gibbs. All the structures at Stowe can be considered follies but this is, surely, the one which most merits the description.*

fashionable, landowners who were lucky enough to have interesting looking ruins set in their surrounding landscape, could use them as eyecatchers in much the same way. Thus at Duncombe Park in Yorkshire there was a ready-made 'folly' in the form of the ruin of Rievaulx Abbey when it was acquired by Sir Charles Duncombe in 1689. He laid out the park so that it contained 12 viewpoints, all of them directed towards the ruin through the trees which grew below the terrace on the hillside. Equally well known is Fountains Abbey, around which John Aislabie's garden at Studley Royal was designed, using it as an eyecatcher.

For those without a convenient ruin nearby, Sanderson Millar would be willing to build you one. Two of his 18th century 'Gothic' creations can be seen at Hagley, where there is an entire 'ruined castle'; and at Wimpole, where a tower stands in a woodland glade surrounded by sparse 'ruins'.

Others decided to treat the existing ruins on their estates differently. During the 1750s, on his estate at Shobdon in Hereford and Worces-

ter, Lord Bateman pulled down a Norman Church and built a new one in its stead. The main centre arch and two of the doors of the Norman church were joined together and made into a folly, so positioned that they were in full view from the house (which no longer exists). It is stories like that which make you glad that we live in an increasingly conservation-minded society today.

Many early follies were designed by gentleman amateurs, one notable candidate being the Hon. Charles Hamilton (1704–1786) who built several on his estate at Painshill in Surrey, including a fine Gothic octagon. He overspent on his own garden and was eventually declared bankrupt, poor fellow. The garden was allowed to fall into neglect, but some efforts have recently been made to restore it to its former glory. All those years ago, as Shoberl tells us, 'Mr. Hamilton indulged the public with a sight

Above: *Portmeirion — a general view of Sir Clough Williams-Ellis' Italianate creation in North Wales, with its colonnaded loggia and campanile, as seen from across the garden.*

of the beauties of this place; and even allowed the use of small chairs drawn by ponies, which were provided by the inns at Cobham'.

The many follies at Painshill bring us to conceits.

CONCEIT

A conceit is a fanciful overall conception, which may include one or more follies, but which sometimes has elements of the macabre, and specifically reflects the character and whims of the person who conceived it. In 1733 Jonathan Tyres transformed the land originally surrounding a farmhouse at Denbighs, on the North Downs above Dorking, Surrey, as described by Shoberl's *Surrey, 1813*: 'The principal scene was a wood of about eight acres which he denominated *Il Penseroso*. It was intersected with many pleasing walks, and in the centre was a small temple loaded with inscriptions of the most grave and solemn kind; while a clock, concealed from view, struck at the end of every minute, and forcibly proclaimed the rapid flight of time'. Other descriptions of this gloomy place tell of an iron gate leading into the Valley of the Shadow of Death, with coffins for gate piers and with the skull of a famous highwayman on one end and a famous harlot on the other. It doesn't sound much fun.

At the opposite extreme is the charming modern conceit created at Mount Stewart, Greyabbey, Co. Down, by Edith, Marchioness of Londonderry between the world wars. Here there is a garden in the shape of a shamrock leaf enclosed by high yew hedges, along the top of which are many topiary figures including a fox hunt in full cry. Inside these hedges is a splendid topiary harp and within the paving at its foot a hand-shaped bed planted with red-foliaged plants — 'The Red Hand of Ulster'.

Yet even more fascinating is the statuary on and around the terracing in the Italian Garden. Here can be seen a Noah's Ark on a plinth with dodos on columns to either side; a dinosaur and a stegosaur share a balustrade with rabbits; curly-tailed lions stand on stone columns; monkeys sit on masks on pillars; and around all these there are cats, gryphons, an owl, a woodpecker, hogs, a fox confronting a giant frog . . . The list is almost endless. These figures are a series of 'portraits' of leading figures of the day who were Lady Londonderry's friends and all members of the Ark

Association over which she presided, but all portrayed as the animals by which they were known in the Association. Lady Astor was 'Nancy the Gnat', Lord Halifax (Edward Wood) was 'Edward the Woodpecker' and Lord Templewood, a great skater, 'Sam the Skate'!

To many, however, the ultimate conceit is the village of Portmeirion in Gwynedd. The dream-like creation of the flamboyant Sir Clough Williams-Ellis, it represents his ideal of an Italian village positioned, somewhat improbably, on a Welsh estuary. Built in the 1920s from the money he made as a successful architect, and without today's problems of Building Regulations and Town and Country Planning Acts, it is still a lovely place to visit and at which to marvel.

DOVECOTE/ COLUMBARIUM/ PIGEON HOUSE

A columbarium gets it name from the Latin word for dove — *columba* — and is synonymous with dovecote. The original purpose for building dovecotes was a purely practical one: they ensured a supply of fresh pigeon meat all the year round. Also their collected droppings must have been a rich source of nitrogen for vegetable and crop production. It was the ancient Romans who built and designed the prototype dovecotes for both pigeons and doves. They built round stone towers with nesting holes built into the walls from top to bottom, and some were large enough to cater for some 5,000 birds. The French use the word *colombiers*.

So far as is known, it was the Normans who introduced dovecotes into Britain during the 11th century, the earliest being massive structures with 1 m (3 ft) thick walls. Over the centuries they became lighter in design and hexagonal, square or rectangular in shape. They often included windows and cupolas. Later, dovecotes were built in brick and many Tudor examples were half-timbered.

The dovecote at the Priory Garden at Dunster, Somerset, with its 540 nesting holes, is supposed to be the oldest surviving in England today. The 15th century dovecote at

Athelhampton in Dorset has 1000 nesting holes and is certainly one of the largest. During the middle of the 17th century it was estimated that there were some 26,000 dovecotes in England alone.

Dovecotes started to become obsolete during the 18th century when crops such as turnips and swedes became available to farmers as winter food for livestock. Before that time all livestock, except those used for breeding purposes, were slaughtered during the preceding autumn. Fresh pigeon meat therefore no longer featured as large on the winter menu, and what a relief it must have been, although I cannot find any trace of a cook book published prior to the 18th century called *A Thousand Ways to Cook a Pigeon*.

Today dovecotes are normally made in wood and painted white, surmounted on a single pole (where the birds are safe from cats) or designed to be attached to a wall, and very attractive they are too. They are welcome additions to any garden so far as I'm concerned, especially if they house fan-tail pigeons.

A pigeon's cooing can only add music to the garden and provide an atmosphere of tranquillity. In a small to average-sized garden of today a dovecote could well become the focal point somewhere at the very end of the garden. It should be visible from a window from where the birds can be seen as they fly in and out and preen themselves.

Luckily a great number of old brick and stone dovecotes still survive today and they can be seen at houses such as Rousham in Oxfordshire; Nymans, Sussex; and Felbrigg Hall, Norfolk.

❧

ICE HOUSE

Ice houses were the forbears of the modern fridge, and although many still exist they have long since been abandoned. They consisted of underground chambers, often brick-lined, and were used for storing ice during the summer. It is known that the Chinese used this very same method for preserving ice many centuries ago

Left: *Nymans Garden — the dovecote framed by topiary hedging. For some time this dovecote was known as a gazebo because of its position set in a wall extending from the house.*

but the idea did not catch on until the mid 17th century in Northern Europe, although ice and snow were preserved in this way in Italy before then.

The ice house built in 1660 in St. James' Park for Charles II is believed to have been the first dug in Britain, and the fashion caught on quickly. Good drainage was essential for an ice house and so they were always dug above the water table on higher ground. Before they were actually filled with ice from nearby lakes and ponds (the ice for the ice house at Chatsworth House was taken from the Long Canal), a layer of branches — probably broom — was placed at the base to assist drainage. A thatch was placed over the top to both shade and insulate the ice during the warmer months. Often trees were planted around them to supply extra shade.

In some cases they were designed as a feature, a 'Gothic' turret or small classical temple, with an upper section which acted as a cool store. Quite a work force of strong men was required to fill an ice house using horse and cart. A Mr. Painter remembers filling the ice house at Buckland House, Oxfordshire, one particularly late spring, in April 1913. 'I remember clearly because it was my 16th birthday. Two men went out in a punt and broke the ring of ice and then got two long poles with iron spikes on the end and pulled the ice onto the bank. Two other men standing on the bank with wooden mallets broke up the ice into small bits and the two who were in the punt had two mesh sieves, wired into a forked stick and they dipped the ice out in the sieves and put it into a wheelbarrow. Six men and wheelbarrows, on a chain, wheelbarrowed the ice up the hill and tipped it. Two more in the ice house shoved the ice in, and two more in the ice house levelled it out. The head gardener, Mr. Gough, heated beer for us and also provided bread and cheese. The ice was wheeled from the ice house to Buckland House every morning and washed before use and the ice lasted practically until the next winter's ice was brought in.'

By the late 19th century ice was being made by machine and it was also being imported

Above: Scotney Castle Garden – the ice house with its unusual thatched roof which gives it the appearance of an elaborate shed, with no hint of the pit it protects.

from Norway. One of the very last estates to use an ice house was Rufford Abbey in Nottinghamshire, as recently as 1936.

Another good example, is to be found at Killerton in Devon. This one is positioned both well up the hillside in a shaded spot and at a considerable distance from the house. Others can be seen at Osterley Park, Scotney Castle Garden and Waddesdon Manor.

HERMITAGE

Hermitages or hermit cells became fashionable during the 18th and early 19th centuries as yet another feature in large gardens. They were built expressly to house hermits — unfortunate creatures who were hired to live in them for years. A usual hermit's contract of the day lasted for seven years, during which time they were not allowed to cut their hair, beard or finger nails. They were not allowed to talk to anyone else, and their job was to be viewed looking decidedly grubby, chewing bones at the entrance to their hermitages and glancing at their onlookers through their dirty matted hair. Food and drink were supplied free from the big house and a sizeable nest egg awaited them once the contract had been honoured. Not surprisingly the vast majority of hermits couldn't stand it for very long and ran away.

Barbara Jones in her book *Follies and Grottoes* tells us, 'Hermits were obtained by advertisement, and it never seems to have been difficult to get one; indeed one young man, Mr Laurence from Plymouth, did not merely answer advertisements but himself advertised in 1810 that he wished to retire as a hermit (to a convenient spot) and was willing to engage (for a gratuity) to any nobleman or gentleman who was desirous of having one. One advertisement demanded a hermit who would live underground invisible, silent, unshaven and unclipped for seven years, in a comfortable room with books, an organ and delicious food. The reward was to be a pension for life of £50 a year, and a hermit accepted, but lasted for only four years.

Above: *Badminton House — the Hermit's Park House, one of the few existing hermitages, designed by Thomas Wright, the astronomer and architect.*

55

Mr Hamilton's terms at Painshill were similar, again the mystic seven years, again no cutting of hair, nails or beard, again food from the house and no speech. But he could walk in the grounds, and was provided with a Bible, optical glasses, a mat, a hassock and an hourglass. The recompense was to be seven hundred pounds, but the chosen hermit was caught at the end of three weeks going down to the pub'.

There must have been a cry of 'Oh dear! It's so hard to find good hermits these days!' As a result, the 'real thing' was often substituted by wax, stuffed or even clockwork effigies.

The hermitages themselves were designed to look dirty, dank and excrementitious, and were built of a crude framework of knotted and gnarled timbers patched with rough plaster or infilled with bark. The floor was often lined with sheep, deer or knuckle bones, or left as bare earth. The roof was normally of thatch. Downmarket hermitages were simple structures of painted canvas over a crude timber framework.

Few hermitages still survive. However the largest still in existence can be found in the park at Badminton House, designed by Thomas Wright, the astronomer and architect. Barbara Jones tells us, 'It is wonderfully preserved, a

fine room rather than a cell, oddly placed out in the deer park . . . The cell is about 20 feet by 24 with a swooping thatched roof. A spike on the top is probably the remains of the cross that finishes most hermitages in the prints. The door frame is the upturned fork of a huge tree and four more big and particularly knotted trunks make the corner posts and three more at each end the steep pediments, which have sections of hollow trees as *yeux de boeuf* round iron gratings. At each side is a curved bay with a two-light pointed window, and everywhere there is a wild jumbled infill of branches, roots, knots and sawn ends. Under the rear pediment, which is curved, is a branch bench with an ogee back lettered in nailheads HERE LOUNGERS LOITER up one curve and HERE THE WEARY REST down the other'.

A hermitage-like structure could be built today for the amusement of children within a large shrubbery or in woodland, but I'm not sure that the local health inspector would be amused if it were used as originally intended.

Above: *Stourhead — the Hermitage, which is more in the manner of an elaborate summer house, with the Pantheon beyond.*

TREE HOUSE

The first recorded tree houses were built as arbours to provide somewhere cool and shaded to sit in. In about 1300, Pietro de Crescenzi published a description of such an arbour in Italy. It must have taken many years to achieve, as first a tree needed to be trained into a shape to accommodate a platform. At a suitable height from the ground the branches were first trained vertically to form the 'walls' and once they had reached a sufficient height were trained back in towards the centre to form the 'roof'.

The commonly perceived idea of a tree house is a small house built within the sturdy branches of a mature tree. One of the oldest surviving examples of this in Britain can be found at Pitchford Hall in Shropshire. It sits up high, resting on the massive branches of an ancient lime. Its framework is very much older than its late 18th century Gothic-style exterior.

ROOT HOUSE

A root house was in many ways similar to a moss house or hermitage, except that the framework was entirely of roots. J.C. Loudon tells us, 'The roots of trees, and especially large roots, including the stool, or the base of the tree after the trunk has been cut down to the ground may be combined together in varying ways, useful, ornamental or curious, in gardening. The idea to be kept in view is that of creating artificial ornaments without much expense, and therefore the roots must never appear to have been left where they are by carelessness or by accident, but placed by design, and with reference to the composition of which they form a part.

'Roots may also be combined together so as to form seats, open or covered huts, grotto-like structures, and grotesque bridges; . . . (they) may be piled up, and connected together by wooden pegs, so as to form arches, arcades, or covered ways or grottoes, or other structures for shelter or repose, the interstices being filled in with moss or heath, and the exterior being thatched with heath . . . .'

Surviving root houses are a great rarity, but one can still be seen at Spetchley Park, Worcestershire.

Above left: *Pitchford Hall — the elaborate 18th century Gothic-style exterior of the tree house, set in the boughs of an ancient lime tree.*
Above: *Spetchley Park — the Victorian root house, with the roots supporting a conical thatched roof.*

MOSS HOUSE

It was during the Victorian era when rustic summer houses were all the rage that the moss house evolved. They were not built to last, often put together by estate workers who used whatever lengths of spare timber there happened to be hanging about at the time.

From the outside a moss house looked as if it had almost 'grown' where it stood, with crude walls of interlocking timbers and a thatched or bark roof which extended out from a central point, supported on rustic poles. Inside, laths were nailed to the timber framework and between them were crammed clumps of moss. The desired effect was walls smothered in patterned mosses. They must have looked rather splendid for the first few days before bits turned brown and started to fall out. Such a damp hollow must also have attracted every gnat and mosquito in the neighbourhood, as well as swarms of other insects. In any case it does seem a terrible shame to denude damp and shaded areas of their mosses. Perhaps it's a good thing that moss houses have not been built for quite some time now.

◦◦◦

GROTTO

The word 'grotto' comes from the Greek *krypte* meaning a crypt or vault. The structures themselves are descendants of the Greek *nymphaea* which were natural rocky caves where offerings were made to nymphs. The Romans copied the idea and built artificial *nymphaea* and decorated them with stucco, mosaic and inlaid shells.

Here yet again we see the familiar pattern emerge of the ancient Romans copying the Greeks, Renaissance Italy copying the Romans, and Europe, often lead by France, copying the Italians. The ancient grottoes of Greece and Italy did, I suppose, serve a practical purpose of supplying somewhere cool to sit but those built later in Europe were built purely as follies, although it has been rumoured that they were sometimes used as hideaways during the days of religious persecution.

Right: *Goldney Hall — Thomas Goldney's spectacularly elaborate grotto, construction of which was begun in 1737.*

In England one of the best preserved grottoes in existence today is Goldney's Grotto in the grounds of Bristol University, started in 1737. Simon Curwen, an American exile visiting the grotto in 1778, wrote: 'We arrived at the door of the grotto, situated under the terrace; the object that presented itself to our view was a lion in a sitting posture, and behind in a dark cave, a lioness, the latter so like life that I could hardly persuade myself to the contrary. The form of the grotto is octangular, its roof semicircular, having a dome with a round window in the centre; the diameter about 20 feet on each side, from the door in front to the mouth of the cave in which the lioness is sitting; to the right and left of the entrance the roof is supported by pillars; covered as its roof and sides are with a variety of shells, stones, spars, petrifications, etc . . . On the left hand, beyond the dome and under a rough cragged stone arch, is a small quadrangular stone basin of water supplied by small streams . . . On the door was a miniature of a female face with a seemingly broken glass covering it . . .'.

What is extraordinary about this description is that the grotto looked very similar indeed when I visited it in 1986, except that the water was supplied by a gushing urn clutched tightly by Neptune.

Of the smaller grottoes, the one at Stourhead in Wiltshire, with its statue of the River God and the glorious view across the lake at water level through a craggy window, is a sight never forgotten. The grotto room at Woburn Abbey, dated at about 1630, is the most extravagantly shell-decorated room anywhere to be seen. Although not strictly a grotto in the *nymphaeum* sense of the word, it is none the less wonderfully preserved, given its age.

⌘

ORANGERY

Orangeries are so called because they were designed to house citrus trees over winter to protect them from the harsh European winter climate. Both oranges and lemons were grown in them so I suppose they might just as well have been called lemonaries.

Left: Stourhead — one of the most extraordinary grottoes is the home of the River God. This section of the landscape is said to represent the Underworld.

It is not absolutely clear when citrus trees were first introduced into Europe but it could have been as early as the early 16th century. Before that the orange had been introduced into Spain by the Arabs during the 12th or 13th centuries, and then into Italy during the early Renaissance. It was in Italy that the method originated of bringing them indoors during the winter and this sparked off the idea to gardeners throughout northern European countries.

The first person known to have grown oranges in England was Sir Francis Carew at his estate in Beddington, Surrey, about whom little is known — his estate is now a public park and sewage farm! Tradition says that Sir Francis received the seeds from Sir Walter Raleigh, but it is far more likely that he imported the fully grown, and sculpted, trees from Italy in about 1560. He also received some from France soon after. He is credited with having built the first orangery in Britain.

Orangeries became very grand edifices during the 17th and 18th centuries and they were often built with solid roofs until it was realized that the extra light from a glass roof was beneficial.

Heating was a problem in those early days, and a complicated system of brick flues was at first adopted. In 1684 at the Apothecaries' Garden in Chelsea the orangery was heated by red hot coals shovelled under gratings in the floor. These clumsy heating methods often resulted in fumes harming the plants and the air becoming too dry. The introduction of hot water pipe systems, an idea brought over from France during the early 19th century, overcame these problems and also supplied better heat distribution.

Sadly, several of the earliest orangeries have fallen into decay or simply disappeared. The majority of those which have survived are now used for different purposes. Sir Christopher Wren's orangery at Kensington Palace now houses camellias; Sir William Vanbrugh's at Kew is a museum and the one at Ham House a tea room. At least they still survive and it is not difficult to imagine their glory in their heyday. One of the most dramatic of all is the one at Wrest Park in Bedfordshire which was built in 1836 on a high grass bank. Other good examples can be seen at Belton House, Lincolnshire; Powis Castle, Powys; Dyrham Park, Gloucestershire; Osterley Park, Middlesex; Ripley Castle, Yorkshire; Montacute House,

Somerset; and Weston Park, Staffordshire. Frampton Court on the River Severn in Gloucestershire boasts an orangery in the Strawberry Hill 'Gothic' style, built in 1760. It gives a wonderful reflection in the formal canal which stretches away from it.

In their heyday orangeries must have been an impressive sight during the colder winter months. In early summer the containerized fruit trees were frequently put out into the open to further embellish the fashionable parterres of the day. In such circumstances they were shaped to round balls or 'lollypops' and then positioned symmetrically to fit in with their formal surroundings. These days imported citrus fruits are easily available all the year round and as a result the orangery has lost its *raison d'être*.

Citrus trees, like most fruit trees, are more likely to produce sizeable fruits on grafted rootstocks. This was one lesson we all learnt as children when faced with disappointing crops produced from domestic pips. You do, however, stand a better chance of success with pips from grapefruit, lemon and lime.

A young grafted tree grown in a container can grow up to 2 m (7 ft) or more if left to its own devices. They do not produce fruit during their first few seasons. Following the example of the old traditionalists, they enjoy being outside in an open and sunny spot where they should be kept freely watered, allowing the compost to dry out completely between waterings. If you haven't got around to building an orangery for yourself they will happily spend the winter in a cool greenhouse where the temperature averages 8–10°C (46–50°F). They are best repotted during the winter if they are root-bound, always ensuring that they have adequate drainage. A good feed whilst they flower will ensure a more prolific fruit crop. Regular mist-spraying will also add to the contentment of the plants, especially when they are in bud, as the mass of tiny water droplets act as a 'lubricant' to help unhinge the bursting buds.

Established plants require large, and therefore heavy, containers. They have to be taken in and out of the greenhouse (or orangery), so containers on wheels are ideal, although in the olden days they were carried on two poles by two sturdy gardeners.

Right: *Saltram — the beautiful wooden orangery built between 1773-5, at the same time as the Adam house.*

STOVE HOUSE

Stove houses were the precursors of the greenhouse and conservatory and the first glassed buildings to have been built to house tender plants during the winter, in the mid-1600s. They were built in those early days with a solid roof. Glass roofs came with the conservatory towards the end of the 18th century.

Often referred to simply as 'stoves', they were so called because originally they were heated by indoor Dutch stoves. These early coke-fired stoves were not ideal by any means as they produced a dry heat and a fair amount of dust, neither of which proved conducive to healthy plant life. Later on, however, hot water pipes replaced the stoves, resulting in better heat distribution, no dust and the added advantage of humidity.

The end of the 18th century was an era when the rich appeared to be in stiff competition with each other to see who could grow many of the new exotic fruits continuously being brought into the country by plant hunters. Pineapples, bananas and mangoes were three favourites.

Insectivorous plants such as the Venus' Fly Trap, *Dionaea*, plants which moved when touched such as the Humble plant (*Desmodium gyrans*) and 'Air plants' (*Tillandsia*), were all used to make up exotic mini-tropical landscapes. Foliage plants were also collected; these included anthuriums, codiaeums and alocasias. Tropical plants with exotic flowers were also often included in stove houses, such as ixoras, allamandas and medinillas.

It must have been a thrilling era of botanical discovery. Of course today all these plants are grown in the various botanic gardens dotted around the country where everyone and not just the rich, can admire them at close quarters.

Stove houses can still be found at several botanic gardens, but they are steadily being replaced by modern, more efficient, structures, such as the new Princess of Wales Conservatory at Kew. The modern aluminium-framed glasshouse is a far cry from its predecessor.

CONSERVATORY

Today a conservatory often describes a glazed extension to a house used for extra living space, where less attention is paid to plants and more to decor. Originally, however, it evolved during the late 18th century from the earlier stove houses and orangeries when it was realized that most plants preferred more light. A conservatory at that time came to describe a large ornate 'greenhouse', designed to house tender plants. It emerged, therefore, as the new sort of plant house with a glass roof.

Some fantastic glass framed giants sprang up all over the country, among the best of these being the Temperate House at Kew and the majestic domed conservatory at Syon Park, Middlesex. Joseph (later Sir Joseph) Paxton's design for the conservatory at Chatsworth House in Derbyshire, which first housed the huge water lily (*Victoria regia*) from Brazil and which is now demolished, inspired him to build the Crystal Palace in 1851. This feat of engineering made him a household name.

Victorian and Edwardian England witnessed an explosion of conservatory building fired by the new wealth of the industrial revolution. They were the 'hallmarks of success', and were stuffed to the gills with the fashionable palms and ferns of the day.

Above: *A stove house built to house the new botanical discoveries brought back by plant hunters.*
Above left: *Castle Ashby — the orangery designed by Matthew Digby Wyatt. Note the rather unusual balustraded roof.*
Left: *Bicton House — the orangery with its Doric colonnaded portico.*

The 1980s, for some a decade of wealth under Mrs Thatcher's government, have witnessed a further surge of conservatory fever. Those based on Victorian designs have so far proved the most popular style, their wooden frames embellished with ogee or round-topped windows, finials, etc. However, the 1970-built greenhouse at Chatsworth certainly broke the mould. It was designed by George A.H. Pearce on the same lines as the glasshouse he designed for the Botanic Gardens in Edinburgh.

FERNERY

Those conservatories which house only ferns are called ferneries. They were particularly fashionable during the Victorian and Edwardian eras and contained every sort of fern imaginable including the tree fern. Individual ferns were sometimes brought into the house in elaborate glass cases.

Outdoor ferneries also became popular at that time, where they were landscaped in amongst stumps, known as stumperies.

Stumperies were also popular with the Victorians and normally consisted of old stumps grouped together. Old rotten stumps proved particularly effective where they had ferns planted within them.

Very few exist today, although the indoor fernery at Tatton Park in Cheshire is well worth a visit.

Above: *Tatton Park — inside the fernery.*
Left: *Chatsworth House — the 'Conservative' Wall designed by Sir Joseph Paxton, this central portion being specifically designed for camellias.*

NYMPHS, NOT GNOMES

STATUARY
OBELISK
SUNDIAL
ASTROLABE
WELL-HEAD
LEAD CISTERN
SARCOPHAGUS
VASE/URN
JARDINIÈRE
FLOWERPOT
UMBRELLO
STADDLE STONE
WEATHERVANE

Left: *Buscot Park — the canal pool in Harold Peto's Italianate garden, showing urns and statues in niches, with a belvedere above the centre of the gatehouse.*

Like garden buildings, garden ornaments come in an astonishing variety, ranging from the humblest ball finial or stone trough to the most majestic of statuary.

Of the latter surely the most remarkable is to be seen at Pratolino, north of Florence. Here the only significant survivor of the great Medici gardens is Giambologna's *Il Apennino* — The Giant of the Apennines — a huge figure with a grotto in his body and inside whose head it is said that four men can stand. Stooping as if with the woes of the world on his shoulders — there is, in fact, a dragon perched there now, but that was the inferior work of a later sculptor — the statue is said to be the human representation of the hills around.

At the other extreme is the stone trough or sink, the former previously used for watering farmyard animals, the latter moved from the kitchen to the garden, and recently so beloved and sought after by those who grow alpines. At

Above: Anglesey Abbey — Fossi's copy of Bernini's statue of David, flanked behind by two splendid Corinthian columns.

Rodmarton Manor, Gloucestershire, where members of the Arts and Crafts Movement pioneered the resuscitation of the craft workshop economy of the Cotswolds, there is a small garden dominated by troughs which is called the Troughery, the concept of treasuring such outdated items being in keeping with the use to which the house is put.

Finials might well have merited a heading of their own, there being an amazing variety of designs for such modest objects. Before they became the great constructions with which we are accustomed today, small obelisks were popular as finials, and excellent examples can be seen atop the balustraded walls at Montacute House.

Possibly the best known of all is the pineapple finial which became popular after the fruit was first imported into Britain in the reign of Charles II. There is a fascinating, oft-reproduced, painting in Ham House, attributed to Danckerts, which depicts John Rose, then the Royal Gardener, presenting the first pineapple grown in England to Charles II. The painting is a veritable feast of garden ornaments, with statues of Romans on balustraded terraces, a fountain, pots filled with succulents around the pool and a large flowerpot (or is it a vase, or even a jardinière?) containing a tree by the King's left shoulder.

***

STATUARY

Marble statuary was first introduced into gardens by the Greeks who chose heroes and gods for their subject matter. The Romans adopted the fashion and whilst they imported a lot of statuary from Greece, they also produced vast numbers themselves. In Renaissance Italy countless statues and other artefacts were unearthed from the ruins of Roman cities and there was such a lot to go round that many ended up as decoration to gardens as overspill.

Eighteenth century gardens in France were richly adorned with marble statues but they never caught on to the same degree in England. Blomfield said, 'Marble statuary is a mistake in an English garden. To attain its full effect it wants full sunlight, a clear dry light, and a cloudless sky. In the soft light and nebulous atmosphere of the North marble looks forlorn and out of place. It does not colour like stone,

and the qualities of which it is most capable — such as refinements of contour and modelling — are simply lost under an English sky'.

He didn't have anything nice to say about bronze statues either: 'They do not lend themselves to the modelling of nature; they do not grow in with nature, as stone or lead'. However, he was very keen on Portland stone: 'It is hard and weathers well, and few if any stones profit so much by exposure to the sun and rain. The harshness of its outlines become softened by time, and it will take on the most delicate colours, from the green stains of the pedestal to the pure white of the statue that gleams from under the deep canopy of yew'.

From the 18th century onwards lead statuary became the fashion. In those days it was relatively cheap, in ready supply and easy to cast. Nymphs, Pan, Cupids, storks, milkmaids, hunters and buccaneers soon appeared to grace the fashionable gardens of the day. They all weathered to a silvery grey which toned in well with our average light conditions, not to mention the normal colour of our skies! Many of the best lead figures seen today are by John Cleeve, who operated from premises near

Green Park, London, in the latter half of the 18th century, having taken over the lead moulds of John van Nost. The well known dancing shepherds and shepherdesses which adorn the balustraded terraces of Powis Castle, have been variously attributed to both gentlemen.

The Victorians produced cast-iron statues which were often rather sentimental, such as the 'faithful dog' and the like.

Terracotta is widely used for statuary in more amenable climes, but British weather, particularly frost and ice, has horrendous effects on it. Even in Tuscany it suffers, but a headless peasant girl in a secret grove can have a certain charm.

Since the turn of this century there have been so many different movements within the art world that it seems a great shame that the majority of affordable pieces of statuary at

Above, left and right: *Melbourne Hall — an amusing example of statuary used to tell a story. In this case the cherubs are first quarelling, then they kiss and make up!*

garden centres are too hideous to contemplate. Stone and lead pieces, especially if they are antique, have not only become prohibitively expensive but also a source of great temptation for burglars. If I had a moor (and was very rich) I would include a Henry Moore sculpture on it. If I had a vista, I might place a Liz Frink at its furthest end. It's all a question of taste.

OBELISK

An obelisk is a tall, four-sided tapering pillar, topped by a pyramid, usually of stone. The word is derived from the Greek *obeliskos* and the Latin *obeliscus.*

Obelisks and single columns stand as memorials to battles or people and are often positioned at the end of an avenue or where they intersect a ride. There are literally thousands of them dotted all over Britain.

They are also sometimes placed in the centre of a tree plantation. Such an example can be seen at Moreton House in Devon where a 4 tonne, 15.5 m (51 ft 4 in) high, Portland stone obelisk sits on a 4.8 m (16 ft) high, 3 m (10 ft) square pedestal. On its top sits a 2.75 m (9 ft) urn. It was erected by Captain John Houlton in 1785–6 to the memory of a friend. The 30.5 m (100 ft) obelisk at Castle Howard, Yorkshire, was designed by Sir John Vanbrugh for Charles Howard, Third Earl of Carlisle and erected in 1714, where it intersects two avenues and commemorates the planting of the plantations there.

At Castletown in Ireland there exists a 42.6 m (140 ft) high obelisk built by Mrs. Conelly in 1739–40. What is surprising about it is that it sits upon an elaborate arched structure. Mrs. Conelly's sister wrote of it in 1740: 'My sister is building an Obleix to answer a Vistoe from the Bake of Castletown. It will cost her 3 or 4 hundred pounds at least, and I believe more. I don't know how she can dow so much and live as she duse'.

Other good examples can be seen at Hagley Park, Worcestershire, where Frederick, Prince of Wales sits atop, and at Blenheim Palace in Oxfordshire.

Tiny obelisks were favoured as finials to cap gate posts and so on during Jacobean times and such an example can be seen at Canons Ashby in Northamptonshire. There are also several on

top of the balustraded Elizabethan wall at Montacute.

Above: *Chiswick House — the obelisk, lacking its pyramidal topping. It was brought to this country by Lord Burlington from Italy.*
Right: *Stourhead — the obelisk vista stopper which commemorates the Hoare family who created the garden.*

SUNDIAL

'Behold I will bring again the shadow of the degrees, which is gone down in the Sun Dial of Ahaz . . .' *Isaiah 38.8.*

Sundials have been in use since at least 1500 B.C. In Britain they were often included in Tudor gardens; a time when there were very few clocks and those there were could not be relied upon for accuracy. They have remained popular garden ornaments, despite the advent of far more accurate clocks and watches. J. C. Loudon in his *Encyclopaedia of Gardening,* 1834, wrote of sundials that they 'should be placed in conspicuous frequented parts, as in the intersection of principal walks, where the note they give of time may be readily recognized by the passenger'.

Loudon was referring to the most commonly found type of sundial with a round horizontal dial face mounted on a pedestal (or more traditionally held up by a statue of Father Time or a kneeling slave), with an upright bar or 'gnomon' which casts the shadow. There are variations on the same theme, such as vertical dials which are made to be mounted on a wall

or pillar. One of the best examples of this exists at Queen's College, Cambridge. It is brightly painted with the signs of the zodiac, with tables of calculations below. Floral dials were sometimes incorporated as part of the decoration in parterre gardens during the 17th century. Plants formed the dial face and often the gnomon as well.

Sundials are found in many a garden today, although a large number have been repositioned haphazardly, rendering them totally inaccurate as well as obsolete. But it matters not. They are still welcome features whether surrounded by lawn, in the centre of circular paving, in the rose garden or on the terrace. After all, even if they cannot be relied upon to time a boiled egg, they never need winding up.

For the record, to correctly position a sundial the gnomon should be aligned at right angles to the dial along the meridian line which is the 12 o'clock line on the face. The angle at which it is set is all important and should be equivalent to that of the latitude of the place in which the garden is set. To check accuracy the shadow cast should fall exactly on the noon line at local noon time. The dial of a horizontal sundial should be fixed perfectly horizontally with the noon figure pointing due north.

Above: *Anglesey Abbey — Time stooping over a sundial.*
Right: *Ascott — a sundial set on a bulbous base with a dolphin and Mercury fountain beyond.*
Far right: *Cholmondeley Castle — sundial in the rose garden surrounded by flowering lavender.*

ASTROLABE

An astrolabe was an ancient instrument used by mariners for determining latitude with the aid of tables listing the sun's declination. Being on the cumbersome side it was rapidly replaced by the sextant when it was invented in 1550. In its earliest and crudest form it consisted of a disc of wood suspended by a ring. Around the disc's edge were marked the degrees of a circle. A pointer along which the sun or a star could be sighted was pivoted on a centre pin. Later they were made of metal and they are most often seen as a circle inside which the hours are marked. Some had a *rête*, consisting of a plate with a map of the stars and the circle of the zodiac on its reverse side. Thus, after measuring the sun's altitude, its position could be noted on the circle of the zodiac and a line drawn to a circle of hours showing the time.

Many gardens feature metal astrolabes positioned on plinths much in the manner of sundials. Among the most outstanding is the gilt one at Hever Castle which is set among the series of small Tudor gardens below the east facade of the Castle. Others can be seen through a moon window at Polesden Lacey in Surrey, and within the walled garden of Haseley Court in Oxfordshire, this being on a particularly tall and elaborate plinth.

Above: *Hever Castle — the astrolabe in Anne Boleyn's Garden, below the east façade of the Castle, is used to show the movement of the heavenly bodies.*

WELL-HEAD

Wells were originally purely practical structures, designed to maintain a regular supply of fresh water to those houses which did not have a stream or river flowing close by. The great majority of English well-heads were simple and undecorated, with many of the finest originating in Venice. Ruskin described them as 'some of the most superb examples of Venetian sculpture . . . (like) colossal capitals of pillars, with foliage at the angles and the shield of the family upon their sides'. Many of these early Italian well-heads found themselves being introduced into British gardens during the 19th century. This, I fear, was a widespread habit at that time. There certainly exists a fine Italian well-head at Portmeirion in North Wales.

Very often these decorative well-heads are positioned at the crossing points of paths in rose gardens and the like. There is, for example, an excellent marble one in the centre of the rose garden at Polesden Lacey.

There are also many dummy well-heads dotted around the country, although some stand above real wells still in use. There is a danger of dummy well-heads looking twee but for guidance you need only to look at some of the finer earlier examples such as those at Old Hall, Langham, Rutland and Canons Ashby, Northamptonshire which are beautifully decorated by handsome wrought iron work.

LEAD CISTERN

The grand old lead cistern was originally designed to hold water. Many great houses still possess them although, because they have deteriorated over the years, they now sit empty in courtyards where they seem to look most at home.

Many cisterns are richly decorated with family coats of arms and other embellishments, and they are often dated. They can, indeed, be very old. In a description of Theobalds in Hertfordshire, in 1598, it is stated of the

Left: Polesden Lacey — the Venetian marble well-head in the centre of the rose garden, with a pergola leading towards a sundial.

summer house that, 'the upper part of it is set round with cisterns of lead, into which water is conveyed through pipes, so that fish may be kept in them, and in summer time they are very convenient for bathing'. It is not made clear whether the fish were removed from the cisterns before the bathers jumped in!

If you want to add an ancient lead cistern to your garden, it is likely to cost you several thousand pounds. They may sit empty in courtyards, but they are highly sought after, especially the most decorative ones. They can always be used as jardinières, where flowerpots can stand on blocks inside them.

SARCOPHAGUS

The sarcophagus gets its name from the Greek *Sarkophagus*, meaning 'flesh-eating'. The original Greek sarcophagi were made of limestone which was thought to consume the flesh of corpses.

A sarcophagus is really more of a collector's piece than a garden ornament, and although many are very ancient and attractively carved, I'm not sure that I would be very keen to have my garden littered with stone coffins. Be that as it may, there exist some fine examples of both Roman and Greek sarcophagi in the garden at

Above: *A rectangular lead cistern, typical of the latter part of the seventeenth century.*

Right: *Cliveden — one of the eight sarcophagi, set against a yew hedge, depicting the Triumph of Dionysus.*

Iford Manor, near Bath, as part of the collection of the late Harold Peto. Hever Castle also sports sarcophagi among a huge assortment of ancient sculpture collected by William Waldorf Astor at the turn of the century. Chatsworth House in Derbyshire boasts yet another.

Perhaps the most remarkable collection of all sarcophagi can be seen at Cliveden, which, like that at Hever, is part of the Astor collection. Here, against a background of great yew hedges on the north side of the forecourt of the house, are no less than eight, all from the classical Roman period. The carvings are astonishingly elaborate and, if one can put their original use from one's mind, worthy of close scrutiny. Among the many characters depicted are Dionysus in his panther-drawn chariot, Indian slaves riding an elephant and a camel, Luna, Hymnaeus and Endymion, Pan, Eros, Psyche, Theseus, Daedalus and King Minos (shades of labyrinth!), to name but a few.

I have not yet seen a sarcophagus used as a planter, thank goodness. What would one do with the lid?

VASE/URN

VASE

Towards the end of the 17th century British garden art became increasingly influenced by the Dutch. One Jan van Nost came to settle in England and produced a great many ornamental vases and statues between about 1686 and 1729. Many landscape architects of the day, particularly London and Wise, appreciated the excellent quality of his work and often included his pieces in the gardens they designed. Luckily many examples still survive today.

Perhaps the most magnificent vase in existence today is the huge 4.5 m (15 ft) high Waterloo Vase in the gardens of Buckingham Palace. It was begun in Milan on the orders of Napoleon, then came to England in an unfinished state before it was decorated for

Right: *Buckingham Palace — the Waterloo Vase makes a spectacular display. Weighing in at an impressive 40 tons of white Carrara marble, it was begun in 1820 on the orders of Napoleon. Since 1906, however, it has resided in the palace gardens.*

George IV. It was then later given to the nation by William IV. Its massive weight and size meant that it proved too unwieldy to be on permanent exhibition in the National Gallery so it was offered back to the Royal Family in 1906, to Edward VII. It has remained in the palace gardens ever since.

The Victorians produced large numbers of cast-iron vases in classical designs but these could not match the beauty of their stone predecessors.

Vases are used to decorate many different parts of the garden in much the same way as urns. If you are ever in North Wales, a visit to Sir Clough Williams-Ellis' village of Portmeirion is very worthwhile. It is full of things to see, including a gatehouse surmounted by elegant stone vases.

URN

Although urns have become sought-after garden ornaments, they were originally monuments to the dead. The vase-shaped, ornamen-

tal garden urn is a lavishly designed descendant of those once used for containing the ashes of the dead. Most great 18th century gardens had at least one where they were used as terminal points in vistas, placed in alcoves, or positioned on balustrading or gate posts.

The landscape gardener and poet William Shenstone (1714–1763) said in his *Unconnected Thoughts on Gardening:* 'Urns are more solemn, if large and plain; more beautiful if less and ornamented. Solemnity is perhaps their point, and the situation of them should still co-operate with it'. Dr. Johnson vehemently disagreed: 'Sir, I hate urns, they are nothing, they mean nothing, convey no ideas but ideas of horror — would they were beaten to pieces to pave our streets!'

Above left: *Cliveden — Queen Anne's Vase, possibly made by Thomas Greenaway of Bath c.1725.*
Above: *Lanhydrock — a bronze urn with thoughtful cherubs, made by Louis Ballin who was goldsmith to Louis XIV.*

JARDINIÈRE

Jardinière is a French word meaning 'a pot or stand for flowers or plants'.

Jardinières were widely used by the Victorians to enable them to display plants *en masse* either in the conservatory or outside. They were often made of delicate fine wire designs and painted white.

Precisely what makes a jardinière a jardinière is difficult to define. It is definitely not a matter of shape for they can be square, rectangular, round, elliptical, even hexagonal. They can also be free-standing, supported on feet, such as lion's paws, or can stand on a solid columnar base. They can even have handles. The choice is enormous.

FLOWERPOT

It is known that plants were grown in large earthenware pots during the reign of Ramses III and when the Romans invaded Egypt they took the idea home with them. The Romans were lovers of plants and were the first to develop gardens as important extensions to their houses. They had a wide range of containers for fruit trees as well as small fish ponds, and were the first users of window boxes in their cramped apartment blocks.

The ancient Chinese, on the other hand, have always been famous for their ceramic pots. In recent years they have started to flood the European markets.

Flower pots, as we know them today, were first manufactured during the early 19th century, often decorated with classical designs. Now plastic pots have largely taken over from terracotta. They are not nearly as attractive, of course, but they are more practical as they are less porous. Garden centres originated in the U.S.A. as recently as the 1930s and it wasn't until some 20 years later that the idea caught on in Britain. During the early days plants were sold in old tins — a far cry from the modern day plastic liners.

There is no doubt that containerized plants have revolutionized gardening as all plants can now be planted at any time of the year provided they are subjected to as little root

disturbance as possible. Before then all planting took place either in the autumn or spring, but recent surveys have proved that the best time to plant winter hardy plants is during the autumn, right up to the end of November.

Top: *A carved stone jardinière with lion's paw feet.*
Above: *A lead jardinière, moulded with panels depicting lovers in a garden, on a raised circular foot.*

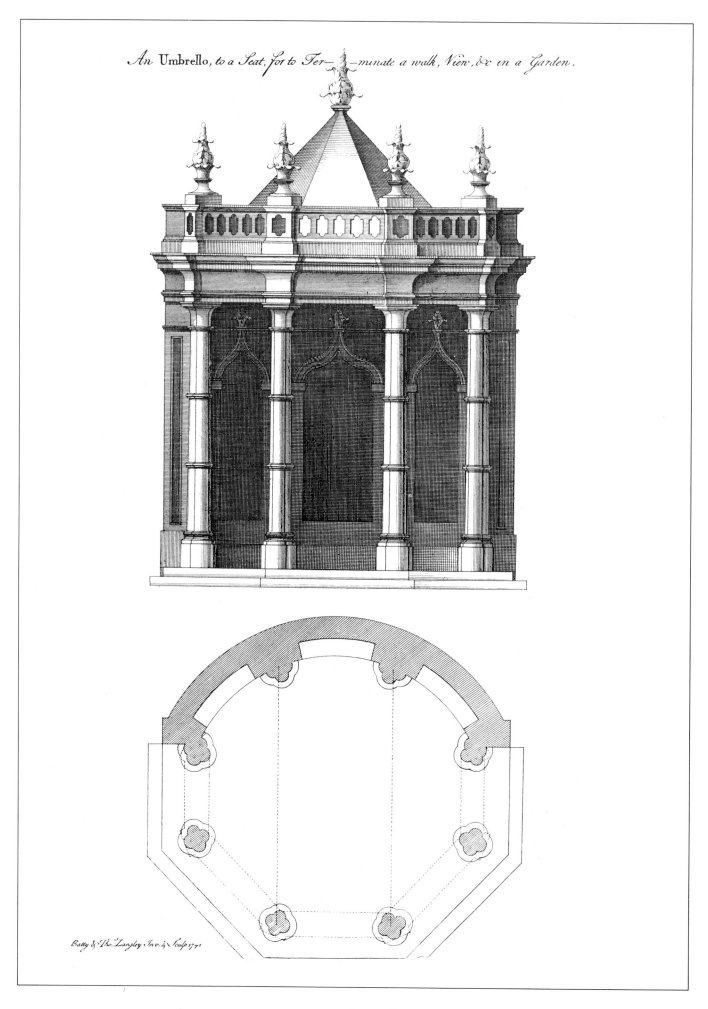

An Umbrello, to a Seat, for to Ter——minate a walk, View, &c in a Garden.

Batty & Tho. Langley Inv. & Sculp 1741

UMBRELLO

Umbrello comes from the Latin *umbra* meaning 'shade'. The Italian *ombrello* was an alternative spelling of umbrella, although it has long been out of use. Umbrelloes were at one time built as umbrella-like canopies over circular seats to supply shade as well as protection from the elements, and were often positioned at a view point. The umbrella canopy was normally made of either tin, wood or canvas.

At Stourhead in Wiltshire the gardens used to include a Chinese umbrello crowned by a pineapple and supported on a central Roman Doric column. Sadly it was demolished quite some time ago. Also no longer in existence, this time through neglect, is the umbrello built as an elegant summer house to the specifications of the Strawberry Hill Committee at Wentworth Castle.

I find it strange that these charming garden features enjoyed such an ephemeral fashion and that they have not been reintroduced. Perhaps it is time. After all, where would we be without the collapsible portable prototypes?

STADDLE STONE

The word 'staddle' comes from the Old English for foundation — *stathol*. Staddle stones always used to be made of stone in the shape and size of 0.6 m (2 ft) high mushrooms. They were originally used for supporting the edges of grain stores to prevent rats from climbing up into them. These days they are used as garden ornaments, often heralding a driveway, and often manufactured in reconstituted cement.

WEATHERVANE

A weathervane is a rotating device to indicate the direction of the wind. One of the first ever recorded weathervanes surmounted the Tower of the Winds in Athens, built by the astronomer Andronicus in the first century B.C. It was in the shape of a Triton, a mythological beast, half man and half fish.

British churches have traditionally always had a cock as a weathervane, as a reminder to the faithful of Peter's denial of Christ. They now come in all shapes and sizes, from witches on broom sticks, to foxes on the run, ships and steam engines. Today they are mostly made of copper or cast aluminium, whereas prior to the 19th century they were hand-crafted in copper sections which were then soldered together and burnished.

Opposite: *A design for an umbrello by Batty and Thomas Langley of 1742.*
Left: *An example of a staddle stone.*
Above: *The famous weathervane at Lord's cricket ground in London, showing Old Father Time.*

REFLECTED GLORY

LAKE
POND/POOL
STREAM/RILL
STEPPING-STONES
FOUNTAIN
CASCADE
BRIDGE
CANAL
MOAT

Left: *Sheffield Park — the magical mirroring effect of water shown at its best on one of 'Capability' Brown's lakes. Sadly, the gales of 1987 have marred this beautiful landscape since the photograph was taken.*

How many times has it been said that water adds an extra dimension to a garden? Even so, it is surely worthy of repetition. Running water adds still more to the picture.

I will always remember my first visit to Versailles. It was a blazingly hot late June day and we had spent some two and a half hours touring the palace while being incessantly jostled by crowds of bored children being dragged round (or perhaps they were doing the dragging) by their teachers. Then, around midday, we stepped out into the boiling heat that was the gardens . . . And not a single one of its famous fountains was playing! The only flowing liquid I saw that day was the cola being dispensed by the many stalls around the parterres, and that went straight down parched throats.

In marked contrast, when I first set foot in the gardens of the Villa Garzoni in Tuscany all the waterworks were playing, the fountains, the cascade and the giant spout from the angel's shell trumpet at its summit. Quite naturally my memories of the latter are far more pleasurable.

Water features take many forms, but they can be reasonably separated into two, informal and formal. The most informal of all are natural rivers, streams and lakes which form part of, or border, gardens. Standing on the terrace at Cliveden, you can see the Thames winding away to your right and without its presence the effect would be by no means so dramatic or beautiful. Its gently flowing waters below you lend a great deal to the pleasure of a stroll as you follow the paths through the wooded escarpment.

It is almost certain that all lakes in gardens have been modified by man — and, in a staggering number of cases, by one man, 'Capability' Brown — but they have, for all that, a gentle air of informality, like the streams which add such charm to the wooded valley of Wakehurst Place. And, however formal the concept behind Japanese water gardens with their interlinking pools, such as those at Cliveden and Compton Acres, the aim is to create an air of relaxed informality.

Formal water gardens, with the exception of castle moats, have come to us from Italy, by way of Holland and France. Their principal features are geometrical pools, fountains, (simple or elaborate), canals and cascades, although there are several splendid examples of informal cascades as well.

One particularly outstanding example of a formal water garden, which does not fit comfortably under any of the following sub-headings, is at Buscot Park in Berkshire. There, between a small formal pool and the lake is a canal walk, a series of square pools interconnected by small cascades, presumably gaining inspiration from stepped canal locks. And, of course, there is the most impressive British example of all, the Water Parterre at Blenheim, below which are two rectangular pools with obelisk centrepieces and beyond them Brown's lake, showing a succession from the most elaborately conceived formality, through simple formality to the contrived informality of the lake, the whole producing a remarkably harmonious effect — a veritable ode to the use of water in gardens.

LAKE

There is something fascinating about a large expanse of water. Somehow a lake soothes the spirit and it is no wonder that the Lake District and the lochs of Scotland attract people in droves to their shores. In 1770 William Whateley wrote: 'In considering the subjects of gardening, ground and wood first present themselves; water is next, which, though not absolutely necessary to a beautiful composition, yet occurs so often, and is so capital a feature, that it is always regretted when wanting; and no large place can be supposed, a little spot can hardly be imagined, in which it may not be agreeable; it accommodates itself to every situation; is the most interesting object in a landscape, and the happiest circumstance in a retired recess; captivates the eye at a distance, invites approach, and is delightful when near; it refreshes an open exposure; it animates a shade; cheers the dreariness of a waste, and enriches the most crowded view: in form, in style and in extent, may be made equal to the greatest compositions, or adapted to the least: it may be spread in a calm expanse to sooth the tranquillity of a peaceful scene; or hurrying

Above right: Stourhead — a print showing the lake and Pantheon, designed by Flitcroft, 1753-4, at a relatively early stage of its development.
Right: Stourhead — the lake, bridge and Pantheon in winter as it can be seen today.

along a devious course, add splendour to a gay, and extravagance to a romantic situation'.

It was during the 17th century that many beautiful artificial lakes were made, one of the most memorable being at Stourhead in Wiltshire. It was created for Henry Hoare II (1705–1785) a couple of decades before 'Capability' Brown began to make his mark in the natural landscape movement. The lake at Stourhead was made by simply damming the river Stour, just as Brown did at Blenheim Palace later in the century by damming the Glyme stream. Both were allowed to fill up along the natural contours of the land, the dams being concealed often behind clumps of trees or hillocks.

Along with Stourhead, which was created from a series of fish pools in what was a bleak valley, and Blenheim, the lakes at Sheffield Park must rank highest in terms of their overall setting. Where Stourhead has only the one and Blenheim two, Sheffield Park has no less than four interconnected by cascades and weirs. Yet again 'Capability' Brown was responsible, if only partially, for their creation, only two of them being attributed to him.

In gardening terms, possibly the greatest tragedy of the gale of October 1987 was the destruction of up to 80 per cent of the astonishing variety of trees which ranged up the slopes of the hills surrounding these lakes, although astonishing efforts are being made to recover the situation. It was not just the stretches of water themselves, but also the trees with their range of colour throughout the year and radiant autumn display, together with their reflections in the placid water, which made the garden a masterpiece of picturesque gardening.

Another outstanding example of Brown's art is at Petworth House, where the serpentine lake around which deer and geese graze, was the subject of many paintings by J. M. W. Turner. Turner was a close friend of the owner, the Third Earl of Egremont, who was a remarkable man for his time and preferred painters and men of letters to politicians.

Luton Hoo, too, is said to be one of his finest achievements, and remains much as he designed it. Here, he created out of the most unpromising of areas two attractive lakes by damming the river Lea in two places.

However much we might now criticize Brown for the destruction of so many formal gardens, it has to be admitted that we also owe

him much. When the balance is weighed, it may well come down in his favour!

Referring back to Petworth, it offers us an interesting case in point, for, with the uninterrupted parkland surrounding the lake, it must be very much as he originally planned it to be. What Brown's contemporaries most disliked about his creations was the nakedness of their shores, as he was very often dealing with flat, or flattened, areas of land, and the owners' desire to be able to see the maximum possible area of water from their houses.

Today we tend to enjoy lakes for the stillness they impart, with the only things to disturb their surface being wildfowl and the occasional leaping fish. Yet this was not always so. Perhaps following on from Louis XIV's penchant for miniature naval battles on the Grand Canal at Versailles, many landowners are known to have kept elaborate barges and sailing ships on their lakes and, indeed, there is one at Longleat now.

At West Wycombe there would appear to have been what we might now refer to as a drunken orgy when the West Portico of the house was dedicated in 1771. The guests are said to have dressed in 'skins wreathed with vine leaves' and repaired to the lake for further merriment, accompanied by 'discharges of cannon' from the boats. I wonder how many of them ended up in the water! At another party held there, the 'captain' of one of the boats was forcibly struck by a large piece of wadding from an opponent's cannon, although how much damage he suffered does not appear to have been recorded.

It has to be said that many lakes are on a far less grand scale and the point when a lake becomes a pond, or *vice-versa*, is ill-defined. Among the many small lakes, of which the choice is almost legion, pleasant ones can be seen at Wakehurst Place, Pusey House and the R.H.S. gardens at Wisley. Some lakes are further enhanced by having small islands in their midst, and on these pavilions or temples were often built. Usually these could only be reached by boat, being perfect havens to adjourn for afternoon tea or other diversions . . .

Examples of this concept are Nicolas Revett's Music Temple at West Wycombe, which was

Left: *Stowe — a winter view of the William Kent-inspired landscape showing the lake and the mansion beyond.*

designed as a setting for *fêtes champêtres*, and the island pavilion at Claremont, which was designed both as an eyecatcher which could only be viewed from certain specific points and as a summer house for fishing parties during the season.

The largest artificial lake in the British Isles is said to be Virginia Water at Windsor, designed by Thomas Sandby during the 1750s. It became larger than originally planned purely by accident, when it was flooded in 1768.

During this and the latter half of the last century most of the 'lakes' built have been reservoirs, Lake Vyrnwy in mid Wales being one of the most renowned. The old and trusted way of using clay to line lakes and ponds on porous soils is still popular, although some of the earliest were made with an army of labourers who firmed straw into the clay with the heels of their boots to stabilize it. This process was called 'puddling in'.

Today many ornamental lakes and ponds are lined with flexible liners, one of the most durable being butyl. It is manufactured in strips which are heat-sealed together where larger areas are to be covered.

∽∾∾∽

POND/POOL

I have always understood ponds to be either informal or natural in appearance, and pools to be formal. The first recorded appearances of either in gardens in Britain were in monastery gardens where they were used as fish-ponds, fish (and especially carp) being a particularly important source of food throughout the year. Fish-ponds spread into the gardens of the nobility in Tudor times, an existing example being at Newstead Abbey, Nottinghamshire, below the lake and Abbey. Again, these were used as a source of food, with pike being added to carp in order to widen the menu.

Leaving fish-ponds in Britain momentarily, we must fly to Italy. There, water-dominated terraced gardens were proliferating towards the end of the 15th century, the lowest of the terraces playing host to formal, usually round, pools with fountain centrepieces. A surviving example exists at the Villa Garzoni in Tuscany, where twin circular pools are the principal features of the wide areas at the foot of the terraces. This fashion spread to Britain and

Top: *Barnsley House — the formal water-lily pool backed by the Doric temple summer house.*
Above: *Hidcote — a view through a hedge door to the bathing pool garden, showing the pool with central statue.*

pools became decorative features. (It was not for almost another two centuries that the goldfish was introduced from the Far East.)

As with all the other elements of such formal gardens, myriads of these pools were swept away as 'Capability' Brown and his followers landscaped our great estates, so it is rare to find pools dating back to before the 18th century which have not been considerably modified. Even at Montacute, which is the most complete example of an Elizabethan garden, the sunken pond in the lawn with its obelisk-finial decorated balustrades matching those which run round its ancient walls, was in actual fact designed by R. S. Balfour in 1894, some 300 years after the originals were built. Another deceptive pool is that in the centre of the parterre at Penshurst Place, which is an essential part of the reconstruction of a 17th century garden design.

As an indication of how fashions can change I can do no better than quote Francis Bacon who, writing in 1625, said, 'Pools mar all and make the garden unwholesome and full of flies and frogs'. Today we are encouraged by conservationists to build pools in our gardens, as a breeding place for frogs which feed on the flies! Oddly, in the same quote Bacon also said, 'for fountains, they are a great beauty and refreshment', giving the impression that fountains and pools were not inseparable in his mind.

Every beautiful garden now has its pools and the following selection is purely arbitrary. With a surround of castellated yew hedges which are reflected in it, that at Knightshayes is simple, but exceptionally attractive; at Easton Neston, Northamptonshire, a bow-shaped *pièce d'eau* is fronted by hedges of golden yew which curl in Archimedean spirals. This is backed by curved hedges in the niches of which stand busts on pillars, the centre of the hedge being cut out to provide a vista across an informal stretch of water and the countryside beyond.

At Barnsley House Garden a Doric Temple summer house is reflected in the water of an almost informal pool covered in water lilies; at Hidcote a circular swimming pool is raised to waist height to bring the reflections of the sky and surrounding hedges closer to eye level; and at Sutton Place, Ben Nicolson's 'White Reliefs', a giant realization in white Carrara marble, is reflected in an unusual shaped pool of widening rectangles set within one another.

One of the most unusual features of some pools, often in a secluded part of the garden, is either a bathing area or bath-house, which were used precisely for that purpose by members of the household or their staff. One

Above: *Easton Neston — the formal circular pool with its yew hedge surround and statuary.*

such, at Wrest Park, has only quite recently been restored, and is constructed of irregularly shaped stones. There is also one at Packwood. At Rousham, in a glade dedicated to Venus with its small informal ponds and cascades, is an ice-cold bath, the overflow from which feeds the rill.

A particularly attractive informal pond, which is used to display a wide selection of bog and water plants, is to be seen at Bressingham Hall, the home of the Blooms; while at Crittenden in Kent an old cattle pond has been transformed into the central feature of the garden.

❧❧❧

STREAM/RILL

STREAM

The simplest form of flowing water is a natural stream and if a garden has the luck to be blessed with one, it can be its most soothing of features. They are particularly to be found in the Victorian 'wild' plantation gardens which were often planted on valley slopes to protect the many exotic trees and shrubs being introduced by the collectors who ranged so widely at that time. A small stream, for example, runs down the Slips, a steep-sided wooded valley at Wakehurst Place, forming at one point a small pond which plays host to numerous water plants. On a hot summer day it is an ideal spot at which to pause and contemplate.

At Bodnant the Dell is formed by the valley of the tiny River Hiraethlyn, a tributary of the Conway. Some apparently natural streams, however, are in fact the work of man, an outstanding example being at Burford House where there is a stream garden, with water being drawn from the River Tame which flows past the garden.

A muddy stream has always flowed through the valley where Hodnet Hall in Shropshire stands, but it has been excavated into a series of lakes, cascades and streams around which plants such as gunnera and astilbes proliferate, giving it a beautifully contrived 'natural' appearance.

RILL

A rill frequently flaunts its unnaturalness. It is a small channel, built of stone or concrete down which water flows, and it is often used as a connecting link between other water features.

Above: *Wrest Park — the restored bath house, constructed of irregularly shaped stones.*
Right: *Wakehurst Place — a view of the stream, in what is now an offshoot of the Royal Botanic Gardens, Kew.*

Sometimes they are camouflaged to look natural, but the majority are positively formal. They are said to have originated in Moorish courtyards and been developed from irrigation channels.

An outstanding example is the winding rill, designed by William Kent, which flows through the octagonal pool at Rousham, then leads you through a woodland walk.

Sir Geoffrey Jellicoe used rills extensively in his garden designs, one example being at Shute House, Wiltshire. With Kent as his inspiration, here the rill flows down through a series of octagonal pools and small cascades, one of the pools having a bubbling fountain worked by gravity (an idea learnt from Kashmir gardens). Jellicoe was always an ardent searcher for ideas, drawing together many disparate art forms and eras, and producing harmonious effects overall.

Above: *Hestercombe — the rill by Lutyens running from the wall pool. This is a concept he developed from the ideas of Gertrude Jekyll.*

STEPPING-STONES

Stepping-stones are one of the simplest and most appealing means of effecting the crossing of a pond, pool or shallow stream. Today we tend to associate them particularly with Japanese water gardens and there is more than one set of them crossing the ponds at Compton Acres in the area around the Imperial Tea House.

However, they have also been adapted by designers such as Sir Geoffrey Jellicoe, the designer of the canal at Wisley R.H.S. garden. The garden for which he was responsible at Sutton Place contains two very different modern examples of the genre. Formal paving slabs on top of stones cross the moat by the east facade, introducing the element of risk that needs to be taken to reach the Paradise Garden; while circular stepping-stones lead to a swimming raft in the centre of the swimming pool, the design of which has inspired by the works of the painter Joan Miro, the pool being known as the 'Miro Mirror'.

Preston Park Rockery, Brighton, has what can only be described as stepping-rocks — they being of considerable size — which make it possible to cross the pool with a reasonable sense of security to admire the goldfish.

FOUNTAIN

The word 'fountain' is derived from the Latin *fontana*, meaning 'pertaining to a spring'. The first fountains, therefore, were purely utilitarian, as a source of water supply which, over the centuries, has evolved into a hydraulic engineering art of the most sophisticated kind.

First let us concentrate on Italy where the same historical pattern emerges of ancient Roman architectural landscaping skills copied, and being indeed further embellished upon, by planners and designers during the Italian Renaissance era. As was so often the case, it was France who stole ideas from Italy, and these slowly filtered through into England.

In the gardens of Italy, during the time of the ancient Romans, water was most usefully exploited by creating various narrow water channels which would supply water for

functional purposes. Homer described such a canal network in *The Garden of Alcinous:*

> 'The plenteous fountains the whole
>   prospect crown'd;
> This through the garden leads its
>   streams around,
> Visits each plant, and waters all ground:
> While that in pipes beneath the palace
>   flows,
> And thence its current on the town
>   bestows;
> To various use their various streams
>   they bring,
> The people one, and one supplies the
>   King.'

Such water channels can easily be identified in the ruins of Pompeii.

But back to Renaissance Italy, where some of the most fantastic fountains were built, not surprisingly perhaps as the countryside surrounding both Rome and Florence is rich in natural springs. In 1429 a manuscript was found in the library of the monastery of Monte Cassino. It was called *De aquis urbis Romae* and had been written by a Roman Commissioner of Water, Sextus Julius Frontinus, during the first century A.D. It contained detailed instructions of the plumbing of fountains, which the Medici princes were the first to put into practice.

At the Villa de Castello, laid out in 1540 for Cosimo I, the central feature in the garden was a tall, three-tiered fountain surmounted by a statue of a woman wringing her hair. Fountains of this kind further inspired landscape architects when building the several magnificent villas of the era such as d'Este and Aldobrandini. Many gardens also included aquatic practical jokes which soaked unsuspecting visitors as they walked around the garden. How awful for them.

Above: *Compton Acres — stepping stones crossing one of the interlinked ponds in the Japanese garden, with an Acer palmatum displaying its autumn plumage.*
Overleaf: *Cliveden — the marble Fountain of Love by Ralph Waldo Story, made in 1897.*

All this flowing water did, however, create problems. One of the greatest of all Italian water gardens, which was famed throughout Europe, was at Pratolino on the old road to Bologna north of Florence. A lunette by Utens (1599) gives some idea of the extent of the waterworks as seen from above, but its water-powered mechanical grottoes under the terraces adjoining the villa come down to us only from the descriptions of fascinated visitors. The problem was that all this flowing water eventually undermined the foundations of the villa and it had to be knocked down in the 19th century. All the waterworks, with the exception of the pool which fronts Giambologna's gigantic 'Giant of the Apennines', were destroyed at the same time.

Italian fountains were admired and copied extensively, but as there were so few other suitable sites in Europe where the water pressure matched that of the Italian hillsides, they seldom had quite the same effect.

One such exception is the sheer magnificence of the fountains at Versailles. Louis XIV, or the 'Sun King' as he later became known, spent over 50 years planning the since unrivalled gardens at Versailles, where one of the most fantastic fountains was designed for his favourite mistress, Madame de Montespan. It consisted of a huge metal tree that spurted water from every branch; and it sat in a rectangular pool lined on the outside with metal bulrushes from which jets of water also sprang.

Some of the very oldest fountains to exist in Europe today are found in Spain. These were built by the Arabs who invaded Spain in the 8th century, and who brought with them styles of fountains from other countries they had vanquished, most notably Persia. One of the most outstanding of these early fountains still in existence is that in the Lion Court at Alhambra. A single jet of water tumbles down into a huge alabaster bowl encircled by marble lions below, and from their mouths pours the water which in turn feeds the channels which radiate out from it.

In England there certainly existed fountains in gardens during the reign of Elizabeth I, but, generally speaking, during the 17th and 18th centuries they remained small and formal. The 'Emperor Fountain' at Chatsworth broke the conventional mould. It was built in 1844 in honour of the Czar's visit to Chatsworth. Sadly,

he never got there to admire the 88 m (290 ft) high jet emerging from an informal rock outcrop in the Canal Pond, but it still exists to delight visitors today. Also at Chatsworth is the Willow Tree Fountain, a smaller but nonetheless exciting alternative to Madame de Montespan's tree fountain at Versailles.

Other fountains which are well worth a specific mention include the great marble Fountain of Love, by Ralph Waldo Story, at Cliveden (1895), with its several naked maidens on a scallop shell supported by rocks; the Atlas Fountain at Castle Howard, acquired by the Seventh Earl of Carlisle at the Great Exhibition of 1851, and installed in the centre of the South Parterre; and that at Ascott

Above: *Chatsworth — the Willow Tree Fountain, the successor of the first Duke of Devonshire's original. Spurting water from its copper branches traps the unwary, and the dell in which it sits is surrounded by powerful jets.*
Above right: *Ascott — the Venus Fountain designed by Ralph Waldo Story.*

depicting a life-size Venus on a shell drawn by sea-horses and attended by winged Cupids, together with a boy struck by one of their arrows. Also, at Blenheim, one of the many works of Achille Duchêne — the spectacular gilded dolphins, supporting a great bowl, in the centre of which stands a lady whose flowing gilded robe fails to cover her nakedness and who holds high a gilded crown from which water plays. In addition, the extensive group of Italian Renaissance-style statuary, each an individual fountain, in the formal pool which is the focal point of the South Front Terrace at Waddesdon Manor; and such fancies as a boy being eaten by a dolphin at Buscot Park and a snake at Sezincote in Gloucestershire.

In humbler surroundings, the Victorians were very keen on fountains and the *nouveau riche* were responsible for many springing up in suburban gardens the length and breadth of the country.

Today, of course, they are as popular as ever as garden features, although many sold at garden centres and the like are a little alarming — I'm thinking particularly of the two children sheltering under the dripping umbrella — but there we are. You may like the idea of water bubbling up through an old mill stone and draining away through the gravel bed below, or indeed the Brussels Boy doing what comes naturally into your pond, but what is simpler or more effective than a single jet of water spurting up in the centre of a circular pool?

❧

CASCADE

Cascade is the alternative word used both in French and English for waterfall. Cascades can take on varying shapes and sizes, both formal and informal. The ancient Romans were recorded as having formal cascades which flowed down marble steps into a pool below, fed at the top by a wall fountain. The most splendid formal cascade in England is at Chatsworth House in Derbyshire, built for the First Duke of Devonshire during the late 17th

century by Grillet, a pupil of le Nôtre. It is precision built with 24 steps, each 7.2 m (24 ft) wide, so that the water runs evenly down each. Like all the other waterworks there, it is gravity-fed from a series of lakes on higher ground. A temple built in 1703 stands on the top of the cascade where dolphins spew, fountains sprout and the stepped, domed roof becomes another cascade. Behind the temple another cascade runs over a bridge under which a road was built in the 19th century for coal wagons to fuel Paxton's Great Conservatory. At the base of the formal cascade the water disappears into the ground, only later to feed further fountains before it again goes underground to drain into the river.

The Chatsworth cascade is very much in keeping with d'Argenville's ideas for the construction of cascades which he said should be elaborated with 'sheets, bubblings, mushrooms, sheafs, spouts, surges, candlesticks, grills, tapers, crosses and vaulted arches of water . . . maritime ornaments as artificial ice, congelations, petrifyings . . . and Naiades, tritons, serpents, sea-horses, dragons, dolphins, griffins and frogs, which are made to vomit and throw out streams and torrents of water'.

Natural fountains or cascades have always fascinated man. It is hard to emulate the skilful hand of Mother Nature but the Hon. Charles Hamilton did an admirable job at Bowood in Wiltshire. There, once 'Capability' Brown had created the lake, Hamilton was asked to build a cascade, no doubt because his own at Painshill in Surrey had been so admired. It is a masterful example of how an informal cascade or waterfall should look: it could have been transported stone by stone from some moorland crag. What is particularly clever about it is that the separate falls of water fan out towards the bottom. The water can be controlled by a sluice gate from the lake, enabling you to have anything from a gentle trickle to a furious torrent.

Above: *Chatsworth — looking down the great stepped formal cascade by Grillet, from the Cascade House to the house itself.*
Above right: *Belton House — an early painting of the cascades, which sadly no longer exist.*

A large cascade can always be built in a modern garden but you will need a sizeable pump to continue recycling the same water unless you are lucky enough to have a natural supply. A smaller submersible pump will be strong enough to circulate water to the top of a small stream, interrupted by small cascades. The pump is normally positioned in the pond at the bottom of the cascading stream, and the whole feature could be lined with a flexible butyl liner, being very careful to disguise its edges with stones and plants.

❧

BRIDGE

The word 'bridge' derives from the Old English *brycg*, and the Old Norse *bryggia*.

Bridges have of course been around for a very long time, perhaps the most romantic example of all being the drawbridge as a means of access to a house over a surrounding moat. Quite a number can still be seen today in many parts of East Anglia, Warwickshire and else-

where, such as Hever Castle in Kent.

One of the finest classical bridges is found at Chatsworth House in Derbyshire. It was designed by James Paine in 1762 on the instructions of the Fourth Duke of Devonshire, as part of his plans to relandscape the old formal gardens. It consists of three large arches and is decorated by classical balustrades and statues on its piers. At least this bridge performs a useful function as part of the drive, which is more than can be said of the Grand Bridge at Blenheim Palace, begun in 1710.

Although it acts as a part of the vista running on towards the Column of Victory, the Grand Bridge is used only as a pedestrian walkway. It is 31 m (101 ft) long and was designed by Sir John Vanbrugh, who also designed the palace itself. Of all the famous bridges in Britain this one must have had the most chequered history. It was originally designed to be much taller, with an arcaded superstructure and drumhead finials, but it looks none the worse without them. At first it spanned a rather unimaginatively designed straight canal with a round lake or basin at one end. This luckily

disappeared when 'Capability' Brown flooded the area by damming the Glyme stream, resulting in the two huge lakes we know today, but semi-submerging the bridge in the process. As Brown's biographer, Dorothy Stroud, put it, 'If these two lakes had been designed as one vast expanse of water the effect would have been tedious. As it is they are both united by Vanbrugh's bridge from which the two parts spread out like the loops of a nicely tied bow'.

Humphry Repton, in his book *Art of Landscape Gardening* describes how a bridge spanning the junction of two lakes, can create the appearance of a river, 'To preserve the idea of a river, nothing is so effectual as a bridge; instead of dividing the water on each side, it always tends to lengthen its continuity by showing the impossibility of crossing it by any other means provided the ends are well concealed'. (By the 'ends' he was referring to the far reaches of the lakes). This certainly describes the effect that Brown so admirably achieved.

Of all the classical bridges in Britain, perhaps the platinum medal should go to the Palladian Bridge at Wilton House in Wiltshire. It was built between 1735 and 1737 by Henry Herbert, Ninth Earl of Pembroke, with the assistance of Roger Morris, after the designs of the Italian 16th century architect Andrea Palladio. It spans the river Nadder which was diverted and widened to accommodate it. It boasts an Ionic colonnade with small temples at either end, and there is something magical about its proportions.

These and other magnificent classical bridges must have spurred on J. C. Loudon in his *Encyclopaedia of Gardening* (1834) to say, 'The Bridge is one of the grandest decorations of garden scenery'.

It was during the 17th and 18th centuries that many other styles of bridge became part of the landscape. All things Chinese became fashionable, and as a result many beautiful and intricate bridges *à la Chinois* were built in wood and stone. Moorish and gothic styles also

Above left: Blenheim — Vanbrugh's bridge, going nowhere in particular and half drowned by 'Capability' Brown's lake.
Left: Stowe — the Palladian Bridge at the head of the octagon lake. Note the piered balustrade and Ionic colonnade.

became popular. After the Treaty of Nanking there followed a similar fashion in everything Japanese. As a result Japanese gardens with bridge-spanned water features appeared all over the place. Excellent examples can be seen at Compton Acres near Bournemouth and at Tatton Park in Cheshire. At the Japanese garden at Heale House in Wiltshire there is a good example of a Nikko bridge painted in the customary red, with a large *Magnolia soulangiana* arching its graceful boughs into the water next to it — Willow Pattern brought to life, but even better!

Rustic bridges were also built extensively during this period, many of them being extremely intricate in design. They were very popular with the Victorians as well.

Lastly, a particular style of bridge I have always admired, but seen all too rarely, is a turf bridge, linking lawns. It means more work during its construction but can make an extremely effective feature.

CANAL

In the architectural landscape meaning of the word a canal is a long, rectangular, formal stretch of water. In Britain many such formal canals were built during the reign of William and Mary, no doubt as William brought the idea over from Holland.

Formal canals were built on a grand scale at Versailles designed by André le Nôtre, the most impressive being the one which starts at the foot of the Grande Allée, and stretches for 1.6 km (1 mile). It is shaped into a cross and the side arms lead to the Menagerie to the south and the Trianon to the north. At its far end it spreads out into a square port.

Although it is not known for certain that le Nôtre actually stepped foot onto British soil, he certainly had a strong influence over some British landscape architects of the time. Charles II apparently fell under his spell when he built the 1.2 km (¾ mile) long canal at Hampton Court, as well as the avenue-lined canal which once ran the length of St. James's Park. The fashion soon spread throughout the country and one of the first to be built in a private garden was at Westbury Court between 1696 and 1705. At Frampton Court on the opposite bank of the nearby river Severn there

exists a charming, if a little neglected, 'Dutch' formal canal with a Strawberry Hill 'Gothic' orangery reflected at one end.

The reflective qualities of these canals, like huge mirrors laid flat on the ground, must have been one of the reasons which inspired landscape architects to first build them. They were built continuously throughout the Victorian and Edwardian eras; indeed Gertrude Jekyll often included one in her designs.

They are still popular garden features today, often positioned opposite a much-used, groundfloor window to further enhance the symmetry of a house. One could well suit your garden but it must be to scale with its surroundings.

MOAT

A moat is a deep trench usually found surrounding a castle or fortified house to keep out uninvited visitors. They are nearly always filled with water, and during mediaeval times and before, were also used to protect livestock from marauders. These days many moats have been incorporated into the design of the gardens where they are often used as formal canals.

The moat at Hampton Court was filled in during the reign of Charles II, but Hever Castle in Kent boasts an inner and outer moat, beautifully restored by William Waldorf Astor at the turn of this century, and now playing host to a spectacular mass of water lilies.

Helmingham Hall in Suffolk, the seat of the Tollemache family since the 15th century, is another splendid example, where two drawbridges are pulled up every night, as they have been since 1510. Helmingham also has a smaller but much earlier moat which surrounds the walled garden. The moat around the house is 18 m (60 ft) wide and is now stocked with several kinds of fish including large pike. Moats were most often built in parts of the country where there existed a high water table, such as East Anglia.

Above: Buscot Park — Harold Peto's highly individual canal walk, one of the most distinctive of all the water features.

One of the most pleasant of all moats surrounds Ightham Mote in Kent. With it we have one of the many confusions with which the English language abounds. One could be forgiven for thinking that Mote was an earlier spelling of moat, but this is not so. It is an alternative spelling of moot, the local council which met in one of the most significant and prosperous houses of the neighbourhood, and is an indication of the antiquity of the house, which exhibits beautiful 14th century half timbering and stone. Connected with it is a particularly pleasant legend that, being a Royalist stronghold, Cromwell's soldiers were determined upon destroying it but they got lost on the way and destroyed another house of lesser value in its stead!

I think that if I were rich, with a valuable collection of furniture and so on, I would be tempted to build a moat around a suitably positioned house. Large mechanical diggers would do the job very nicely and a tough flexible liner such as butyl would make an excellent job of keeping it water-tight if the soil proved porous. On a practical note, care would have to be taken with underground pipes and

cables, but I do not see these problems as insurmountable. Just imagine by how much your insurance premiums would be reduced!

Top: *Scotney Castle — the 14th century moat and castle seen in springtime.*
Above: *Ightham Mote — an engraving of the moat in 1894.*

GIRDLE
OF STONE

PLANTING WALL
BEE-BOLE
CLAIR-VOYÉE
MOON WINDOW
HEATED WALL
CRINKLE-CRANKLE

Left: *Edzell Castle — the planting wall laid out by Sir David Lindsay in 1604. It is thought that the niches in the walls were once used either as nesting boxes or bee-boles.*

Stone is the age-old, wall-building material but bricks have been around for many thousands of years. Earth, mud, chalk or cob (clay and straw) were also old and traditional building materials for walls.

Walls were, originally, defensive structures designed to keep out marauders and they are still sometimes built for that purpose today. Even in this enlightened age, we are sadly still afflicted by vandals. The use of walls in gardening, however, would seem to have originated in mediaeval monasteries where they surrounded and protected the vegetable gardens. At the time of the dissolution, during Henry VIII's reign, the era of 'British Garden Naissance', most of these monasteries passed into the hands of the nobility. Brick walled-in gardens were first built extensively as they complied with the grander fashions of the day. Sadly many succumbed to 'Capability' Brown's bulldozer mentality, and here I think anyone would be justified in calling him a vandal. Luckily some survived, mellow and weathered as they are now.

The bricks used during the Tudor era were around one-third thinner than the modern brick of today; an altogether neater shape. Throughout the centuries efforts were made to further enhance the bricks by glazing, carving and even embossing them. Their colour too was often subtly changed by varying the composition of the clay. During those early days patterns were often introduced into walls by contrasting the occasional black one with the terracotta, a technique still used sometimes (and not often enough) today.

It is both as a support for, and a background to, plants or sculpture that walls really come into their own as decorative, rather than purely functional, elements of a garden. To walk through the entrance of Sissinghurst Castle and see the beautiful herbaceous borders with roses and other climbers clambering up the walls behind them, is a constant delight; and those protecting the rose garden at Kinross House are equally memorable, particularly when the roses are in full, glorious bloom. At Hever Castle a wall is used as the background for William Waldorf Astor's large collection of Roman statuary, but I find the example at Pusey House, Berkshire more to my taste. Here curving walls of rusticated stone have decorated niches which play host to marble busts on truncated columns, the whole effect being delightfully harmonious.

In truth, almost every garden has its walls, these being only a few random examples. You may well find, or have found already, your own particular favourite.

Finally, kitchen garden walls, many of them built by the Victorians, still remain, but sadly are mostly neglected and forlorn. This I find strange considering we live in an age of conservation (sadly, not conversation), but one day some bright spark will find a less labour-intensive use for them.

❧

PLANTING WALL

Planting walls are best built of either stone or brick which incorporate pockets of soil for planting. In a stone planting wall each stone is laid at a slight gradient to encourage water to percolate in towards the plants' roots, so giving the face of the wall an irregular, rustic appearance. On brick planting walls, slates are often placed under each soil pocket for the same reason. These walls are sometimes built with a shaft of soil down the centre from top to bottom, with gravel at the base to encourage efficient drainage.

The deep rose-coloured sandstone walls surrounding the beautifully restored 'pleasance' at Edzell Castle in Angus are not I suspect, true planting walls, for the patterns of square holes decorating them may originally have been designed for nesting boxes. However authorities differ on the matter since some do claim that they were specifically designed for the planting of flowers. Either way, it is gratifying to know that flowers, not bird droppings, tumble from them today.

❧

BEE-BOLE

From Tudor times right up until the 19th century, either arched or square niches, or 'bee-boles', were built into south-facing walls near to the ground. They were normally about 0.6 m (2 ft) wide and 1 m (3 ft) high, and acted as shelters for the old straw bee-skeps before modern wooden hives were introduced. These old skeps were very fragile and needed some sort of special protection from the elements,

particularly rain. Though now obsolete, bee-boles remain as conversation pieces, or the home of a treasured ornament.

There exists a fine example of a series of bee-boles on either side of the well known wrought iron gates at Packwood in Warwickshire.

❧

CLAIR-VOYÉE

A *clair-voyée*, as the literal translation from the French suggests, is an opening (normally in a wall), through which the view is extended on further to some other feature on the landscape, such as a church steeple. They were often positioned at the end of walks.

These openings always contained an iron work, often very elaborate, grille, good examples of which can be seen at Portmeirion in north Wales. There exists a fine example of a 'stretched' clair-voyée at Hampton Court which really looks like a series of what we know today as iron railings, but interrupted by elaborate piers.

The fashion for clairs-voyées came to England during the reign of William III, from Holland. J. C. Loudon in his *Encyclopaedia of Gardening*, (1834) says: 'King William [III] . . . gave vogue to clipt yews, with magnificent gates and rails of iron, not infrequent in Holland, and about this time . . . introduced

into France, and, in reference to the opaque stone walls which they supplanted, called them clairs-voyées'.

Other good examples of clairs-voyées can be seen at Wotton House, Buckinghamshire; Easton Neston, Northamptonshire, and Syon House, Middlesex.

Top: *Packwood House — the wrought-iron gates built in the middle of the 17th century, flanked on either side by bee boles built into the walls.*
Above: *Huntercombe Manor — a wrought-iron clair-voyée grille.*

MOON WINDOW

A moon window is a perfectly circular opening in a wall, varying in size, sometimes built as a round gate. You nearly always see brick moon windows (in brick walls) as they are more easily built than in stone.

The Japanese often built moon windows through which a carefully trained plant, often a conifer, would emerge. A moon window is a most attractive feature to suit practically all garden designs. Its secret of success lies in its shape; the most simple of geometric lines.

Excellent examples of moon windows can be seen at Polesden Lacey. Here the viewer looking through them into the walled garden has his eye drawn to a male statue from one, and an astrolabe from another, the circular frame being effective for both. There is also another lovely example at Biddestone Manor, Chippenham, which is especially striking at wisteria time.

At West Green House in Hampshire there is a spectacular example of a modern interpretation of a moon window, this being a moon gate through which even the tallest can pass. Looking from the *jardin potager*, it frames an eye-catcher in the form of an open temple.

HEATED WALL

It had long been known that tender plants, particularly exotic stone fruits, could be best grown on south-facing walls, but in the early 18th century the invention of so-called 'hot walls' helped greatly in that they prevented the damage that late frosts could cause to the blossom.

It would appear that the first heated outdoor walls were built in 1718, but the earliest surviving one, at Packwood, was designed in 1723. These original hot walls were heated by means of flues set in the brickwork which were connected to charcoal stoves. At Packwood what appears at first sight to be an unusual gazebo set at the corner of two walls is, in fact, the old furnace house.

Later Victorian examples had cast-iron pipes built into the walls and the water which circulated through them was heated by coke boilers, which were also discreetly hidden.

The elaborate 'hot water wall' at Shrubland Hall in Suffolk, although no longer heated in this way and with the boiler long gone, still stands as a magnificent memorial to this era.

Left: Polesden Lacey — a moon window through which is framed a discus thrower in the centre of the lavender garden.
Right: Packwood House — the gazebo-like furnace house in a corner of the heated walls, designed in 1723.

CRINKLE-CRANKLE

This is the name given to wavy or serpentine walls, also called 'ribbon' walls. In Europe they were built mainly in Holland, where they are known as *Slangemuren* ('snake walls'). At least 14 are recorded there, and in England they are found mostly in East Anglia and the South West. Outside Europe the best known are at the University of Virginia, Charlottesville, built by Thomas Jefferson in 1826.

It is not clear when the word 'crinkle-crankle' came into common usage. The dictionary definition of the word 'crinkle' is 'to twist . . . curl' and the word crankle, 'a turn, winding . . . to bend', and they are listed separately. 'Crinkle-crankle' could have evolved from 'crinkum-crankum', meaning 'intricate or crooked', through either phonetic mispronunciation, or perhaps intentional pun.

Why were they built? Well, in a climate as uncertain as that of the British Isles, every effort was made to find the most effective method of ripening fruit grown out of doors. Plant hunters were continually bringing new and 'exotic' fruits home to our shores. John Tradescant the Elder, introduced the apricot from the Algerian coast as early as 1621, for example, and few could afford to build stove houses or conservatories, never mind run to the cost of heating them. Peaches and figs were two other fruits which benefited from the protection of a wall, especially in inland areas. It is possible that the thinking behind their construction was to create a microclimate in each of the concave recesses where heat was trapped to promote the ripening process. The length of planting space was also increased.

As far back as 1594 Sir Hugh Platt, who lived at Bishop's Hall in Bethnal Green, compiled a book of 'experiments' which he chose to call *The Jewel House of Art and Nature*. In 1608 Platt wrote 'Quince growing against a wall lying open to the sunne and defended from colde windes eate most delicately; This secret my Lord Darcie brought out of Italy'. In a later edition of his book *The Garden of Eden* there is a description of how Sir Francis Walsingham 'caused divers Aprococke [*sic*] trees to be planted against a south wall' with their 'branches trained like vines'. As a result it was claimed that the fruit ripened some three weeks earlier than those on orchard trees owing to the reflection of the sun. Also mentioned in this book is a description of growing fruit which possibly could have conceived the crinkle-crankle: 'If every tree were planted in a Tabernacle, or such concave as were aptest for the receiving and reflecting of

the Sun-Beams upon the fruit . . .'.

Perhaps the most surprising facts about a crinkle-crankle wall are that it is longer lasting and requires less bricks than a normal straight wall, so long as it doesn't exceed a certain height. It is more stable because of its shape and this meant that it could be built the thickness of a half-brick, whereas a straight wall has to be built one brick thick, with additional piers. J. C. Loudon in his *Encyclopaedia of Gardening*, published by Longman, Hurst, Rees and Brown in 1834 describes this clearly: 'The wavy or serpentine wall has two avowed objects; first the saving of bricks, as a wall in which the centres of the segments composing the line are 15 ft apart may be safely carried 15 ft high and only 9 in in thickness from the foundations; and a 4 in wall may be built 7 ft high on the same plan. The next proposed advantage is shelter from all winds in the direction of the wall . . . '. Most writers of the day agreed that serpentine walls should run from west to east.

Those for whom money was no object nearly always settled for a conventional, or straight wall, so it could be said that the crinkle-crankle was the 'poor man's wall'. They were usually built in the gardens of small manor houses and rectories. However this was not always the case. At Heveningham Hall in Suffolk, which as I write is in a sad state of decline under the ownership of an absentee Arab landlord, there exists a splendid wavy wall. Two other good examples include a 5 m (17 ft) high beauty at West Horsley Place in Surrey and another at the Everton Court Hotel, Lymington.

During the latter half of the 18th century, when crinkle-crankle walls were being built in sizeable numbers, some thought that the advantages of the trapped heat in the recesses were outweighed by the damage caused to outer tender shoots by strong winds which rebounded from side to side. Designs for angular, zig-zag and square fret walls were drawn up but seldom if ever built. Half-circle walls were however built; one exists at Wraxall Abbey.

It would make a pleasant change to see a few crinkle-crankles being built today. After all, we have already gleaned from the above that they are cheaper to build than straight walls.

Left: *A splendid example of a crinkle-crankle wall, also known as a serpentine or 'ribbon' wall.*

PATTERNS
FOR
PLEASURE

STEPS

TERRACE

BALUSTRADE

PARTERRE/KNOT GARDEN

POTAGER/HERB GARDEN

MOUNT

BOSKET

QUINCUNX

SUNKEN GARDEN

EXEDRA

PLANT SCULPTURE

HEDGE · MAZE/LABYRINTH · TOPIARY
ESPALIER · CORDON · FAN
PLEACH · PLASHING

TUNNEL

TRELLISWORK/TREILLAGE

PERGOLA

ARBOUR

SEAT

AVIARY

TROMPE L'OEIL

HA-HA

BOWLING GREEN/
CROQUET LAWN

PATH

PATTE D'OIE

ROND-POINT/RONDEL

AMPHITHEATRE

ALLÉE/AVENUE/VISTA

In this final chapter we bring together those features of a garden which are designed to lead you through it, to display it to its best effect or purely to please the eye. Until this point, flowers and plants have merited only an occasional passing mention, but henceforward they gain in prominence. For what would a parterre be without its flowers, an avenue without its trees, or a maze without its hedges? And it is here that we meet our greatest' problem — what to include and what to exclude?

The Victorian formal garden was developed from, and is often still referred to as, the parterre, which leads into the formal rose garden with its arched pergolas. Sunken gardens, hedges and topiary lead to the single-coloured and theme gardens of those, say, at Sissinghurst and Hidcote. Paths pass between massed herbaceous borders or climb over rockeries. The cut-off point we have selected is purely arbitrary — where we believe that the flowers themselves so dominate the feature as to be the most significant part of it. There is, almost certainly, more than sufficient material for a book of similar length using such discarded subject matter.

⌒⋙⌒

STEPS

Steps are one of the easily ignored features of a garden. Unless we have the misfortune to be physically disabled, when even the shortest flight can represent an impenetrable obstacle, if we perceive them at all it is as a means to an end and no more.

A short flight may lead us through a wall or balustrade down to a formal or sunken garden; longer, balustraded flights from terrace to terrace; or rough-hewn ones will guide us into the peace of a wooded valley through which a stream meanders. Yet on a hot summer day, when our explorations have taken us to the furthest limits of the garden, we may find ourselves confronted with having to climb tier after tier to get back to the house and a cup of tea. At this point, even the fittest of us will now

Previous pages: *Shrubland Hall — the great terraced staircase designed by Sir Charles Barry in the early 19th century, and styled after the one at the Villa d'Este.*

notice those steps; and suddenly to be confronted by the 93 log-edged steps which climb through Winkworth Arboretum, even in the autumn when the Japanese maples lining them are in full, glorious, colour, can come as a more than mild shock to the system.

Yet steps in themselves can be an attractive feature; a lovely example of a relatively untesting flight being the brick ones at Chilham Castle in Kent. At Haddon Hall the stone steps with ball-capped balustrades, which lead us down to the pool-centred rose garden, could hardly be more perfectly proportioned in length and breadth. Edwin Lutyens' circular steps at Great Dixter in East Sussex are pure inspiration.

Yet it is probably the more majestic that remain longer in the memory and of these, the steps at Luton Hoo are an outstanding example, a great curving sweep leading us down from the house onto the upper terrace. They may not be the Spanish Steps, but they are mightily impressive all the same.

The steps at the Villa Garzoni in Tuscany are splendid. Their great advantage is that as you enter the garden from the bottom, you are able to climb the terraces before the day warms up. That means of course, that you need only to descend them to leave the garden. But it is not this fact alone which so attracts me to them, rather their decoration. Perched on the balustrades which line them are numerous terracotta statues of monkeys in a variety of entertaining poses; if and when exhaustion does set in, there is plenty for you to pause and admire — that is if the glories of the garden itself which are spread out below and above you are not attractions enough.

⌒⋙⌒

TERRACE

Steep slopes in gardens can mean severe problems and the most widely used solution is the terrace, this being a flat area, usually artificially constructed, which is either paved or grassed or plays host to pools, knots, parterres or formal gardens. The word 'terrace' itself is, in fact, 12th century French, when it meant precisely the same thing it does in English today. However the country in which the terrace first proliferated is Italy.

During the Italian Renaissance garden explosion, designers took their example from

the terraces of the hillside villas of the Romans, and produced extensive terraces linked by grand stairways, flanked by white marble balustrading. These were used as viewpoints from which to admire the lower gardens, especially the parterres. Their expertise at terracing was virtually forced upon them, for so very many Italian gardens were built in the hills around Rome and Florence, or later around the shores and on the islands of the north Italian lakes. The most outstanding example of the latter is Isola Bella on Lake Maggiore. Most great French gardens, on the other hand, were built in the relatively flat lands surrounding Paris and along the valley of the Loire, so terraces were not used so extensively.

Terracing reached its peak in Britain in the hill country in the north and west, in Wales and Scotland in particular, and that is where many of the best examples can be seen today, for they escaped the sweeping relandscaping of 'Capability' Brown. He was responsible for doing away with many English terraced gardens during the 18th century and introducing swathes of lawn which came right up to the house in their stead. Thankfully his successor, Humphry Repton, restored the terrace as a useful link between the house and the garden.

Possibly the most outstanding example of terracing in Britain is at Powis Castle in Central Wales, yet even here Brown recommended that they be levelled. Thank heavens he did not always get his way! There is a series of terraces, begun in about 1700, with a drop from the house to the valley below of 30m (100ft). Here balustrades play host to lead statues, the lowest level being, unusually, an orangery. Surprisingly, although they represent the Italian influence, they were designed by a Dutchman, William Van Nassau-Zylestein, whom William III created Earl of Rochford. The original gardens on the terraces had much Dutch influence although there is little sign of that today. The house reverted to the Powis family about 20 years later and the finishing of the great terracing project almost bankrupted them.

Further north at Bodnant is a more modern terraced garden (begun in 1875) which is equally spectacular with a view of the River Conwy and the mountains beyond.

Above: *Powis Castle — the great terraces designed by William Van Nassau-Zylestein, created First Earl of Rochford. Begun in 1700, they are decorated with lead statues by Van Nost and the lowest terrace contains an orangery.*

Of the terraced gardens in Scotland, the one at Drummond Castle in Perthshire is particularly impressive, especially as the terraces afford views of the great St. Andrew's Cross formal garden which, like all of its kind, can best be appreciated from above.

But this is not to say that excellent examples of terracing do not exist in England. That at Cliveden should not be ignored and one of the most spectacular series of terraces of any garden in this country is at Shrubland Hall in Suffolk, styled after the famous Villa d'Este by Sir Charles Barry at the beginning of the 19th century. Here, a series of stone balustraded steps and terraces — there are 100 steps in all — descend to a large round pond from an elaborate baroque portico.

The terrace is still built today in sloping gardens, although the word is sometimes used erroneously to describe a patio.

※

BALUSTRADE

The word 'balustrade' comes from the Latin *balaustium*, and we derive the word directly from the Italian *balaustrata*. It got its name from the fact that it resembled the double curving calyx tube of the pomegranate flower.

A balustrade consists of balusters which support the coping and is often interrupted by piers surmounted by urns or other shapes such as obelisks. All balustrades were made of carved stone (such as granite) until quite recently, whereas today they are made mostly of reconstituted cement.

Balustrading was used in large grand gardens where they dictated formality. In England we copied the balustrade design from the Villa Borghese in Rome. Its function was (and still is) to compartmentalize a garden into formal and informal areas, where they border steps, terraces (and sometimes even bridges).

Balusters come in many varied shapes, the most popular being the one copied from Italy, i.e. delicately scrolled. It is a feature used quite extensively today, but I feel that some people get carried away with a wish for *folie de grandeur* by using it to embellish their modern houses. It can look out of place, even pretentious, and can clash quite dreadfully with the architecture of the house.

Parapet screening is an alternative to balustrading as it is less formal and can always be used where balustrading would look out of place. However it was also used in grand gardens, a good example being at Blickling Hall, Norfolk. Both balustrades and parapet screening invite climbing plants to partially swamp them, especially where they are surmounted by walls. Wisteria, *Vitis davidii* and both climbing and rambler roses are perfect subjects as they can be trained in between the balusters and over the coping.

Good examples of balustrading can be seen all over Britain including at Montacute House, Somerset; Shrubland Hall, Suffolk; Blenheim Palace, Oxfordshire; Mellerstain, Gordon, Scotland; Haddon Hall, Derbyshire, and Balcaskie, Fifeshire.

※

PARTERRE/KNOT GARDEN

The precise difference between knot gardens and parterres would appear to have challenged all writers on the subject and defeated the great majority of them. I would not dare to be so foolish as to claim to have reached a thorough resolution of the conundrum, but a brief history might assist our understanding.

The very earliest designs, which could be conceived of as patterned gardens, appeared in illustrations of Italian monastery gardens in the 13th century. In a monastery in Turin built for hermits for example, each monk had his own separate house with a garden beside and behind it, many of these being laid out in relatively simple patterned designs. As the Italian Renaissance gathered pace, this concept spread to the gardens of the nobility although not, initially, on a grand scale. So called 'knots' — they would appear to have got their names because the patterns were interwoven or 'knotted' — were relatively small, if often intricate, and were designed to be viewed from above, usually from a raised path or the top of a wall which ran round them.

Soon the Dutch became attracted to the concept and it is believed that they spread to England in early Tudor times. Though still small and usually rectangular, the more intricate the pattern the better they were considered to be. In Britain designs featuring heraldic beasts became particularly popular and many were made of coloured compounds and gravels

with simple low box borders, possibly for ease of maintenance. This method of construction was also used for mazes.

A knot garden is a grouping of more than one knot to produce a more elaborate effect. It was the French who took hold of this concept, and arrogantly thrust the parterre on to the receptive world in the 17th century, using the Italian Renaissance gardens as the basis of their majestic endeavours. Gardens were suddenly conceived as a whole rather than as a series of disparate parts — the walled Tudor garden was, essentially, a compartmentalized affair with no relationship between its parts — with the house as the focus.

Bringing together two concepts, the knot and the quadripartite crucifix form conceived by the Persians, they developed the broad spaces of the parterre lying directly below the windows of the house, from where it could be viewed. What is important to make clear is that a parterre — meaning literally 'on the ground' — originally referred to the overall design concept, including the areas of grass which separated and complemented the knots. Only in more recent times does it appear to have been assumed that the words were synony-

mous, the older knot garden being superseded by the French parterre. It would appear that the concept of the knot was absorbed into the concept of the parterre and, this being on a far grander scale, it suited the rapidly expanding gardens of the 17th century.

I would now like to turn to the designs themselves and some of the plants and materials used for them. These formal layouts in geometric designs were often edged using shrubs such as box, or herbs and aromatic plants such as thrift, santolina, rue, germander or rosemary. In some cases the centres were filled with low growing, compact annuals as in the case of *parterres de compartiment* or grassy areas bordered by flower beds, known as *parterres à l'anglaise*, the latter, I fear, having once been described as 'the plainest and meanest of all'!

Simple patterns were improved and enlarged upon, and by the early 18th century, the zenith

Above: *Montacute House — the obelisk-finialled balustrade surrounding the pool which was built as a replacement for the knot garden by R.S. Balfour but designed to match the walls behind which are some 300 years older.*

of the French parterre era, designs became extremely elaborate with 'branched and flourished' work with sprigs, tendrils, frets, wreaths and interlacings. The most detailed were the *parterres de broderie* which consisted of intricate, embroidery-like designs laid out in box which stood out in relief against a background of various colours, such as yellow (sand), black (coal dust), white (chalk, plaster or lime) or red (brick dust). They must have been a wonderful sight in 18th century France, complete with an army of gardeners forever primping and pruning to keep them in pristine condition.

Where are the outstanding examples which can be seen today? Unfortunately there are no examples of original knots still in existence in Britain, for they were swept away by the several succeeding garden fashions, but in this age of conservation some have been reconstructed. One of the simplest is at Barnsley House in Gloucestershire where, against a background of grey gravel, a geometrical knot using lavender, santolina, box and rosemary, has been laid out. A second simple knot, at Moseley Old Hall, was designed by Miles

Hadfield, the author of the definitive work '*A History of British Gardening*' (1960), using box and gravel. Far more colourful is the cruciform group of four knots forming a sunken knot garden, its box-hedged enclosures infilled with colourful bedding plants, at New Place, Stratford-upon-Avon. Lastly, at the ruined Edzell Castle in Angus there is a restored so-called 'pleasance', a beautifully conceived series of relatively intricate box-edged knots.

As with the knot garden, most parterres were swept away by the 18th century landscape gardening movement and, of those which survived, many are now formal or rose gardens, with Victorian-inspired plantings, rather than parterres proper.

Probably the largest in Britain and, potentially, the most impressive is at Cliveden. Unfortunately this was a rather late design in

Left: *Moseley Old Hall — the reconstructed knot garden of box and gravel, designed by Miles Hadfield in 1960.*
Above: *Drummond Castle — the great Victorian formal garden laid out in the design of a St. Andrew's cross.*

the green *parterre à l'Anglaise* fashion and has been restored as such, whereas I feel that it could do with some more colour. The Victorians clearly thought so too, for when Queen Victoria stayed there it is said that the head gardener arranged one night that all the flowers decorating it were changed so that she awoke in the morning to a different blaze of colour.

At Oxburgh Hall can be seen a beautiful *parterre de broderie* derived from a French design of the very early 18th century, and the Great Garden at Pitmedden, Aberdeenshire, reconstructed in 1952, is equally colourful and on a far grander, almost French, scale.

Possibly the most spectacular of all parterres in Britain are those at Blenheim. On the east front is one designed for the Ninth Duke of Marlborough by Achille Duchêne in the early 20th century, but on very traditional lines, while the most famous of all is the Water Parterre.

This astonishing creation, with its curving water basins and scrolled patterns of low box hedging, we also owe to the Ninth Duke and Duchêne. What a great shame it is that he ran out of money before they set to work on reconstructing Henry Wise's original Great Parterre on the south front which was almost 0.8km (half a mile) long.

During Victorian times the fashion for parterres reawoke, but most of these can be more accurately described as formal gardens. Without a shadow of doubt the most dramatically impressive of all these is at Drummond Castle in Perthshire, where one can look down from the terraces on a gigantic St. Andrew's Cross elaborated with an astonishing variety of patterns, including two multiple box-delineated crowns.

POTAGER/HERB GARDEN

POTAGER

In simple terms a potager is a French vegetable garden, but it has come to mean a great deal more than that and to be almost inextricably interwoven with knots, metaphorically speaking.

Under the influence of Louis XIV's gardener, Jean de la Quintinie, who created the *Potager du Roi* at Versailles, many formal and highly decorative potagers were laid out in

France and, to a far lesser extent, in Britain, their object being as much to please the eye as to provide food for the household.

By far the most outstanding example of a potager today is at the Château of Villandry on the Loire, where Dr. Carvallo, the founder of the *Demeure Historique*, reconstructed a formal French 16th century garden. On the lowest of the three shallow terraces is the potager. Within relatively simple designs, their borders in yew and box, are grown a wide variety of vegetables and herbs.

At first sight such a setting for lettuces and the like can strike one as being incongruous, but slowly the concept grows on one and it develops a certain charm. Nothing quite like it exists in Britain. There is however a small *jardin potager* at West Green House in Hampshire. The reconstructed knot at Barnsley House, has been referred to as being a potager, using as it does lavender, santolina and rosemary. Even if it is not accurately described it leads us naturally to herb gardens.

HERB GARDEN

Gardens of herbs have been grown throughout history, for their products both flavoured foods and were the sources of pleasant aromatic scents which could be used to hide those less pleasant. Indeed potagers were used in much the same way, their clippings being strewn over the floors of houses to make them less foul smelling.

One of the largest herb gardens can be seen at Hardwick Hall, but in recent times much smaller ones have become popular decorative adjuncts, under the influence of Gertrude Jekyll and the Arts and Crafts Movement. Remembering the one at Knole where she grew up, Victoria Sackville-West constructed a most attractive one at Sissinghurst Castle. Here, within a low yew enclosure — shades of potagers — the herbs have been selected more for their colour contrasts than perhaps their culinary use. It is a charming corner of a very beautiful garden.

Left: *Barnsley House — the freshly planted potager, its design based on 17th century French precepts.*

MOUNT

A mount is an artificial hill built within a garden. It could be said to be the descendant of the *ziggurat*, or the stepped pyramid of the ancient Sumerians.

In Britain the first mounts were defensive features within walled fortresses, allowing the defenders to look out over the walls with less physical danger to themselves than when standing on the walls.

During Tudor times they were still built, but as ornamental features, topped by an arbour or small building from where the garden and the view beyond could be admired. These smaller buildings were no doubt the first gazeboes (p. 39). Royal mounts and those belonging to the very rich were often surmounted by a banqueting house. Sir Francis Bacon in his *Essay on Gardens* of 1625, wrote of his ideal garden: 'In the very middle, a fair mount, with three ascents, and alleys, enough for four to walk abreast; which I would form in perfect circles, without any bulwarks or embossments; and the whole mount to be thirty feet high, and some fine banqueting house with some chimneys neatly cast, and without too much glass'.

In Italian Renaissance gardens mounts offered views of knot and parterre gardens and were always included as part of the overall design where the terrain was flat. More often that not they were built of stone or brick covered in earth and planted up with trees and shrubs. Some were terraced, with steps leading up to the summit in a straight line and some had a spiral path.

Back in Britain the mount built for Henry VIII at Hampton Court in 1533 is said to have had a foundation of over a quarter of a million bricks over which soil was laid and planted with hawthorns. On its summit stood a 'lantern-arbour', a three-storey building of which the lead cupola was surmounted by a heraldic lion weathervane, reached by a spiralling path, as is the summit of the mount in the Queen's Garden at Kew.

Quite surprisingly mounts were still being built as late as the 18th century, Alexander Pope's garden at Twickenham, constructed in and around 1744, having no less than three, two small ones at the end of the bowling green and a much larger one overlooking groves of trees, together with the orangery and stove house.

The 'Mount' at Claremont is not a mount in the traditional sense of the word, being a landscaped hill on top of which Vanbrugh's castellated Belvedere is positioned.

BOSKET

The word 'bosket' is the anglicized version of the French *bosquet*, which describes a block of woodland, or a small plantation or thicket that supplies contrast as well as a dark background for the intricate and colourful patterns of the parterre.

At Versailles very elaborate boskets were planted but examples in England tended to be simpler and not on such a large scale. At Blenheim Palace a bosket was planned to adjoin the great south parterre and was intended to include a grotto. However, Sarah, First Duchess of Marlborough, ordered its destruction before it was completed. How I would have hated having her as a client.

Like the parterres which they were designed to complement, British boskets were swept away by the landscape gardening movement of the 18th century and there is no evidence that any originals still exist. To see one you need to venture to the mainland of Europe. At the reconstructed garden of the Château of Vaux-le-Vicomte, east of Paris, a bosket has been planted to back the east parterre, while avenues lead through older, neatly planted, boskets in the gardens of the Schönbrunn Palace on the outskirts of Vienna.

QUINCUNX

A quincunx is a group of five trees planted in a square or lozenge shape. Today this method of laying out trees in this pattern is only used in the planting of orchards. I cannot do better than to quote Sir Thomas Browne in *The Garden of Cyprus; or, The Quincuncial Lozenge; or Network Plantations of the Ancients; Artificially, Naturally, and Mystically Considered*, (1658) in which he defines a quincunx ' . . . the rows and orders so handsomely disposed, of five trees so set together, that a regular angularity, and thorough prospect, was left on every side. Owing this name not only unto the quintuple number

of trees, but the figure declaring that number, which being double at the angle, makes up the letter X, that is, the emphatical decussation, or fundamental figure'. Well, there you are!

By careful planting of these groups, vistas can be produced not only straight through a wood but also along both diagonals. There are relatively small scale quincunces reproduced at Westbury Court and Sudbury Hall but, as with boskets, none of those originally planted in the 17th and early 18th centuries in Britain would appear to exist still.

❧

SUNKEN GARDEN

The joy of a sunken garden is that it creates a small private world which can be overlooked so that the design in all its relatively diminutive glory can be admired and appreciated to the full. The colours of the flowers and foliage, the reflections in the pool — for sunken gardens almost always have one — the texture and shape of the paths and paving.

The originals were, most probably, the Tudor knot gardens which were sunk in relation to their surrounding walks, for only from above could their intricate designs really be appreciated. Henry VIII's sunken garden at Hampton Court was originally designed as a knot garden, but today it bears the unmistakeable imprint of the Victorian age, for the heyday of the sunken garden came at the end of the 19th and beginning of the 20th centuries under the advocacy of Gertrude Jekyll and Edward Lutyens. They were responsible for several attractive ones, of which outstanding examples can be seen at Folly Farm, Sulhampstead, where a sunken pool is surrounded by rose gardens, and at Marshcourt in Hampshire.

The sunken garden at Knole, as it was in the early 1900s inspired the Hon. Victoria Sackville-West to build one at Sissinghurst. The one at Great Dixter originated through the same influence for, although it was designed by Nathaniel Lloyd, the owner of the house, he employed Lutyens as his architect. Surrounded by low walls over which plants tumble, with its

Above: *Dunham Massey — a bird's eye view of the garden as originally designed, showing a spirally pathed mount to the left front of the house, overlooking twin boskets.*

central lily pond and its richly planted borders, it is, without doubt, a strikingly attractive example.

EXEDRA

The word exedra comes from the Greek *ex*, meaning 'out', and *hedra* meaning 'seat'. The Greeks would appear to have had two uses for the word, the first being, 'The portico of the palaestra or gymnasium in which disputations of the learned were held amongst busts of the ancients'; the second, 'The vestibule of a private house used for conversation.' Both seem to have an association with leisurely postprandial discussion of abstruse theories before afternoon slumber sets in.

In architectural terms, the word exedra is now used to describe a curved wall forming the vertical surface of an apsidal end to a room, while in gardening terms it refers to a curved or semi-circular background to a display of statuary. Most commonly this background is a hedge, but it can also be of stone.

The best known hedge-backed exedra is that designed by William Kent at Chiswick House, although now extensive tree growth makes it somewhat different from the original design. The statues of Roman emperors and vases which it displays were taken from Hadrian's Villa at Tivoli. Undoubtedly the dark background serves to display marble statuary to very good effect.

Facing the orangery across the Italian garden at Belton House is Sir Jeffry Wyattville's stone exedra supporting marble busts, a positive throwback to the original Greek meaning of the word. I would also propound that the so-called 'Temple of British Worthies' at Stowe, the niches of which include busts of Queen Elizabeth I, Bacon, Shakespeare, Hampden, Locke, Newton, Milton and William III, is, in reality, a large exedra. It is surely not a temple in any reasonable interpretation of the word?

Above left: *Packwood House — the sunken garden with its rectangular formal pool.*
Above: *Chiswick House — the fine hedge-backed exedra designed by William Kent.*

PLANT SCULPTURE

Man has always held the belief that he can improve nature and he has been engaged in shaping trees and shrubs unnaturally at least since Roman times, if not before, when topiary was popular. Some of the earliest sculpted trees in Britain were the oranges imported by Sir Francis Carew from Italy and France in about 1560, but it was towards the end of the 17th century and into the 18th that the clipping of all forms of trees proliferated to an astonishing, almost obsessive, extent.

It was at this time that George London and Henry Wise developed their 100-acre plant nursery at Brompton Park in West London, this now being the site of Imperial College and the Science and Natural History Museums. Their nursery supplied plants to those gardens in their care and as they were, in succession, Royal Gardeners to Charles II, William and Mary and Queen Anne, they were able to dictate fashion. Their speciality was sculpted trees and the fashion for them spread throughout the land.

This was a time when many of the more famous topiary gardens were laid out, including Levens Hall, and practically every form of evergreen, including some mature conifers were shaped. Even deciduous trees such as the stately English elm, (so few of which, sadly, survive), were subjected to such treatment, being reduced to nothing but boles with tiny heads. Some councils now do much the same, supposedly in the interests of safety.

Inevitably such extremes resulted in opposition and towards the end of Queen Anne's reign, when London died and Wise sold the nursery, they were ridiculed in print by, among others, the philosopher, Joseph Addison, who wrote, 'Our British gardens . . . instead of humouring nature, love to deviate from it as much as possible. Our trees rise in cones, globes and pyramids. We see the marks of the scissors upon every plant and bud. I do not know whether I am singular in my opinion, but, for my own part, I would rather look upon a tree in all its luxuriancy'. He went further, going on to suggest that nurserymen like to make a profit from whatever they have in stock regardless. One must ask oneself whether things have changed!

HEDGE

Hedges are the simplest of all forms of topiary, both in terms of maintenance and decorative character.

In Roman times the most frequently used hedging material was laurel — perhaps they appreciated a regular supply of laurel leaves with which they could crown their victors? Other popular materials at that time were cypress and box.

During the Renaissance box was used extensively as edging for knots and potagers while, with its extensive advocacy by John Evelyn, yew was equally popular for mazes and labyrinths in particular. During the time of London and Wise plant sculpture and hedges proliferated — not least for the reason that there were nurseries such as theirs making it possible to obtain readily large supplies of one and the same species. There are still splendid examples dating back to their time at Levens Hall, which support its more elaborate topiary.

Above: *Chatsworth — The serpentine beech-hedge allée, leading from the ring pool to the bust of the 6th Duke of Devonshire, inspired by the crinkle-crankle wall.*

As their popularity grew, so did the variety of trees and shrubs used and these were not restricted to conifers and evergreens. Beech and hornbeam were two other frequently used deciduous trees. St. Paul's, Waldenbury has splendid beech hedges lining its radiating avenues; and Hidcote a hornbeam hedged allée through its arboretum. Yew was used extensively again during the Gertrude Jekyll-inspired late Victorian movement, and many of the delightful small enclosures at both Hidcote and Sissinghurst use it as it gives a particularly good dense dark background for herbaceous borders. At Hidcote they even allow *Tropaeolum speciosum* to climb up yew hedges, leading the unwary to believe, if only momentarily, that they have suddenly burst into flower!

Possibly the most spectacularly unusual hedges in Britain are at Chatsworth. There the beech hedge allée leading from the ring pond to the bust of the Sixth Duke of Devonshire is in a double serpentine form, inspired by the crinkle-crankle wall, this having been planted as recently as 1953.

Today the variety of materials that are available for hedging is vast and there is little excuse for sticking to privet or leylandii. Perhaps we should follow the example of the Duchess of Devonshire who used no less than 3500 plants of golden box for her parterre-inspired west front garden planted at Chatsworth in 1960. Apparently when she ordered them the incredulous response of the nursery was that no one had wanted golden box since 1914.

As a specific point of interest, the tallest hedge in Britain is of beech, which runs alongside the Perth to Blaigowrie road for 550 m (600 yds), at Meikleour in Scotland. It is 26 m (85 ft) tall and about 240 years old.

MAZE/LABYRINTH

The origin of both the maze and labyrinth is lost in antiquity and mythology, and it is believed that they originally had some sort of either religious, mathematical or even magical significance. Ancient mazes cut into chalk do still exist on Southern downland hillsides.

The word labyrinth evolves from the Greek *labrys*, the sacred double axe. Undoubtedly the most famous of all labyrinths was the legendary one made by Daedalus for King Minos of Crete which led Theseus to the Minotaur. Like all legends efforts to reinterpret this one have produced far less exciting an explanation. It has been suggested that the labyrinth simply meant the Royal Palace of King Minos since the *labrys* was kept there.

The word 'maze', on the other hand, has Scandinavian origins and would appear to descend from Norse mythology. The *Shell Garden Book*, edited by Peter Hunt, states that: 'The distinction between a labyrinth and a maze seems to be this: that a labyrinth involved passages, while the maze is made up of paths — the one is three-dimensional, the other only two. The terms are confused in their use, and often regarded as interchangeable. The distinction is important, though, for in gardening the ancestors of the present labyrinth (i.e. a hedged maze) seem to be two: the hedged enclosure (sometimes called an arbour) which provided privacy within the garden at a time when there was none inside the house, and the knot garden. In the knot garden patterns were employed which were geometrical and included mazes (in the two-dimensional sense) of low shrubs and herbs . . .'.

The hedged maze, or labyrinth, traditionally planted with common yew or one of the taller growing boxes, emerged as a garden feature during the 17th century, during the latter half of which the famous maze at Hampton Court was laid out by our old friends London and Wise. It is thought to have been made originally of hornbeam which must have been quite an unusual choice. Perhaps they had excessive stocks of hornbeam in their nursery at the time.

As has been mentioned above, not all mazes were designed to lose people. At Hatfield House in Hertfordshire there exists a delightful low box maze set into gravel taking the form of a knot maze.

Grey's Court in Oxfordshire plays host to an attractive modern interpretation of one of these low mazes with a particularly delightful history. It is called The Archbishop's Maze, in honour of the current Archbishop of Canterbury who, at his enthronement, declared his belief that everyone should help one another to solve the secret of the maze of life. Its seven

Right: *Glendurgan — the laurel-hedged maze winding its way around the slope of the hillside. Mingled with the surrounding wood, this maze has a whitebeam as its centrepiece.*

rings of paths, representing the seven days of creation, total 0.4 km (¼ mile) in length and the design represents the Crown of Thorns, the solution being found by crossing straight over each of the diamond shaped thorns and following the Path of Life. It is particularly apposite since turf mazes, of which there is an example at Wing in Leicestershire, are believed to have had some specific religious significance.

The great majority of mazes and labyrinths are planted on level ground and a particularly outstanding example is the yew maze, composed of 1000 trees, at Hever Castle, in its splendid setting of an angle of the mediaeval moat. I suppose the point might be made that by studying its solution by viewing it from the battlements before entry one might be said to be able to cheat!

Possibly the most unusual, however, is that set on the steepest part of the slope in front of the house at Glendurgan in Cornwall. Constructed of ever-curving hedges of close-clipped laurel, it is the maze which most blends with its surroundings.

Very few mazes are laid out today as they require such a lot of maintenance; but I would imagine they could be a very useful source of entertainment for parents and their children, not least as a means of safely 'losing' each other for a short time.

TOPIARY

Topiary is the art of shaping suitable trees and shrubs into decorative shapes, or 'living' statues. It has been suggested that the word derives from *Topiarius*, a gardener in ancient Rome during the time of Cicero, who was reputed to have excelled in this art.

Unearthed murals at Pompeii clearly illustrate unnaturally shaped plants, and Pliny wrote extensively about them. He describes walks clipped into the shapes of animals, obelisks, ships and 'letters expressing the name of the master'.

Above: *Levens Hall — a view of some of the ancient and elaborate topiary work which was begun c.1692.*
Right: *Keir — a topiary arbour of clipped yew.*

We next hear of topiary in mediaeval gardens where small trees were sometimes clipped into tiered shapes as the centrepiece for geometric flower beds. They were also often positioned at the top of mounts. Topiary certainly emerged as a popular garden feature during Tudor England.

It was in Renaissance Italy that topiary was first used extensively and elaborately. A 15th century picture of the Medici Villa at Ceffagglio shows clearly a topiary arbour in one corner of the garden. Colonna, a 15th century monk, had a garden full of topiary where a variety of plants were trained and clipped into weird and wonderful shapes. Intricate knots bordered with marjoram or rue were filled with pansies, primroses and violets. Santolina, box, and myrtle planted in pots were clipped into a variety of shapes. The garden at Villa Quaracchi was famous for its collection of topiary figures, ranging from apes to cardinals. It was commonplace to find cypress and bay shaped into cylinders, spheres, cones and spirals.

John Evelyn initially recommended that Mediterranean cypress be grown in Britain but, after a couple of hard winters, all of these died and they were never developed for topiary purposes here.

The golden age of topiary in England was during the late 16th and 17th centuries. The topiary gardens at Levens Hall in Cumbria date back to that time.

Another outstanding example, if of a slightly later date, is John Fetherston's Yew Garden at Packwood House, the first plantings being around 1660, where the trees are said to represent the Sermon on the Mount — although even this is disputed by some authorities. However the main planting of yews here took place much later in Victorian times when there was a revival in the art of topiary. Being on heavy clay, which becomes compacted by the feet of the visitors, these are particularly difficult to maintain in good condition. To add to their troubles they have also suffered badly from scale.

In both these cases the topiary can be said to dominate rather than blend into the garden, this being a feature of gardens developed at the time when London and Wise were in the ascendant.

Another excellent example from Edwardian times can be seen at Hidcote. Here topiary is used less extensively; what Vita Sackville-West described as the 'smug broody hens, bumpy doves and coy peacocks' in the White Garden are ideal examples of the smaller cottage garden style of topiary.

In Europe common yew is used for large topiary shapes. After problems with cypresses, John Evelyn strongly advocated the yew and it is believed that he considerably influenced its extensive use. Contrary to popular belief it is not such a slow-growing plant as it is made out to be. If it is generously watered and fed throughout its first few seasons a decent-sized peacock can be achieved after about five years. Box is often used for small topiary but it tends to become loose with age. Supporting wires are often used to keep large topiary figures neat and to reduce the likelihood of snow damage.

Getting away from the classical geometric shapes, true fantasy comes to life in the gardens of Ladwe, Maryland, U.S.A., where a hunting scene has been re-enacted with hounds in full cry racing across the lawn, followed by a horse and rider jumping a gate in hot pursuit. There is a similar scene outside the front door of Usk Castle, Gwent. The topiary chessmen at Hever

Castle in Kent and the box bells at Heale House in Wiltshire should not be missed either.

Today the enjoyment of topiary has spread to even quite modest-sized gardens, where passing motorists can enjoy the delights of battleships, Eiffel Towers and the like. I have a very modest golden privet ball in my front garden which suits the period of the house very well (17th century). It shines out on sunny days, silhouetted as it is against a large and ancient yew.

Other good examples of topiary can be seen at: Antony House, Cornwall; Haseley Court, Oxfordshire; Ascott, Buckinghamshire; Knightshayes Court, Devon; Chilham Castle, Kent.

ESPALIER

There are quite a few ways of training fruit to allow a longer stem length, at a convenient height for harvesting, and one of them is called 'espalier'. It is a French word which is derived from the Italian *spalliera*, meaning ' a support for the shoulders'.

It is one of the oldest methods of training fruit trees and was commended by John Evelyn in the middle of the 17th century. In 1719 the nurseryman Henry Wise supplied no less than 150 evergreen oaks to the Duke of Chandos for his garden at Canons in Middlesex which were planted espalier-wise in an avenue, although this is considered by some to have been a misuse of the word, and the famed naturalist Gilbert White of Selborne records in his diary that one of the regular jobs for January was the new staking of espaliers.

Today it has become a word to describe a method of training fruit trees such as apple and peach in horizontal layers at regular intervals one above the other, secured on wires against a wall or between posts out in the open.

CORDON

This describes another method of training fruit where one, two or three branches only are grown obliquely, allowing several trees to be grown in a restricted space, usually along a wall. The fruits most commonly treated in this manner are apples and pears.

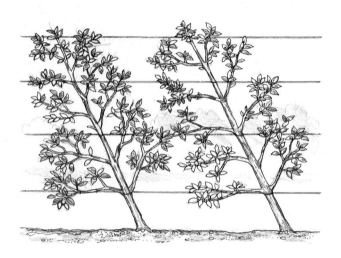

FAN

This describes the shape of a fruit tree which has been trained into a fan-shape, with branches radiating out from a short, main trunk tied onto horizontal wires or bamboo canes. It is possible to grow apples and pears in this manner, but those most commonly trained thus are peaches and similar stone fruits.

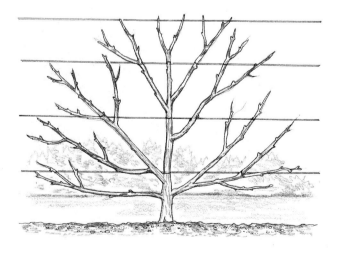

Left: *The training of fruit trees in horizontal layers is known as an espalier.*
Top: *An example of a well-trained cordon hedge.*
Above: *A method of growing fruit trees into a fan shape.*

PLEACH

This describes the shape of a tall, narrow, square hedge on the top of bare trunks; a straight line of square 'lollypops'. Lime, beech and hornbeam are perfect subjects for pleaching, planted about 1.8 m (6 ft) apart and trained onto taut wires or canes running the length of the allée.

Pleached allées were particularly popular in Tudor times, sometimes being allowed to develop into full tunnels for the extra shade they imparted. With the decline in interest around plant sculpture in general, and the development of the landscape movement, many were destroyed. However they regained popularity in late Victorian times and there exist good examples of pleached lime allées at Sissinghurst Castle in Kent — bordered on either side by an ocean of spring flowers, and therefore not to be missed in the spring.

There is also an excellent example of a pleached hornbeam allée at Hidcote which, like that at Sissinghurst, is maintained in perfect condition by the National Trust, despite the considerable effort involved.

Above: *Hidcote — the pleached hornbeam allée looking towards the twin gazeboes, the open door of one of which can just be seen.*
Above right: *Cut-back trees form plashing.*

PLASHING

The object of plashing was to achieve precisely the opposite object of a tunnel. Where an avenue of trees threatened to join their branches together and close up a vista they would be cut back and interwoven on the sides facing the avenue to form vertical hedge-like faces, although the other sides of the trees were not necessarily cut back in the same manner to balance the weight of foliage. This must have made them unstable in high winds, disregarding the sheer difficulty of maintaining the effect as the trees grew taller. There is, however, at least one example of plashing extant, at Hall Barn, Beaconsfield. Here the plashed trees open out the vista which ends at an obelisk commemorating the completion of the garden in 1730.

TUNNEL

The ultimate extension of all forms of plant sculpture is a tunnel in which one either bores through a hedge or plants are so manipulated as to join together over one's head. Undoubtedly the latter are the more spectacular and of these I feel drawn to the yew tunnel at Melbourne Hall south of Derby. Planted by

London and Wise in about 1704, it is 90 m (290 ft) long and believed to be the longest of its kind in Europe. Yet it is not so much its age and length, but the manner in which the dark branches intertwine and give it a vaguely sinister feel which most impresses. One could, if only temporarily, imagine oneself in the phantasmagorical world of Tolkien and the ents.

So called 'tunnel arbours' were popular in the Elizabethan era. Built on wooden rods, one of the earliest forms of trellis-work, and hung with roses, vines and ivy, they were designed to provide shaded walks for the ladies of the house at a time when to gain a tan was considered near sinful. Perhaps, with the current scares about the ozone layer and skin cancers, they will regain their popularity.

In the 16th century, through the advocacy of John Evelyn, pleached lime trees were particularly popular because of their sweet scent — one such can be seen at St. Paul's, Waldenbury — but they did have an unfortunate propensity for dripping their black sticky secretion on the

unwary dawdler and species such as beech and hornbeam soon replaced them.

Later developments included the remarkable 100-year-old apple tunnel at Tyninghame, Scotland, now sadly cut back, where massed trees were trained to form a near perfect curve, and the May spectacular of the laburnum walk at Bodnant.

❧

TRELLISWORK/ TREILLAGE

Trellis is one of the earliest forms of garden structure; there is evidence that it existed in Egyptian gardens in 1000 B.C.

Simple thin criss-cross timbers tied together in either diamond or square patterns, are an old and trusted support for climbing plants. I would imagine that the *pergula*, or sheds used by the ancient Romans must have been built of them in formal or informal styles. Trellis panels of 1.8 m (6 ft) lengths enjoy a healthy turnover at modern day garden centres as they are used mainly for heightening boundary walls and fences. Three 1.8 m × 0.6 m (6 × 2 ft) panels make a simple yet effective surround to a

---

Previous pages: *Melbourne Hall — the sinister yew tunnel planted by London and Wise in 1704.*
Above: *Bodnant — the laburnum tunnel in all its glory.*

138

Treillage has been popular since the 17th century, its great advantages being that structures made from it can be designed and built quickly, and it gives an 'instant' effect, whereas hedges and tree screens of course last very much longer. Its disadvantage is that it is short-lived, and therefore only printed designs show us what was built during those early years. Luckily the Victorians used wrought iron for their treillage arbours and so on, and some survive today. John Belcher said of treillage: 'It can be altered and shifted at pleasure until the desired effect is obtained in a way which more solid and valuable materials prohibit'.

The 1970s and '80s should be recorded in history as an era of garden renaissance, when so many new ideas for garden design and ornamentation have recently come onto the market. Simple trellis trompe l'oeil panels are easily acquired, to be positioned at the far end of the smaller garden or courtyard to give it more apparent depth. This is just one way of using trompe l'oeil in the garden.

bench, or arbour. Their uses are many.

When trellis is woven into more elaborate designs to form trompe l'oeil panels, domes on the top of pergolas, or shapes like obelisks for example, it is then referred to as 'treillage'. This French word can be translated loosely into English as meaning 'trelliswork' or 'lattice-work'.

The laths which make up trellis are normally of chestnut, oak or ash. During Victorian days laths were fastened together with wire; today they are more flimsy and often stapled together. On large structures such as pergolas and summer houses the Victorians used to incorporate thin wire supports painted to look like laths to give it strength.

Dezallier d'Argenville in his book *The Theory and Practice of Gardening* lists many uses for treillage: 'Arbours, porticos, galleries, cabinets, summer houses, salons, niches, and shells adorn'd with columns, pilasters, cornices, pediments, jambs, panels, vases, corbels, frontispieces, domes, lanterns and other ornaments of architecture'.

Above: *The intricate use of wrought iron is shown in this Victorian treillage.*

❧❀☙

PERGOLA

The word 'pergola' comes from the Latin for a shed, *pergular*, yet another example of a word that has changed its meaning throughout the ages. Sheds in existence during the days of the Holy Roman Empire may have been simple structures with climbing plants for a roof, but their origins must have gone back a good deal further than that as an obvious way of supplying shade (normally with vines) in hotter climates.

Today in Europe the pergola has evolved as a purely ornamental garden feature, confirmed by the dictionary definition, 'A structure with climbing plants along a walk'. The pergola could also be said to be a development of the pleached allée of Tudor times, where young trees of hornbeam and wych-elm were trained over an arched walkway.

Strictly speaking, pergolas are not usually objects of beauty in their own right, but merely supports for climbing plants. After all, you seldom see attempts being made to ornament them; there is little point if climbing plants are to eventually smother them. But then there's

absolutely no reason at all why you shouldn't let your imagination run riot and make yourself an ornate pergola but you will have to avoid rampant climbers if indeed you choose to grow any up it at all.

Pergolas can take on several shapes to serve different purposes. For instance, a dead straight series of matching rounded arches will give you a trompe l'oeil effect when viewed from one end as they appear to be getting smaller in the distance where a focal point can always be positioned. This eye-catching feature must be to scale; if it is too large it will foreshorten your vista. This simple rounded arch effect should support climbing plants of tidy habit, or anyway plants such as apple or pear which can be pruned right back so that they hug the hoops and maintain the basic shape. Apples are sometimes grafted where they meet in the middle, thus becoming a living arch.

The 'solid' tunnel effect is achieved by growing and training other climbing plants of a more rampant habit over a pergola. A glorious floriferous tunnel is easily established with *Laburnum* × *watereri* 'Vossii' as can be seen at the stunning 'Laburnum Walk' in the gardens of Bodnant in North Wales. *Robinia hispida* is rumoured to be the future fashionable replacement for laburnum, with its delightful hanging 'pink' racemes. Wisteria also works very well, especially *W. floribunda* 'Macrobotrys Alba' which has extra-long hanging white flowers, an excellent example of which can be admired alongside the formal canal at Wisley. The purist may choose grapes, but would be advised to choose one of the German-bred, mildew-resistant varieties of *Vitis vinifera*. If you are after a 'curtain' effect with good autumn colouring then one of the parthenocissus species will be right for you. The true 'Virginia Creeper' *(P. quinquefolia)* seldom fails to delight.

These more invasive climbers demand a heavier support. Pergolas with great thick stone or brick legs supporting massive wooden beams across the top, like overfed warriors with battering rams at the ready are oppressive, I find. 8 cm × 8 cm (3 in × 3 in) timbers used as uprights as well as horizontals with chamfered

Left: *The Royal National Rose Society's Garden — a pergola rampant with roses 'Chaplin's Pink Champion' and 'Vera Dalton'.*

141

ends make a less clumsy structure, or better still columns supporting a treillage roof.

Roses are a favourite on pergolas but they have the disadvantage of thinning out below once they have discovered the sunnier delights up on top. They should therefore be accompanied by one of the less rampant honeysuckles or a wall shrub to plug this gap. Pergolas give you a good excuse to try out a variety of climbing plants you have always wanted to grow and very often a varied mixture grown haphazardly over the same structure gives a delightful effect. Tender fruiters such as Kiwi (*Actinidia chinensis*) will however require the warmth and protection of a warm and sunny wall if they are to fruit.

The simplest pergola is one built of horizontal bamboo canes betwen upright rustic timbers. Quite recently the black, hooped or ogee, tubular, plastic-coated modules have come onto the market, and these can be lined up to create an effective pergola walk to suit any modern style of garden.

Do you have the space for a pergola? If in doubt you might consider running one along a side wall or fence preferably opposite a window with a focal point at its furthest end. It is surprising how much larger a pergola can make a small garden seem as within it is a separate 'outdoor room' with a completely different ambience.

The introduction of a pergola is a quick way of defining areas at a far lower cost than a wall. If you can position it so that it frames the view or hides an eyesore, all the better. Isolated buildings can be linked by pergola walkways, like the garage to the house for instance and the end result is a more harmonious landscape.

Although it may seem obvious, a pergola should be a minimum 1.8 m (6 ft) high, its width being dictated largely by the climbers you wish to grow up it, so shall we say anything between 0.9-1.8 m (3-6 ft). However, it must be in scale to the garden.

ARBOUR

The word 'arbour' is derived from the Anglo-French *herber*, which in turn came from the Latin *herbarium* meaning 'grass, herb'. It appears that the word changed its meaning because of the confusion with the Latin for tree,

i.e. *arbor*. An arbour therefore describes either a grass plot, herb garden, or a retreat or bower of trees or climbing plants. It is the latter definition that I have always understood the word arbour to mean, i.e. a seat which is shaded by trees or climbing plants or recessed within a high hedge. Of the latter there exists a 200-year-old example at Antony House in Cornwall where the yew hedge is about 9 m (30 ft) high. An alternative to yew could be one of the taller growing boxes, i.e. *Buxus sempervirens* 'Handsworthensis' — after all there are few more magical scents than that given off by box bathed in warm sunlight. Wrought-iron treillage was also used for the construction of arbours, the most famous being the blacksmith, Robert Bakewell's, 1710 imitation of an Elizabethan treillage arbour in wrought-iron at Melbourne Hall in Derbyshire.

Most gardens, however small, can afford such a valuable feature. An arbour becomes a safe and secluded place for quiet meditation or study, away from the stresses of life; a place which poses no threat to one's peace of mind.

In mediaeval times an arbour consisted of a simple bower with a seat below cushioned with turf. They were often positioned on the top of mounts. They were certainly popular during the Victorian era when they were fashioned in fine metal.

In its simplest and perhaps most delightful context an arbour can consist merely of a bench in a leafy glade where shafts of light play mottled games. Otherwise, more contrived if you like, it is a bench surrounded by a climber-clad framework, or a slice out of a pergola walk This framework can be a simple affair consisting of taut wires overhead supported by upright timbers, trellis panels (one on the top and one either side), or an arrangement of rustic poles. Rather smart ogee arbour designs have recently come onto the market; your budget will decide your choice. Even the simplest of arbours eventually become beckoning objects of beauty once covered in climbing plants, so you mustn't be put off by their nakedness to begin with.

The position you would choose for an arbour would be the same for a more substantial gazebo, i.e. preferably with a view on offer. It

Right: *Melbourne Hall — Robert Bakewell's 1710 imitation of an Elizabethan treillage arbour in wrought iron, known colloquially as 'The Birdcage'.*

can of course become the focal point of the garden, especially if it is built of ornate design. In a small garden it can face east when it becomes a cool place to sit for breakfast, and a shaded spot for tea, during a hot summer. A deep and generous arbour will supply shade to those who do not like eating lunch *en plein soleil*.

Now to the climbing plants for your arbour which play such an important role. If you want scent and thick cover you can choose from 'Common Jasmine' (*Jasminum officinale*), *Solanum jasminoides*, *Trachelospermum jasminoides*, Virgin's Bower (*Clematis flammula*), honeysuckle and others. For dappled, scented shade you have many roses to choose from (but avoid the over-rampant *Rosa filipes* 'Kiftsgate' as well as mildew-prone varieties such as 'Zéphirine Drouhin', Pineapple Broom (*Cytisus battandieri*), and so on. Unscented, quick-smotherers include *Clematis montana*, Virginia Creeper (*Parthenocissus quinquefolia*) and ornamental vines. The famous Mile-a-Minute or Russian Vine (*Polygonum baldschuanicum*) needs a severe annual haircut in the spring if you are to enjoy its show of white flowers in late summer and autumn.

Above: Bodnant — a seat on a raised plinth backed by curved exedra-like hedges and framed by Italian statuary.

❦

SEAT

Surely one of the greatest joys of a garden is to be able to sit in it and enjoy the fruits of one's labours. To allow the aching limbs to recover while watching a fountain splash gently or breathing in the scents around you.

A garden seat must therefore have several features. It must be decorative and blend well within the overall design, be positioned to give the optimum view and it must be comfortable. All these requirements are brought together to perfection in the gardens of the Villa Garzoni in Tuscany. There numerous individual terra-cotta seats are placed in advantageous positions throughout the garden, blending well with the surroundings. And they are so formed that they mould perfectly to the posterior.

The problem in Britain is that our weather is not always conducive to sitting out in the open totally unprotected and at Rousham William Kent provided the near ideal solution. Here, by the old bowling green, stand several white painted wood, elegantly treillage-covered seats which, somewhat confusingly, are referred to as 'green seats'. It is believed that they were always white and got their name from being positioned by the bowling green. What,

perhaps, is miraculous is that such relatively flimsy structures should have survived for 250 years. Most surviving wooden seats are much younger.

The earliest unprotected seats were in stone or turf, the amphitheatre being an obvious extension of either of these, but cast-iron became very popular in Victorian times and many of these can still be seen, excellent examples being at Portmeirion and Wilton House, Wiltshire.

Perhaps one of the best positions for a seat is with a well-clipped hedge backing, especially if the hedge is curved to give protection from the wind. At Pyrford Court, near Woking there is a curved Italian stone seat in just such a position and at Bodnant there is a seat painted a subtle bluish-black, on a slightly raised plinth, with a double hedge backing and statues in niches to either side.

AVIARY

It might seem a little contrary to include aviaries in this chapter rather than within the 'Garden Buildings' section of the book, but there is a degree of logic here. In Elizabethan times many domed arbours were elaborately constructed of treillage and these could be converted instantly into simple aviaries by throwing nets over the tops of them. Precisely how the practice developed is uncertain but there is some evidence that Robert Bakewell's famous wrought-iron arbour at Melbourne Hall was netted over during the 19th century.

Besides doves, initially kept for food and later for ornamental purposes, other exotic birds have for a long time been popular as a focal point of interest in gardens. It is said of the Duke of Chandos's garden, Canons, in Middlesex, in 1720, that it played host to barrow ducks, storks, wild geese, whistling ducks, flamingoes, ostriches, blue macaws, Virginia fowls, songbirds and eagles which drank out of special stone basins.

Because of their light construction and rather fragile nature, well-preserved aviaries are now rare and the keeping of exotic birds for ornamental purposes is strictly frowned upon unless they have been bred in captivity. However some 19th century aviaries do still exist, of which possibly the outstanding example is the pheasantry at Waddesdon Manor,

Above: *Dropmore House — a wrought-iron treillage Gothic aviary, built in the middle of the 19th century.*

Buckinghamshire. On a foundation of brick and stone, it is built entirely of wrought and cast iron formed into the most elaborate of rococo designs.

❧

TROMPE L'OEIL

The French word *trompe l'oeil* can only be translated somewhat clumsily into English as meaning 'something that deceives the eye'.

Trompe l'oeil initially developed as a form of artistic illusion where the impression of three-dimensional depth is created on a flat surface. The effect is believed to have been developed by the Romans, but it was finely developed by Mannerist and Baroque painters, the leader of which was Tiepolo. By ingenious use of tricks of perspective the suggestion was made that the painted figures were three dimensional and that they were leaning over balconies and the like. One of the best known examples of this in Britain is the violin, apparently hanging from a peg, on the door of the music room at Chatsworth. The blue ribbon which connects the violin to the peg is even tied with the most convincing of bows, and the shadow is quite remarkable.

Trompe l'oeil effects are widely used in gardens, both on a grand scale where avenues are so planted as to give the impression of increased length by the manner in which the trees lining them are planted, down to the very smallest where a subtly positioned mirror can make a tiny suburban garden appear twice its size. Possibly the best known trompe l'oeil effect of all is produced by the ha-ha.

At Stourhead, between the grotto and the Pantheon, the building is made to appear further away by planting trees towards it in diminishing tones of green, proving that even colour alone can be used as a means of deception.

Murals can play an important role too, as they can transform an otherwise oppressive wall into a beautiful scene, to give the garden one further dimension. The old trick of painting an avenue of columnar conifers disappearing

Left: *One of the best examples possible using a mural as trompe l'oeil. Believe it or not, the steps are painted on a flat wall.*

into the distance with a focal point at the far end always succeeds in 'pushing' the wall further back.

A delightful example of a trompe l'oeil can be found in the London home of Roy Alderson. It is almost impossible to believe that it has been painted onto a flat wall, apart from the balustrades and the statue which are only one foot proud of the wall. This is the work of a man with exceptional talent, Roy Alderson, whose philosophy on his garden was 'To form an amalgam of garden and drawing room so that it was difficult to tell where one began and the other ended.' The jasmine is encouraged to give the impression it is tumbling down the steps.

Mirrors in the smaller garden are a most effective way of deceiving the eye, although the more short-sighted dismiss them as gimmicks.

If they are properly protected against the elements they last for a long time and need only the occasional clean — a job which takes up far less time, and is much cleaner, than most other garden chores. An arched mirror bordered by brick slips gives the impression that the garden continues on through an arch. Where lawn meets the bottom of the mirror it gives the impression that it runs on through it. A strimmer can be used to keep the grass in trim where it touches the mirror. A mirrored wall would double the size of a small garden, just as it succeeds in a bathroom. After all, there are so many design techniques which apply both to 'in'terior as well as 'ex'terior decoration.

Trompe l'oeil can also be achieved by thoughtful design in small gardens where one doesn't want to be continually reminded of how small one's allotted space really is. Screens or barriers dividing up the garden with a vista through them to the end of the garden can hide many surprises within. In the garden I designed for Chelsea Flower Show 1988 the small 20 × 50ft plot contained many such devices with shapes based on the simple circle to help destroy the sharp lines of the rectangular plot.

❧

HA-HA

A ha-ha is a ditch with a sloping earth side meeting a vertical wall of stone or brick to allow the garden an uninterrupted view of the surrounding countryside. It has both practical

Above: Castle Howard — a splendid example of a ha-ha showing how, from a distance, it would provide an uninterrupted view across different levels of land.

eye upon coming near it, and makes me cry Ah! Ah! from whence it takes its name.'

The first British garden designer to use ha-has was Charles Bridgeman, who became Royal gardener in 1728, although those attributed to him are criticized as not being proper ha-has since they have no ditch on the far side of the vertical brick face.

Many ha-has were built by 'Capability' Brown and his school as they proved such an efficient way of opening up the 'natural landscape'. In Britain they were being built on a large scale during the 18th and early 19th centuries and were also a popular feature with the Victorians. In *Mansfield Park*, which Jane Austen wrote in 1814 she said: 'A rage for improvement . . . affected country residences by the thousand. It was indeed a period when every house of any pretentions had its walls (except those of the kitchen garden) swept away and a ha-ha substituted.'

Ha-has varied in length from the very long, to a mere short wall built just beyond vista gaps through hedges or walls. Luckily many still survive. One of the finest examples of a stone ha-ha can be seen at Lacock Abbey in Wiltshire, and there is a magnificent brick ha-ha at Audley End in Essex.

Another excellent example can be seen at Charlecote Park in Warwickshire; this one is brick built with a path running along the top and a very gently sloping ditch. At Killerton in Devon, the sweeping view across the fields below the hillside is much as it was always planned to be and the ha-ha still prevents the grazing cows from entering the garden and causing damage.

At Claremont in Surrey the slow but steady degradation of a ha-ha can be observed. At its far southern end the original brick wall is still in place, if somewhat the worse for wear and partially overgrown. However for the most part, the ha-ha is now no more than a shallow grass ditch which would prevent nothing from crossing it. Also the vista which it was designed to open out is much changed. The slope of the hill from which it was to be viewed now plays host to many trees which block much of the view.

A ha-ha really comes into its own where it divides a lawn and a field especially if it is kept grazed short. At our old house in Wales I remember my father keeping sheep in the field on the other side of the lawn from the ha-ha. As

and view enhancing properties; whilst it keeps out livestock, it also eliminates the need for a wall or fence, thus giving the impression that the garden and the field or park beyond run into each other without anything between.

The word 'ha-ha' is supposed to have crept into the English language as a result of the exclamation of surprise muttered by a surprised visitor who, upon seeing one for the first time, said 'Ah . . . Ha!' I find this more plausible than the other theory that it got its name as it made people laugh when they saw them — or perhaps they actually fell right into them?

Oddly, however, the first English reference to a ha-ha is in a 1712 translation of a French book about gardens which states, 'We frequently make through views, called, Ah, Ah . . . with a large and deep ditch at the front of them, lined on both sides of them to sustain the earth, and prevent the getting over, which surprises the

a result the grass textures blended well into each other and gave the impression that the lawn continued on for a greater distance than in reality.

Ha-has are still built today, often with open stone steps set into them for easy access into the field beyond. They do of course cost more than a fence but a deeper dig into your pocket (and the ground) could result in all the difference being made to your garden.

❧

BOWLING GREEN/ CROQUET LAWN

The traditional game of bowls as we know it today is played on a precisely defined square of flat grass, 37–38 m (40–42 yd) square, surrounded by a shallow ditch with green banks beyond. Yet it has many variants ranging from north country crown green bowls, through west country skittle alleys to the North American developed ten-pin bowling. It is, therefore, not surprising that bowling greens take more than one form.

The first evidence of any form of bowling is from a 6th century B.C. Egyptian tomb where a painting depicts a game using balls and stone pins. Later, in mediaeval Germany, a similar game is believed to have constituted part of a religious rite. Can that be so far removed from the modern indoor bowls arena with its banked seats of spectators on either side worshipping the players?

Bowls proper originated in Scotland in the 16th century and spread from there throughout the British Commonwealth to which, rather like cricket, it has remained principally restricted. According to Francis Bacon (1561–1626), who was the first prolific writer on gardens, bowling was reputed to be good for the 'Stones and Reines'.

Bowling greens became very popular in British gardens with the development of the formal French style, usually being used, like boskets, to balance the decorative parterres and

Above: *Wrest Park — the bowling green and bowling green house with its elegant Doric portico.*

give the eye a rest. Surprisingly all evidence suggests that they were neither actually designed to play bowls upon nor used at any time for the game. They simply became known as bowling greens because they so closely resembled those designed specifically for the purpose. The confusion may have occurred because the French word for those counter-balancing areas of grass was *boulingrin* which came to be translated as 'bowling green', although the counter-argument says that the French got the idea from us and that *boulingrin* was the nearest they could get to a phonetic spelling of bowling green.

The form of bowls played in the early Middle Ages was much more closely allied to skittles and that is why we see grass bank-lined bowling alleys in some gardens. Hampton Court played host to several of these flanked by yew trees and there is still one to be seen at Trinity College, Cambridge. The green restored at Claremont sweeps dramatically downhill from the Belvedere and, if bowls was ever actually played on it, it must have been a particularly exciting, if also exhausting, form of the game.

CROQUET LAWN

Croquet developed much later, in Ireland in about 1850, but was popular in England by 1860 and became a favourite family or party game of the Victorians, many areas of lawn being developed on which it could be played. The correct size of a croquet lawn is 32 m × 26 m (35 yd × 28 yd). It was, I suppose, more suited to ladies in sweeping crinolines than bowls, although bowling green tea-parties were also a popular feature of 19th century entertainment.

Left: *Rousham House — looking across William Kent's parterre-style bowling green to a lion and horse sculpture eye-stopper.*

ᘓᗢᘉᗢᗩ

PATH

History reveals that the ancient Chinese were masters in the art of both path laying and construction. Theirs were both intricate and sophisticated, using materials such as mosaic, shingle and brick which they stamped into the soil. The end result often took on the appearance of a closely woven carpet. They were lain in such a way as to meander around the garden where eye-catching plants and statuary were positioned alongside to arrest the visitor from time to time. Their paths often portrayed animals and insects — deer, lions, butterflies, etc. — as well as the more classic geometric patterns. This kind of twisting path suited the busy Chinese garden style where the visitor was led on a wildly snaking route over water, up and down hills and around rocks. This way of revealing the garden by degrees is a charming idea often used today.

In pre-'Capability' Brown England, straight paths were a feature of formal gardens. These were swept away by Brown, at least all those he could lay his hands on. 'Nature abhors a straight line', he was quoted as having said.

Paths can become exciting garden features. A curving brick path running through long grass where native wild flowers are encouraged to grow looks most effective — something I admire about the gardens at Great Dixter, near Northiam in East Sussex. Brick can be laid end to end or in a pattern such as herringbone, either laid flat (or 'frog-down' as it's known in the trade), or 'on edge'. Brick paths suit most garden styles.

In woodland areas, round stepping-stones, slices of the trunk of fallen trees, fit well into their surroundings. Mown paths cut through areas of long grass give an effective contrast between rough and smooth. Gravel gives a reassuring scrunch under foot, but it should always be contained within a bordering brick or wooden edge, and preferably laid on to a polythene membrane to suppress weeds.

It is always more practicable to use local materials which can be mixed in with whatever other materials you happen to have. For example, an occasional outcrop of pebbles or

Right: *Great Dixter-York stone path in a random pattern alongside a Gertrude Jekyll-inspired herbaceous border.*

flint will alleviate the monotony of the path. 'Crazy' paving paths look a mess if the joins are too wide, and delightful if each piece slots into its neighbour like a jigsaw. Granite setts and York stone are two other favourites of mine. Where lawns become worn a path can be laid at soil level so as not to interfere with the mowing.

Luckily the day of the mean concrete path bordering the edge of the square and rectangular garden is numbered as more sophisticated garden design is being adopted today.

~~~

PATTE D'OIE

Patte d'oie, literally translated from the French, means 'the foot of a goose'. It describes the layout of paths or vistas which radiate fanwise, just like the toes of a goose's foot. The French formal tradition dictated that they should be laid out with geometric precision, a protractor being more important to the designer than the plants through which it passed.

A patte d'oie is normally positioned near to the house at the bottom of some steps or near to a terrace, to give the visitor several vistas through various parts of the garden as well as a choice of route. Frequently there was an element of surprise in their positioning, the visitor being drawn through a gate in a wall to find himself confronted by the sudden dramatic choice of equally appealing routes to take in his explorations.

The patte d'oie at Hampton Court was laid out on a massive scale in the late 17th century when 403 common limes were planted to form each radiating avenue. Sadly many of these now statuesque trees were destroyed during the late 18th century as well as by the never-to-be forgotten storm of October 1987. It is important to emphasize that a patte d'oie is shaped into a semi-and a rond-point into a full circle.

ROND-POINT/RONDEL

ROND-POINT

A rond-point is a circular area or clearing from which allées and avenues spread out to give the visitor several vistas of other parts of the garden or park. Possibly the best known are those in the gardens of Versailles, each having a pool and fountain centre piece, but most are by no means so elaborate, being simply the points where a series of allées or avenues converge. To appreciate a rond-point to its full effect, you need to see it from a helicopter. Clearly the designers of gardens in the 17th and 18th centuries must have had such in mind for their paintings always looked down upon the rond-points from far above.

When Haussman redesigned Paris for Napoleon III he used the rond-point as one of the principal features, the *Place de l'Étoile* being a major example. How difficult it is to appreciate such a feature from ground level is shown in Gustave Caillebotte's impressionist masterpiece, 'Paris Street — Rainy Weather', which depicts a crossing of the *rue Leningrad* as seen from one of the streets, but fails to give any real idea of the rond-point which, in fact, it illustrates.

RONDEL

A rondel differs from a rond-point principally in terms of scale, the hedged rondel at Sissinghurst being a delightful example, especially as it can be viewed from the top of the tower, from which point it can be fully appreciated. Here a circle of neatly clipped and beautifully tended hedges has four hedge-lined paths leading from it, each at 90° from the last. Another example of a rondel which springs to mind is the one included among the extensive topiary work at Levens Hall.

Right: *Sissinghurst — a round yew hedge acting as a rondel to give the visitor different vistas and choice of direction. Such cleverly laid out compartments in this garden make it seem very much larger than in reality, as the visitor enjoys snatched views as he meanders along.*

AMPHITHEATRE

We are all well acquainted with the Roman amphitheatre, its essential characteristics being an elliptical arena surrounded by tiered stone seats, in which Charlton Heston in *Ben Hur* befriended lions and at the same time competed for the hand of the fairest of maidens. Today many of these ancient structures still stand after 2000 years of the depradations of man and the weather, bearing mute evidence to the abilities of their builders. Some are no longer mute, however, that at Arles in Provence being used for bullfights, if less gory affairs than those across the Pyrenees, while that at Verona resounds all summer to the greatest of operatic sopranos is spectacles such as Verdi's *Aida* which may well rival the originals for which it was constructed.

An amphitheatre need not be a complete ellipse or circle; it can also be semi-circular, like those at Orange, also in Provence, and Fiesole in Tuscany, both of which are still used for the performance of plays. And it need not be an ancient structure.

Visitors to the Vittoriale, Gabriele d'Annunzio's hillside estate overlooking Lake Garda, can stand on the terraces of the one he had built in the 1920s for the performance of his own plays. On a mid-summer day the reflected heat from the white stone can be oppressive, but in the evening it must be a pleasant place, for if one becomes bored with the play one has the entire vista of Lake Garda to admire. Together with the advantage that the thunderstorms brew up on Monte Baldo above the far shore giving one due warning.

It is, of course, very clear why amphitheatres have not become popular in Britain. Being essentially open-air structures, they are not particularly conducive to our climate. Yet there are a few in our gardens, designed presumably so that large numbers of guests can sit together and admire the view.

In gardening terms an amphitheatre is a curving series of grassed tiers set in a hillside and the most outstanding example is that at

Right: *Claremont Landscape Garden — Charles Bridgeman's amphitheatre, recently reconstructed with loving care by the National Trust, as seen from across Humphry Repton's lake.*

Claremont in Surrey which has recently been restored, although unfortunately the great gale of October 1987 did considerable damage to the view seen from it, many of the trees on the slopes behind the lake having been destroyed or badly damaged. It was a highly original design by Charles Bridgeman, who is considered to have been one of our first professional gardeners to have attempted to escape from the rigid formality of the 17th century. It is not a single curve, but consists of two opposing curves meeting at a level circle of grass in its centre where paths also cross, and pictures of its original conception show that it was intended that white wooden seats should be positioned for those who did not wish to sit on the grass.

ALLÉE/AVENUE/VISTA

An allée or alley describes a long straight ride or walk which cuts through wooded areas bordered by rows of evenly planted trees or hedges. The difference between an allée and an avenue is one of scale, an avenue being much larger and more extensive. An allée can also be a walk within the garden proper while an avenue is a drive in the park beyond. The word allée, since anglicized to alley, has not been dropped since it was used to describe the vast avenues in the gardens of Versailles which were laid out by André le Nôtre under Louis XIV. At Versailles the allées were 14.6 m (48 ft) wide and often over 0.8 km (½ mile) long. They criss-crossed the gardens where they were intersected by huge fountains. These great allées were bordered by two or three rows of trees, namely limes, elms or oaks. They were sometimes planted so that they became narrower at the far end to the palace to give the impression that they were longer than in reality.

Allées or avenues were planted in Britain from Tudor times onwards. At Bramham Park in Yorkshire there exist some fine examples of beech-lined allées despite the fact that they were severely damaged in the gales of 1962.

Avenues of common lime were widely planted in Britain during the 17th and 18th centuries as the Dutch found it such an easy plant to propagate, which resulted in large quantities of them arriving on our shores. They are not everyone's cup of tea as they sucker, and drip honeydew throughout the latter half of

the summer. However a scented lime avenue in full flower during the summer is full compensation, but it is an avenue for the country. Both Charlecote in Warwickshire and Cliveden on the Buckinghamshire and Berkshire borders have mature avenues of common lime, to mention but two.

The horse chestnut makes a handsome avenue and is a wonderful sight when covered in flower candles. The common horse chestnut (*Aesculus hippocastanum*) with white candles is sometimes interplanted with hybrid (*A.* ×

Left: *Chatsworth — a pedestal surmounted urn framed in blue sky forming a beautiful focal point at the end of an allée.*
Above: *St. Paul's Waldenbury — looking down one of the beech hedge-lined allées toward the lake and temple.*

159

cavnea) Briotii with red candles which appear later, so that the flowering period is extended. These days sterile, conkerless horse chestnuts, i.e. *A. h. Naumannii* are planted by local authorities because so many children have been involved in car accidents while gathering conkers.

It was the Victorians who planted many coniferous avenues as their neat shapes suited their orderly minds. The magnificent avenue of Monkey Puzzle (*Araucaria araucana*) at Bicton Park in Devon, planted in 1840, stands as a memorial to this era. There are also some lovely examples of Cedar of Lebanon (*Cedrus libani*) avenues throughout the country.

Allées and avenues could, I suppose, be called contrived views or vistas especially if they have an eye-catching focal point at the very end. Most grand gardens and parks have vistas running through them as a means of forcing the visitor's eye in a certain direction. The famous vista at Stowe in Buckinghamshire immediately springs to mind where the straight drive follows the undulating contours of the land resulting in the house appearing then disappearing as you approach it. Although 'Capability' Brown destroyed many avenues in

his time, he liked them to perform a certain function: 'An avenue is most pleasing when it climbs up a hill and, passing over the summit, leaves the fancy to conceive its termination'. The 4.8 km (3 mile) long, 18 m (60 ft) wide undulating avenue of common limes at Clumber Park near Worksop in Nottinghamshire, with trees planted in double rows, is still an important feature today.

Today great efforts are made nationwide to replant avenues where they have become diseased or unsafe. Elm avenues killed off by Dutch Elm disease are being replaced by Nothofagus, which prefers the milder, wetter areas of the country such as the South West. The Chilean Robel Beech (*N. obliqua*) has been used recently to form an avenue in Windsor Great Park.

If I had the space for an avenue to anchor my house to the surrounding countryside, modern or otherwise, I would have no hesitation in planting one.

Above: *Bodnant — a magnificent view looking out over terraces onto the river Conway into the distance.*

PART III

GLOSSARY

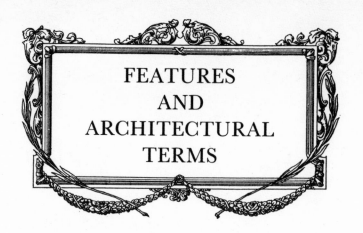

FEATURES AND ARCHITECTURAL TERMS

This glossary contains definitions, in specifically garden terms, of all the features covered in *Elegance and Eccentricity*, together with details of the principal architectural terms found in the book.

Following each feature in the glossary is a compilation of some of those gardens currently open to the public which we consider to have outstanding examples of that feature. Necessarily such selections are a matter of personal taste. Those gardens that are also mentioned in the main body of the book have been set in **bold type.**

Following each definition of the architectural terms, we have listed, where possible, those historic houses and gardens that have excellent examples of the style that has been described. Some of these are also mentioned in the main text of the book but have not, in this instance, been set in bold type.

Not all gardens mentioned in the book are open to the public, but care has been taken to ensure that those listed within this glossary are open at least some of the time during each year. Their opening dates and times are mostly covered in one or more of the first three books listed in the bibliography.

It is, however, very important to recognize that many of the private gardens which open under the aegis of the National Gardens Scheme do so for as little

as only one day a year, although some can also be visited by prior appointment. It is highly advisable to check with their owners, by telephone or by written application, before attempting to visit them.

ALLEY/ALLÉE

A relatively narrow hedge or tree-lined walk within a garden, the hedges or trees usually being clipped or sculpted. An alley is normally distinguished from an avenue (q.v.) both by being inside, rather than outside, the perimeter of the garden proper and by their relative size. The original French allée was widened both metaphorically and physically by those at Versailles, which many people would now perceive to be avenues.

Bramham Park, Wetherby, W. Yorks. (*Beech*)
Brockenhurst Park, Brockenhurst, Hants. (*Ilex and Bay*)
Chatsworth, Bakewell, Derbyshire. (*Serpentine, Beech-hedged*)
Hatfield House, Hatfield, Herts. (*Pleached Lime*)
Hidcote Manor Garden, Hidcote Bartrim, Nr. Chipping Campden, Glos (*Pleached hornbeam*).
Jenkyn Place, Bentley, Hants. (*Beech-hedged*)
Levens Hall, Nr. Kendal, Cumbria. (*Beech*)
St. Paul's, Waldenbury, Whitwell, Nr. Hitchin, Herts. (*Beech-hedged*)

AMPHITHEATRE

A curved or semi-circular stepped gallery, usually of turf, providing an extended area from which large numbers of people can comfortably admire a view (Note — Straight-tiered galleries, such as that at Dartington Hall, do not, strictly speaking, constitute an amphitheatre.)

Claremont Landscape Garden, Esher, Surrey. (*Exceptional*)
Cliveden, Maidenhead, Bucks. (*Very small within a wooded area*)
Dartington Hall Gardens, Dartington, Devon. (*But see above*)
Hackwood Park, Basingstoke, Hants.

ARBOUR

A shady retreat usually, but not exclusively, containing a seat. It can either be cut out from inside a tree, be formed from trained trees, be constructed of treillage with climbing plants trained over it, or be an ornamental structure of metal or stone. (Note — Walks lined with pleached trees, such as that at Ham House, are sometimes referred to as arbours. These are more suitably called alleys if the trees line both sides, or shaded walks if only one.)

Antony House, Torpoint, Cornwall. (*Yew*)
Ashridge, Berkhamsted, Herts. (*Trained tree arbours*)
Drummond Castle Gardens, Muthill, Tayside. (*Yew*)
Hatfield House, Hatfield, Herts. (*Trellis*)
Melbourne Hall, Melbourne, Derbyshire. (*Wrought-iron by Robert Bakewell*)

ASTROLABE

An obsolete instrument used by mariners for determining their position on the earth's surface with the aid of the position of the sun or stars.

Haseley Court, Little Haseley, Oxfordshire.
Hever Castle, Edenbridge, Kent. (*In the Tudor Garden*)

Polesden Lacey, Dorking, Surrey. (*In the walled garden*)

AVENUE

A road or walk planted with trees to either side. In the strict sense of the word an avenue should be outside the perimeter of the garden leading to the house, but many can now be seen within gardens where, because of the sheer size of the trees alone, they cannot be considered as alleys. (q.v.)

Anglesey Abbey, Nr. Cambridge. (*Chestnut*)
Ashridge, Berkhamsted, Herts. (*Unusual — Liquidambar*)
Bicton Park, Bicton, Devon. (*Monkey Puzzle*)
Brockenhurst Park, Brockenhurst, Hants. (*Double rows of lime and chestnut*)
Cliveden, Maidenhead, Bucks. (*Lime*)
Clumber Park, Nr. Worksop, Notts. (*Double rows of limes*)
Cranborne Manor, Cranborne, Dorset. (*Double rows of beech and copper beech*)
Drummond Castle, Muthill, Tayside. (*Beech*)
Levens Hall, Kendal, Cumbria. (*Sycamore*)
Nymans, Handcross, West Sussex. (*Limes — remarkably little damaged by the storm of October, 1987 which created havoc in this garden.*)

AVIARY

A large cage or any building used for housing birds. The most striking examples from the 18th and 19th centuries were constructed of intricate wrought-iron treillage. Some treillage arbours are reputed to have been converted to aviaries simply by throwing nets over them.

Harewood House, Leeds, W. Yorks. (*Modern*)
The London Zoo, Regent's Park, London. (*Although strictly outside the limits of this book, this zoo has the largest collection of aviaries of all ages and styles in the country*)

Sudeley Castle, Winchcombe, Glos.
Waddesdon Manor, Aylesbury, Bucks. (*Outstanding*)

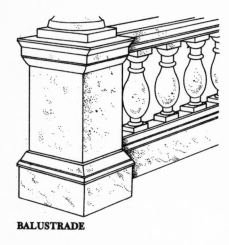

BALUSTRADE

BALUSTRADE

A balustrade consists of a series of balusters which support a coping and stand on a low wall. The more lengthy stretches of balustrading are interrupted with piers which are used for supporting many forms of garden ornaments. Strictly speaking, a balustrade should have balusters in the double curving shape of the calyx of the pomegranate flower since it is from this that the word derives.

Balcaskie, Fifeshire.
Blenheim Palace, Woodstock, Oxford.
Blickling Hall, Aylsham, Norfolk.
Haddon Hall, Bakewell, Derbyshire.
Harewood House, Leeds, W. Yorks.
Hatfield House, Hatfield, Herts.
Heale Gardens, Middle Woodford, Salisbury, Wilts.
Mellerstain, Gordon, Borders, Scotland.
Montacute House, Yeovil, Somerset.
Newby Hall, Ripon, N.Yorks.
Powis Castle, Welshpool, Powys.

BANQUETING HOUSE

As its name implies, a banqueting house was specifically designed for the consumption of food. In fashion during Elizabethan times, they were usually elaborate garden buildings of some size reflecting the style of the main house and usually positioned at the corner of a walled garden.

Blickling Hall, Aylsham, Norfolk. (*c.1620 by Robert Lyminge*)
Hampton Court Palace, Hampton Court, London. (*Overlooking the Thames*)
Montacute House, Yeovil,

Somerset. (*The twin pavilions, as they are now generally called, are thought to have been built as banqueting houses*)
Rievaulx Terrace, Helmsley, N. Yorks. (*One of the twin temples here is known as 'The Banqueting House' since it is laid out for banquets, but it is not one in the strict sense of the term since that is not the purpose for which it was originally built*)

BAROQUE

A florid and exuberant style of art and architecture distinguished by flowing lines and curves, which originated in Italy at the beginning of the 17th century. As originally used in France the word implies elements of exaggeration and the grotesque.

Shrubland Hall, Ipswich, Suffolk. (*The Baroque portico at the top of the steps*)
Waddesdon Manor, Nr. Aylesbury, Bucks. (*The Aviary*)

BEE-BOLE

A niche in a wall designed for the storage of bee-skeps in the winter. They are usually set at ground level or at no great height for the skeps to be easily lifted into them. (Note — Bee-skeps were made of straw and were rendered obsolete by the invention of the wooden beehive in the 19th century.)

Erddig, Wrexham, Clwyd
Packwood House, Hockley Heath, Warwickshire.
Tilty Hill Farm, Duton Hill, Dunmow, Essex.

BELVEDERE

A structure from which a view could be admired. Most frequently turrets added to houses, belvederes were also built as separate structures in gardens. Note — There would appear to be no positive distinction between a belvedere and a gazebo (q.v.). However the latter are usually more decorative and less military in appearance.

Claremont Landscape Garden,
Esher, Surrey.
(*See also Gazebo for further examples*)

BOSKET

An ornamental plantation of trees usually backing on, and specifically designed to complement, a parterre. The more ornate and extensive of boskets had enclosures within them and/or were interfaced with paths leading to rond-points with fountain centrepieces.

As far as we know no boskets survive in the British Isles to original designs. However traces of the 17th century boskets can still be seen in the park of Felbrigg Hall, Nr. Cromer, Norfolk, and one is being reconstructed at Ham House, Richmond, London.

BOWLING GREEN

Three separate forms of bowling green can be seen in gardens.
  1. A precisely defined square of flat grass, its dimensions being 37-38 m (40-42 yd), surrounded by a shallow ditch with grass banks beyond it on which the game of lawn bowls is played.
  2. A flat area of grass within and part of a parterre, its simplicity being used to complement the elaborate design of the parterre itself. These were never designed for any game to be played on them.
  3. A grass alley with banks to either side on which a game allied to skittles was played. These latter are also called bowling alleys.

Berkeley Castle, Nr. Bristol, Glos. (*Bowling alley*)
Chatsworth, Bakewell, Derbyshire.
Claremont Landscape Garden, Esher, Surrey. (*A bowling alley leading down to a bowling green*)
Nymans Garden, Handcross, West Sussex.
Rousham House, Steeple Aston, Oxfordshire.
Trinity College, Cambridge,
Cambs. (*Bowling alley*)
Wrest Park Gardens, Silsoe, Beds. (*Parterre bowling green*)

BRIDGE

A structure taking a path or road across a stream, river or dry valley.

Abbots Ripton Hall,
Huntingdon, Cambs. (*Chinese Chippendale*)
Blenheim Palace, Woodstock, Oxfordshire. (*Very grand!*)
Castle Howard, York, N. Yorkshire. (*Magnificent setting between the Temple of the Four Winds and the Mausoleum*)
Chatsworth, Bakewell, Derbyshire. (*Classical*)
Heale Gardens, Middle Woodford, Salisbury, Wilts. (*Japanese 'Nikko'*)
Prior Park, Widcombe, Bath. (*Palladian bridge*)
Pusey House, Faringdon, Berks. (*Chinoiserie*)
Sezincote, Moreton-in-Marsh, Glos. (*Indian, with bulls atop its balustrade*)
Shugborough, Stafford, Staffs. (*Chinoiserie*)
Stowe, Buckingham, Bucks. (*Palladian*)
Wilton House, Salisbury, Wilts. (*Palladian*)
Wrest Park Gardens, Silsoe, Beds. (*Chinoiserie*)

CANAL

A long formal stretch of water, rectilinear in shape.

Bramham Park, Wetherby, W. Yorkshire.
Brockenhurst Park, Brockenhurst, Hants.
Buscot Park, Nr. Faringdon, Oxfordshire. (*Very unusual 'canal walk'*)
Folly Farm, Sulhampstead, Berks.
Forde Abbey, Chard, Dorset. (*The 'long pond'*)
Jenkyn Place, Bentley, Hants.
R.H.S. Gardens, Wisley, Surrey.
Westbury Court, Westbury-on-Severn, Glos.
Wrest Park Gardens, Silsoe, Beds.

CLAIR-VOYÉE

CASCADE

The word cascade is synonymous with waterfall, but in gardening terms is usually applied to the more extensive and elaborate of waterfalls.

Athelhampton, Athelhampton, Dorset.
Blenheim Palace, Woodstock, Oxfordshire.
Bodnant Garden, Tal-y-Cafn, Gwynedd.
Bowood House, Calne, Wilts.
Chatsworth, Bakewell, Derbyshire. (*Stepped cascade and the 'Cascade House'*)
Harewood House, Leeds, W. Yorks.
Hodnet Hall Gardens, Hodnet, Shropshire.
Leonardslee Gardens, Horsham, W. Sussex.
Sheffield Park Gardens, Sheffield Park, E. Sussex.
West Wycombe Park, West Wycombe, Bucks.

CASTELLATED/ CASTELLATIONS

Battlements or turrets surmounting a building or walls, imparting the impression that they were intended for defensive purposes.

Castle Howard, York, N. Yorks. (*The walls to either side of the Pyramid Gate*)
Claremont Landscape Garden, Esher, Surrey. (*The Belvedere*)
Lanhydrock, Nr. Bodmin, Cornwall. (*The gatehouse*)

CHINOISERIE

Imitations of Chinese art forms in buildings, bridges, follies and the like. Having made their first appearance in the latter half of the 17th century, Chinoiserie designs became popular during the 18th.

Biddulph Grange, Biddulph, Staffs. (*Pavilion*)
Pusey House, Nr. Faringdon, Oxfordshire. (*Bridge*)
Shugborough, Stafford, Staffs. (*Bridge*)

CASTELLATIONS

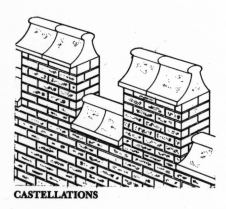

COLONNADE

Wrest Park Gardens, Silsoe, Beds. (*Bridge*)

CLAIR-VOYÉE

Simply translated from French as 'clear view', this describes either a decorative fence, usually in wrought-iron, on top of a low wall which permits a view into or across a garden, or a grille in a wall through which a garden may be admired.

Hampton Court Palace, Hampton Court, London.
Kinross House, Kinross, Tayside. (*The clair-voyée 'Fish' gate*)
Portmeirion, Portmadoc, Gwynedd. (*Many grilles*)
Syon House, Brentford, London.
Wotton House, Nr. Aylesbury, Bucks.

COLONNADE

A row or series of columns surmounted by an entablature. Entablature is the part of the order above a column and includes the architrave (the beam), frieze (a horizontal band of sculpture between the architrave and the cornice) and cornice (a horizontal projecting moulding above the frieze).

Wilton House, Nr. Salisbury, Wilts. (*The Ionic colonnade of the Palladian bridge*)

COLUMBARIUM

Derived from the Latin 'columba' for a pigeon, the word columbarium is now virtually synonymous with dovecote (q.v.) but it should, in all probability, be most strictly applied to the simplest round stone structures which were specifically built for keeping and breeding pigeons as a source of food.

Charleston Manor, Westdean, Litlington, East Sussex. (*Norman columbarium*)
Cotehele House, Calstock, Cornwall.
(*See Dovecote for further examples*)

CONCEIT

Although the words conceit and folly are treated by many as being synonymous and interchangeable there would appear to be a subtle difference which challenges definition. Unlike a folly, a conceit is not a single structure but rather a fanciful overall conception which may contain one or more follies. It is even more likely than a folly to reflect the character and whims of its designer and frequently has elements of intended humour or the macabre.

Biddulph Grange, Biddulph, Staffs.
Mount Stewart, Newtownards, Co. Down, Northern Ireland. (*Animal sculpture*).
Painshill Park, Cobham, Surrey.
Portmeirion, Portmadoc, Gwynedd.
Stowe, Buckingham, Bucks. (*A conceit of temples*)

CONSERVATORY

An extensively glazed building in which tender plants are grown. In modern times the word has come to be used for a lean-to structure against a house, but in its original sense it was a far less modest structure, separate from the house and of considerable size and height, often with a domed or curved roof.

Alton Towers, Alton, Staffs.
Ashridge, Berkhamsted, Herts.
Chatsworth, Bakewell, Derbyshire. (*In particular the 'Conservative Wall' for camellias*)
Flintham Hall, Nr. Newark, Notts.
Montacute House, Yeovil, Somerset. (*Now houses ferns — see under 'Fernery'*)
The Royal Botanic Gardens, Kew, Surrey.
Syon Park, Brentford, London.
Wallington, Cambo, Northumberland.

CORDON

A method of training fruit trees to grow on oblique stems, allowing several trees to be grown in a restricted space.

Examples of all methods of training fruit trees can be compared at the R.H.S. Gardens at Wisley, Surrey.
Dove Cottage, Clifton, Ashbourne, Derbyshire. (*Interesting gooseberry cordon hedges*)

CRINKLE-CRANKLE

A wall built in a serpentine fashion, the bays formed by its curves providing shelter for fruit trees, particularly stone fruits, the blossoms of which can be damaged by late frosts.

Deans Court, Wimborne, Dorset.
Heveningham Hall, Halesworth, Suffolk.

CROQUET LAWN

A flat expanse of grass, the correct dimensions of which are 32 × 26 m (35 × 28 yd), designed and laid out for the game of croquet. The game is played with wooden mallets with which wooden balls are hit through metal hoops.

Bodnant, Tal-y-Cafn, Gwynedd. (*On the terrace*)
Castle Drogo, Chagford, Devon.
Chartwell, Edenbridge, Kent.
Jenkyn Place, Bentley, Hants.
Old Hall, Stiffkey, Norfolk.

CUPOLA

A small dome crowning a roof or turret.

DORIC

The simplest of Greek orders of architecture which evolved on mainland Greece. Doric columns tend to be shorter than Ionic (q.v.) ones, swell towards the middle and taper towards the top to prevent them from looking cumbersome. They are less sophisticated, emphasizing their structural strength, and Doric colonnades lack a continuous sculpted frieze.

The Parthenon is said to

CUPOLA

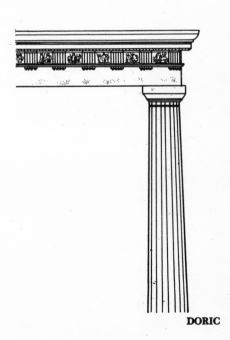

DORIC

exhibit Doric perfection.

Anglesey Abbey, Nr. Cambridge, Cambs. (*Two Doric-pillared open temples*)
Barnsley House, Barnsley, Nr. Cirencester, Glos. (*'Doric Temple' summerhouse*)
Blickling Hall, Aylsham, Norfolk. (*18th century Doric temple*)

DOVECOTE

Originally designed as a building in which pigeons were kept and bred as a source of food (see also Columbarium), dovecotes developed into houses for ornamental doves and pigeons, both the buildings and birds being for purely decorative purposes.

Athelhampton, Athelhampton, Dorset.
Crathes Castle, Banchory, Grampian.
Felbrigg Hall, Nr. Cromer, Norfolk. (*Octagonal — very large*)
Gunby Hall, Burgh-le-Marsh, Lincs.
Heale Gardens, Woodford, Salisbury, Wilts.
Nymans Garden, Handcross, West Sussex. (*This used to be referred to as a gazebo*)
Rousham House, Steeple Aston, Oxfordshire.
Snowshill Manor, Nr. Broadway, Glos.

ENTRANCE GATE

Any structure designed to give access to the grounds or garden of a house, while usually preventing undesirables from gaining that access by some form of locking device. They range from the simplest double piers supporting a wrought-iron gate to the most majestic of castellated gatehouses.

Blenheim Palace, Woodstock, Oxfordshire. (*East Gate*)
Castle Howard, York, N. Yorks. (*Pyramid and Carrmire Gates, together with the magnificent wrought-iron gates to the right of the entrance to the grounds*)

Charlecote Park, Warwick, Warwicks.
Cranborne Manor Gardens, Cranborne, Dorset.
Compton Acres, Poole, Dorset. (*Japanese 'Torro' Gate*)
Hampton Court Palace, Hampton Court, London. (*Lion gates*)
Lanhydrock, Nr. Bodmin, Cornwall.
Nymans Garden, Handcross, West Sussex. (*Italian-style brick gate in the walled garden*)
Pusey House, Faringdon, Oxfordshire. (*Elaborate wrought-iron gates between simple stone piers*)
St. Osyth's Priory, St. Osyth's, Clacton, Essex. (*Fortified Tudor*)

ESPALIER

A method of training the branches of fruit trees in 'horizontal' layers one above the other and securing the branches by wires against a wall or posts.

Examples of all methods of training fruit trees can be compared at the R.H.S. Gardens at Wisley in Surrey.

Barnsley House, Barnsley, Cirencester, Glos.
Barrington Court, Ilminster, Somerset.
Erddig, Wrexham, Clwyd.
Haddenham Hall, Haddenham, Bucks. (*Espaliered apple walk*)
Hatfield House, Hatfield, Herts.
Jenkyn Place, Bentley, Hants.

EXEDRA

A curving, usually semi-circular, background to a display of statuary. Most frequently seen as a dark hedge designed to complement and contrast with white marble, they can also be constructed of stone.

Belton House, Nr. Grantham, Lincs.(*Stone*)
Chatsworth, Bakewell, Derbyshire. (*Hedge-backed*)
Chiswick House, Chiswick, London. (*Hedge-backed*)
Stowe, Buckingham, Bucks. (*The so-called 'Temple of British Worthies'*)

FAN

The training of fruit trees into fan shapes with branches radiating from a short trunk and being tied onto horizontal wires or bamboo canes.

Examples of all methods of training fruit trees can be compared at the R.H.S. Gardens at Wisley, Surrey.
Erddig, Wrexham, Clwyd.
Hatfield House, Hatfield, Herts.

FERNERY

Strictly speaking a partially glazed but heavily shaded structure designed to maintain ideal conditions for growing ferns. The word is now used to describe any building which may originally have been an orangery, stove house or conservatory, that has been adapted to house ferns.

Highclere Castle, Nr. Newbury, Hants.
Montacute House, Yeovil, Somerset.
Tatton Park, Knutsford, Cheshire.

FINIAL

A formal ornament surmounting any structure, particularly balustrades, pavilions and the like. Popular subjects are simple balls, pineapples, obelisks and fleur-de-lys.

Canons Ashby House, Canons Ashby, Northants. (*Obelisks on gate posts*)
Montacute House, Yeovil, Somerset. (*Obelisks on balustraded walls*)
(**Note** — Almost every garden of any significance has finials.

FLOWERPOT

Any pot in which flowers are grown. (Note — The point at which a flowerpot becomes a jardinière (q.v.) would appear to be indefinable.)

Barnsley House, Barnsley, Cirencester, Glos.

Great Dixter, Northiam, East Sussex.
Hever Castle, Edenbridge, Kent. (*Italian terracotta*)
Powis Castle, Welshpool, Powys. (*Victorian baskets*)
Tintinhull House, Yeovil, Somerset.

FOLLY

A folly can be said to be any costly structure showing folly in its builder. (Note — In its widest sense the word includes many of the features covered separately in this book, in particular such buildings as temples, mausoleums, hermitages, moss and root houses. Also, although not fitting within the strict sense of the word, 'natural' ruins such as those of Fountains and Rievaulx Abbeys are generally accepted as follies when they are used as eyecatchers for gardens.)

Arthur's Hall, Cirencester Park, Glos.
Castle Drogo, Chagford, Devon. (*The Wendy House*)
Castle Howard, York, N. Yorks. (*The Pyramid*)
Fountains Abbey, Ripon, N. Yorks.
Hagley Hall, Nr. Stourbridge, W. Midlands. (*Sanderson Millar mock ruins*)
Lanrick Castle, Perthshire. (*A 60 ft stone 'tree'*)
Lyme Park, Disley, Stockport, Cheshire. (*Octagonal lantern tower*)
Reninshaw Hall, Bolsover, Derbyshire. (*Gothic 'Eagle House'*)
Rievaulx Abbey, Helmsley, N. Yorks.
Rockingham, Roscommon. (*Two sham castles*)
Shugborough, Stafford, Staffs. (*Athenian Stuart's Triumphal Arch*)
Stowe, Buckingham, Bucks, (*The 'Gothic' Temple*)
Wimpole Hall, Nr. Cambridge, Cambs. (*Sanderson Millar mock ruins*)

FOUNTAIN

Both a jet of water designed to spout for ornamental purposes

FINIAL

GOTHIC

and the structure from which it issues forth.

Ascott, Wing, Bucks. (*Venus on a shell*)
Blenheim Palace, Woodstock, Oxfordshire. (*Several*)
Buscot Park, Faringdon, Oxfordshire. (*Boy on a dolphin*)
Castle Howard, York, N. Yorks. (*Atlas fountain*)
Chatsworth, Bakewell, Derbyshire. (*Several*)
Cliveden, Maidenhead, Bucks. (*Fountain of Love*)
Holker Hall, Cark-in-Cartmel, Cumbria. (*Italian*)
Nymans Garden, Handcross, West Sussex. (*Italian marble in walled garden*)
Reninshaw Hall, Bolsover, Derbyshire. (*Spectacular single jet framed by yew hedges*)
Sezincote, Moreton-in-Marsh, Glos. (*Snake fountain*)
Shrubland Hall, Nr Ipswich, Suffolk.

GAZEBO

An ornamental building, often attached to a garden wall, from which a view can be comfortably admired. (See also Belvedere.)

Abbotswood, Stow-on-the-Wold, Glos. (*Designed by Lutyens*)
Bronhyddon, Llansantffraid-ym-Mechain, Powys.
Hazelby House, North End, Newbury, Berks. (*Trellis gazeboes*)
Hidcote Manor Garden, Hidcote Bartrim, Chipping Campden, Glos.
Melford Hall, Nr. Sudbury, Suffolk. (*Octagonal 'garden house'*)
Packwood House, Hockley Heath, Warwicks.
Pitmedden, Oldmeldrum, Aberdeen, Grampian. (*In an angle of the walled garden*)
Pollok House, Glasgow, Strathclyde. (*Two on the upper terrace which are also referred to as pavilions.*)
Poundisford Park, Pitminster, Nr. Taunton, Somerset.
Westbury Court Garden, Westbury-on-Severn, Glos.
Wyken Hall, Stanton, Suffolk.

GOTHIC

A mediaeval style of architecture, the most distinctive characteristic of which was the pointed arch. The Gothic revival in the 19th century was notable for the extent of its exaggerated use of such effects.

Abbot's Ripton Hall, Huntingdon, Cambs. (*Gothic treillage rondel*)
Barnsley House, Barnsley, Nr. Cirencester, Glos. (*Gothic summerhouse*)
Bramham Park, Wetherby, W. Yorks. (*Gothic folly temple*)
Pitchford Hall, Pitchford, Shropshire. (*The Tree House*)
Reninshaw Hall, Bolsover, Derbyshire. (*Gothic 'Eagle House'*)
Stowe, Buckingham, Bucks. (*The Gothic Temple*)

GROTTO

A man-made, or man-improved, picturesque cavern, frequently decorated with shells and/or statuary, and often associated with water. (Note — 'Grotto rooms', like those at Woburn, are rooms that are decorated with shells.)

Ashridge, Berkhamsted, Herts.
Chatsworth, Bakewell, Derbyshire.
Claremont Landscape Garden, Esher, Surrey.
Crowe Hill, Widcombe, Bath, Avon.
Goldney's Grotto, Goldney Hall, Clifton Hill, Bristol.
Ince Castle Gardens, Saltash, Cornwall. (*Shell House*)
Stourhead, Stourton, Nr. Mere, Wilts.
Studley Royal, Ripon, N. Yorks.
Waddesdon Manor, Nr. Aylesbury, Bucks.
Woburn Abbey, Woburn, Beds. (*The 'Grotto Room'*)

HA-HA

A ditch bounding a garden, with a vertical face on the garden side. It is so designed to keep stock out of the garden while deceiving the eye by appearing to extend it, and is by far the best known form of Trompe l'Oeil (q.v.) in gardens. The optimum effect is achieved when the ground level at both sides of the ditch is equalized.

Audley End, Saffron Walden, Essex.
Castle Howard, York, N. Yorks.
Charlecote Park, Warwick, Warwicks.
Claremont Landscape Garden, Esher, Surrey.
Grey's Court, Henley-on-Thames, Oxfordshire.
Killerton, Nr. Exeter, Devon.
Lacock Abbey, Lacock, Wilts.
The Old Rectory, Farnborough, Berks.
Sezincote, Moreton-in-Marsh, Glos.
Upton House, Edge Hill, Warwicks.

HEATED WALL

A hollow wall through which heated air is fed or through which hot water pipes run. Their object was to protect the more tender plants grown against them from the ravages of the weather and, in particular, late frosts. (See also Crinkle-Crankle)

Bodelwydden Castle, St. Asaph, Clwyd.
Packwood House, Hockley Heath, Warwicks. (*Includes a gazebo-like furnace house*)
Shrubland Hall, Ipswich, Suffolk.

HEDGE

A fence of trimmed bushes or low trees, either forming the boundary of a garden, or separating one part of a garden from another, or edging paths, knots and the like, or acting as background contrast for some other garden feature.

Ascott, Wing, Bucks.
Athelhampton, Athelhampton, Dorset.
Blickling Hall, Aylsham, Norfolk.

Chatsworth House, Bakewell, Derbyshire.
Crathes Castle, Banchory, Grampian.
Hidcote Manor Garden, Hidcote Bartrim, Nr. Chipping Campden, Glos.
Knightshayes Court, Nr. Tiverton, Devon.
Levens Hall, Kendal, Cumbria.
Penshurst Place, Tunbridge Wells, Kent.
Sissinghurst Castle, Sissinghurst, Kent.

HERB GARDEN

A part of the garden set aside for the cultivation of culinary herbs. Although sometimes severely utilitarian, many are designed to please the senses of sight, smell and touch.

Acorn Bank, Temple Sowerby, Penrith, Cumbria.
Badminton House, Badminton, Avon.
Buckland Abbey, Tavistock, Devon.
Hardwick Hall, Chesterfield, Derbyshire. (*Particularly extensive*)
Jenkyn Place, Bentley, Hants.
Knebworth House, Knebworth, Herts. (*Quincunx pattern, designed by Gertrude Jekyll*)
Norton Priory, Runcorn, Cheshire.
Sissinghurst Castle, Sissinghurst, Kent.
Swanington Manor Gardens, Swanington, Nr. Norwich, Norfolk.
Wyken Hall, Stanton, Suffolk.

HERMITAGE

A garden retreat built to play home to a hermit who was employed to live in it. To maintain the deception hermitages were usually as rough and unkempt in appearance as their intended inhabitants.

Badminton House, Great Badminton, Avon. (*Hermit's Park House*)
Bicton Park, Bicton, Devon.

ICE HOUSE

A building designed for the storage of ice before the advent of refrigeration. Set high above the water table, it consisted of a deep pit protected by thick walls. The pit was filled by ice from the lake in the gardens at the approach of spring, assuring the house of a supply during the summer months. Usually severely practical in design, they were occasionally ornamented to accord with the style of other nearby garden structures.

Attingham Park, Shrewsbury, Shropshire.
Harewood House, Leeds, W. Yorks.
Hatchlands, East Clandon, Surrey.
Heveningham Hall, Halesworth, Suffolk.
Killerton, Nr. Exeter, Devon.
Osterley Park House, Osterley, London.
Scotney Castle Garden, Lamberhurst, Kent.
Sutton Park, Sutton-on-the-Forest, N. Yorks.
Tapeley Park, Instow, Devon
Waddesdon Manor, Nr. Aylesbury, Bucks.

IONIC

The second of the Greek orders of architecture which evolved in Asia Minor and the Aegean Islands. Ionic columns tend to be tall and slender in comparison with their shorter, more massive, Doric (q.v.) cousins, and Ionic colonnades are surmounted by continuous sculpted friezes.

Wilton House, Nr. Salisbury, Wilts. (*The Ionic colonnade of the Palladian bridge*)

JARDINIÈRE

An ornamental pot or stand in which flowers are either grown or displayed.

Harewood House, Leeds, W. Yorks. (*Basketwork style*)
Jenkyn Place, Bentley, Hants. (*In the 'Sundial' garden*)

Knightshayes Court, Nr. Tiverton, Devon.
Sezincote, Moreton-in-Marsh, Glos.
Sissinghurst Castle Garden, Sissinghurst, Kent.

KIOSK

A pavilion (q.v.), normally of either hexagonal or octagonal shape, most frequently in a Near Eastern style, usually positioned as a resting place on the tour of a large garden. In modern times buildings in this style are often used for the dispensing of refreshments. (Note — Interestingly, the old red telephone kiosk has recently become a collectable garden feature.)

Claremont Landscape Garden, Esher, Surrey.
Gunby Hall, Burgh-le-Marsh, Lincs. (*Hexagonal 'summerhouse'*)
Nymans, Handcross, West Sussex.
Sezincote, Moreton-in-Marsh, Glos. (*A particularly elegant, modern interpretation*)

KNOT & KNOT GARDEN

A knot is a bed laid out in a relatively intricate pattern, this usually being outlined by a low clipped hedge of box, yew or lavender. The area within the pattern is filled with coloured gravels, sands etc. or plants. The patterns are designed to be viewed from above for the best effect.

A knot garden is a garden constructed of several knots.

Barnsley House Garden, Cirencester, Glos.
Cranborne Manor Gardens, Cranborne, Dorset.
Edzell Castle, Edzell, Tayside. (*The 'Pleasance'*)
Hatfield House, Hatfield, Herts.
Lanhydrock, Nr. Bodmin, Cornwall.
Little Moreton Hall, Congleton, Cheshire.
Moseley Old Hall, Wolverhampton, Staffs.

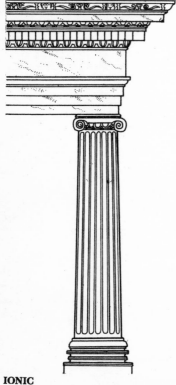

IONIC

New Place, Stratford-upon-
Avon, Warwicks.
Swanington Manor Gardens,
Swanington, Nr. Norwich,
Norfolk.
Tudor House Museum,
Southampton, Hants.

LABYRINTH

The words labyrinth and maze
(q.v.) have today become
virtually synonymous and
interchangeable: the *Pocket Oxford
English Dictionary*, for example,
describes a maze as a labyrinth
and a labyrinth as a maze.
Technically, however, any maze
of which the structure blocks the
view of the intending solver is a
labyrinth. Thus many 'mazes',
as we know them, are actually
labyrinths.

(*See Maze for examples*)

LAKE

A relatively large body of water
of natural appearance.
(Notes — 1. Most lakes in
gardens are, in point of fact, man-
made, streams having been
dammed to form them. 2. The
dividing line between a lake and
a pond (q.v.) is difficult to
determine, often being dictated
by its size in relation to the size
of the garden in which it lies.
Thus a lake in one garden might
well be referred to as a large pond
in another.)

Blenheim Palace, Woodstock,
Oxfordshire.
Blickling Hall, Aylsham, Norfolk.
Claremont Landscape Garden,
Esher, Surrey.
Harewood House, Leeds, W.
Yorks.
Hever Castle, Edenbridge, Kent.
Luton Hoo, Luton, Beds.
Petworth House, Petworth,
West Sussex.
Sheffield Park Gardens,
Sheffield Park, East Sussex.
Stourhead, Stourton, Nr. Mere,
Wilts.
West Wycombe Park, West
Wycombe, Bucks.

LEAD CISTERN

A lead tank designed for the
storage of water. Although
sometimes plain, many were
decorated with mythological
scenes or coats of arms.

Helmingham Hall, Ipswich,
Suffolk.

LOGGIA

An open-sided room attached to
a house, or an arcade, having
one or both of its longitudinal
sides open, which is set apart
from the house. The designs of
the latter are usually Italianate
and they are positioned either as
viewpoints or eyecatchers.

Antony House, Torpoint,
Cornwall.
Cranborne Manor Gardens,
Cranborne, Dorset.
Folly Farm, Sulhampstead, Berks.
Hever Castle, Edenbridge,
Kent.
Misarden Park Garden,
Misarden, Stroud, Glos.
Penheale Manor, Nr.
Launceston, Cornwall.
Shrubland Hall, Ipswich,
Suffolk.
Tintinhull, Yeovil, Somerset.
Wilton House, Salisbury, Wilts.

LOZENGE/
LOZENGE-SHAPED

A rhomboidal or diamond-
shaped figure, usually with
heraldic connotations.

Cranborne Manor Gardens,
Cranborne, Dorset. (*The lodges
which support the gatehouse*)

MAUSOLEUM

A magnificent, some might say
ostentatious, family tomb often
used as an eyecatcher.

Bodnant Garden, Tal-y-Cafn,
Gwynedd.
Blickling Hall, Aylsham,
Norfolk. (*Pyramidal*)
Castle Howard, York, N. Yorks.
The Royal Mausoleum,
Frogmore Garden, Windsor
Castle, Berks.

MAZE

The true ancient maze was a puzzle pattern set in turf with a religious or magical significance. With the development of knots, many were designed as mazes and thus the familiar hedged maze arose, this, technically speaking, being a labyrinth. (q.v.)

Chatsworth, Bakewell, Derbyshire.
Glendurgan, Mawnan Smith, Cornwall.
Grey's Court, Henley-on-Thames, Oxfordshire.
Hampton Court Palace, Hampton Court, London.
Hatfield House, Hatfield, Herts.
Hever Castle, Edenbridge, Kent.
Leeds Castle, Nr. Maidstone, Kent.

MOAT

A water-filled defensive ditch surrounding a castle, hall or house. Today moats are often made more decorative and less strategic by the addition of colourful fish and water lilies.

Baddesley Clinton, Solihull, Warwicks.
Bodiam Castle, Nr. Robertsbridge, East Sussex.
Charlecote, Warwick, Warwicks.
Helmingham Hall, Ipswich, Suffolk.
Hever Castle, Edenbridge, Kent.
Ightham Mote, Ivy Hatch, Kent.
Little Moreton Hall, Congleton, Cheshire.
Oxburgh Hall, Oxborough, Norfolk.
Scotney Castle, Lamberhurst, Kent.

MOON WINDOW

A perfectly circular opening in a wall permitting a view of the garden beyond and often framing some particular feature within it.

Biddestone Manor, Biddestone, Nr. Corsham, Wilts.

Polesden Lacey, Dorking, Surrey.
Portmeirion, Portmadoc, Gwynedd.
West Green House, Hartley Wintney, Hants (*Moon Gate*)

MOSAIC

An art form in which designs are reproduced by joining together minute pieces of materials such as glass or stone of diverse colours.

MOSS HOUSE

A modest garden building constructed of wooden slats, between which moss was pressed. They were popular in Victorian times.

It is believed that none still exist as they soon disintegrated unless continually maintained with fresh supplies of moss.

MOUNT

An artificial hill built within a garden, usually designed to command a view over a specific feature such as a knot garden.

Claremont Landscape Garden, Esher, Surrey. (*The Belvedere is positioned atop what is referred to as 'The Mount', but this is a natural, not an artificial, hill*)
Little Moreton Hall, Congleton, Cheshire. (*Near the knot garden*)
Nymans, Handcross, West Sussex. (*Overlooking the bowling green*)
Packwood House, Hockley Heath, Warwicks.
Stanway House, Stanway, Glos. (*Terraced*)

OBELISK

A four-sided tapering stone pillar topped by a pyramid, used either as a finial (q.v.) atop a balustrade or, on a much grander scale, as a memorial to some personage or event, these latter frequently being positioned as eyecatchers or vista stoppers.

Arlington Court, Barnstaple, Devon (*Celebrates the 1887 Jubilee*

OBELISK

of Queen Victoria)
Blenheim Palace, Woodstock, Oxfordshire.
Canons Ashby House, Canons Ashby, Northants. (*Obelisk finials on gateposts.*)
Castle Howard, York, N. Yorks.
Farnborough Hall, Banbury, Oxfordshire.
Hall Barn, Beaconsfield, Bucks.
Holkham Hall, Wells, Norfolk.
Montacute House, Yeovil, Somerset. (*Finials on Elizabethan walls*)

OGÉE

A sinuous line consisting of a double continuous curve as in the letter 'S', particularly used for a moulding consisting of such a section.

Hermit's Park House, Badminton, Greater Badminton, Avon. (*The back of the bench under the rear pediment*)

OGIVE/OGIVAL

Derived directly from the French, meaning a pointed arch. Gothic (q.v.) arches are ogival in shape.

ORANGERY

A solid-roofed building with heavily glazed walls into which the sculpted citrus trees so popular in the 17th and early 18th centuries were moved in the winter for protection. Later examples have glass lights in the roof for greater illumination.

Belton House, Nr. Grantham, Lincs..
Blickling Hall, Aylsham, Norfolk.
Chatsworth, Bakewell, Derbyshire.
Hestercombe House, Cheddon Fitzpaine, Taunton, Somerset.
Lyme Park, Stockport, Greater Manchester.
Osterley Park, Osterley, London.
Powis Castle, Welshpool, Powys. (*Unusual as it is built into the lowest terrace*)
Saltram House, Plymouth, Devon.

Sezincote, Moreton-in-Marsh, Glos. (*Attached to and curving away from the house*)
Wrest Park Gardens, Silsoe, Beds.

PAGODA

A highly ornamental, multi-storeyed, pyramidal building, Far Eastern in style, the concept being borrowed by the Chinese from sacred Indian towers and used by them for storing relics of Buddha.

Alton Towers, Alton, Staffs.
Chastleton Glebe, Chastleton, Nr. Moreton-in-Marsh, Oxfordshire.
Cliveden, Maidenhead, Bucks.
Compton Acres, Poole, Dorset.
Linden Hall, Carnforth, Lancs.
The Royal Botanic Gardens, Kew, London.

PALLADIAN

An architectural style derived from the drawings and buildings of Andrea Palladio, a 16th century Italian architect. It was introduced to Britain by Inigo Jones during the early part of the 17th century and revived in the early 18th century, from which time most surviving Palladian-style garden buildings originate.

Castle Howard, York, N. Yorks. (*The Temple of the Four Winds*)
Stowe, Buckingham, Bucks. (*Palladian Bridge*)
Wilton House, Nr. Salisbury, Wilts. (*Palladian Bridge*)
Wrest Park Gardens, Silsoe, Beds. (*Pavilion*)

PARTERRE

A formal sweep of patterned beds contrasted and complemented by areas of grass to form an harmonious entity. Developed by the French during the second half of the 17th century, the patterns were initially based on those of knots (q.v.), but eventually became far more extensive and ornate.

(Note — During the Victorian

OGEE

PALLADIAN

PARTERRE

age there was a renewed fashion for formality in garden design, many of the resulting gardens being referred to as parterres, but their fussy use of bedding plants did not accord well with the elegance of the originals. We, therefore, prefer to call these Victorian parterres 'formal gardens'.)

Blenheim Palace, Woodstock, Oxfordshire. (*Both the East Front and Water Parterres*)
Blickling Hall, Aylsham, Norfolk. (*Victorian, but very unusual. Yew hedges shaped as grand pianos form the basis of the design*)
Cliveden, Maidenhead, Bucks.
Drummond Castle Gardens, Muthill, Tayside. (*Formal garden in dramatic St. Andrew's Cross shape*)
The Great Garden, Pitmedden, Udny, Grampian
Ham House, Richmond, London.
Hatfield House, Hatfield, Herts.
Oxburgh Hall, Oxborough, Norfolk.
Penshurst Place, Tunbridge Wells, Kent.
Westbury Court Garden, Westbury-on-Severn, Glos.

PATH

Any footway designed to lead you through the garden, from the simplest of muddy tracks to the most formal of paved paths crossing a terrace or leading around a parterre.

Barrington Court, Ilminster, Somerset. (*Paved paths within the walled garden*)
Castle Drogo, Chagford, Devon. (*The main axial path emphasizes the theatricality of Lutyens' design*)
Great Dixter, Northiam, East Sussex.
Hidcote Manor Garden, Hidcote Bartrim, Nr. Chipping Campden, Glos. (*Many attractive brick paths, but also some made of crushed staddle stones (q.v.)*)
Mottisfont Abbey, Mottisfont, Hants. (*Lined by low hedges leading through the rose garden*)
Newby Hall, Ripon, N. Yorks. (*Unusual stone paths leading through*

woodland)
Pusey House, Faringdon, Oxfordshire.
Wakehurst Place, Ardingly, West Sussex.

PATTE D'OIE

Literally translated from the French as 'goose's foot', this describes a number of alleys, avenues or vistas radiating in a fan pattern from a central point.

(Note — It is important to emphasize that a patte d'oie forms a semi-circle while a rond-point forms a full circle. Confusion over this point often creeps into publications.)

Ham House, Richmond, London. (*Radiating walks edged with hornbeam hedges*)
Hampton Court Palace, Hampton Court, London. (*Radiating avenues lined with common limes*)
St. Paul's, Waldenbury, Whitwell, Nr. Hitchin, Herts. (*Beech hedge-bordered alleys*)

PAVILION

An ornamental garden building usually exhibiting Eastern elements, such as a curved roof, in its design.

Athelhampton, Athelhampton, Dorset.
Biddulph Grange, Biddulph, Staffs. (*Chinese*)
Claverton Manor, Bath, Avon. (*Octagonal*)
Hidcote Manor Garden, Hidcote Bartrim, Nr. Chipping Campden, Glos. (*The twin gazeboes are often referred to as pavilions*)
Mereworth Castle, Kent. (*Italianate pavilion*)
Montacute House, Yeovil, Somerset. (*Although now generally referred to as pavilions, the two buildings set in the walls are thought to have been built as banqueting houses*)
Stowe, Buckingham, Bucks. (*The twin Boycott pavilions*)
Tintinhull House, Yeovil, Somerset.

Wrest Park Gardens, Silsoe, Beds. (*Palladian*)

PERGOLA

A construction consisting of uprights, their tops interconnected by horizontal beams, which act as a support for climbing plants and frames and a walk below.

Bodnant Garden, Tal-y-Cafn, Gwynedd. (*Laburnum tunnel (q.v.)*)
Chartwell, Edenbridge, Kent. (*Vine*)
Gunby Hall, Burgh-le-Marsh, Lincs. (*Fruit trees*)
Heale House Gardens, Woodford, Salisbury, Wilts.
Hestercombe House, Cheddon Fitzpaine, Taunton, Somerset. (*Very long, stone pillars*)
Mompesson House, Salisbury, Wilts. (*Honeysuckle and philadelphus*)
National Rose Society's Garden, St. Albans, Herts.
Polesden Lacey, Dorking, Surrey. (*Roses*)
The Priory, Kemerton, Nr. Tewkesbury, Hereford and Worcester. (*Roses and vines*)
R.H.S. Garden, Wisley, Surrey. (*Wisteria by the canal*)

PIER

A solid support, usually constructed of brick or stone and usually rectangular, as distinct from a circular column.

Chatsworth, Bakewell, Derbyshire. (*The piers of the classical bridge*)
Hampton Court Palace, Hampton Court, London. (*The piers of the clair-voyée*)
Pusey House, Nr. Faringdon, Oxfordshire. (*The piers supporting the elaborate wrought-iron gates.*)

PLANTING WALL

A wall incorporating niches which can be filled with soil and in which plants can be grown.

Edzell Castle, Edzell, Brechin, Tayside. (*Although possibly not a planting wall in the strict sense, this is a fascinating and very attractive structure*)

PLASHING

To a farmer plashing is a method of hedging in which the branches are cut back and interwoven. This technique was adopted and modified for use in Victorian gardens and also extended to the training back of trees lining avenues in order to maintain an open vista.

Hall Barn, Beaconsfield, Bucks.

PLEACH

A form of plant sculpture in which certain trees — notably lime, hornbeam and beech — are shaped into square 'lollypops' on bare trunks. Pleached trees are usually planted to either side of a path forming shaded alleys and are trained onto taut wires stretching between them to help to maintain their shape.

Bateman's, Burwash, East Sussex. (*Lime*)
Chatsworth, Bakewell, Derbyshire. (*Lime*)
Ham House, Richmond, London. (*Hornbeam*)
Hatfield House, Hatfield, Herts.
Hidcote Manor Garden, Hidcote Bartrim, Nr. Chipping Campden, Glos. (*Hornbeam*)
Peover Hall, Knutsford, Cheshire. (*Lime*)
The Royal Botanic Gardens, Kew, London. (*Lime*)
Sissinghurst Castle, Sissinghurst, Kent. (*Lime*)

PLINTH

The lowest square member on which a column stands, or a raised base supporting an ornament such as a vase, urn, statue, sundial or astrolabe.

Haseley Court, Little Haseley, Oxfordshire. (*The elaborate plinth for the astrolabe*)

POND

The words pond and pool (q.v.)

are virtually synonymous, but for the purposes of this book we have believed it useful to attempt to establish a distinction between them. Throughout the text, therefore, a pond is informal, of irregular shape, natural in overall appearance, with plants tumbling round its edges thus further disguising any hint of geometrical form.

(Note — The dividing line between a pond and a lake (q.v.) is difficult to determine, often being dictated by its size in relation to the garden. Thus a large pond in one garden might well be called a lake in another.)

Bressingham Hall Gardens, Diss, Norfolk.
Cliveden, Maidenhead, Bucks. (*Japanese Garden*)
Compton Acres, Poole, Dorset. (*Japanese Garden*)
Crittenden House, Matfield, Tonbridge, Kent.
Heale House Gardens, Woodford, Salisbury, Wilts.
Hodnet Hall, Market Drayton, Shropshire.
Longstock Park, Nr. Stockbridge, Hants.
Penheale Manor, Nr. Launceston, Cornwall.
Rosemoor, Torrington, Devon.
Tatton Park, Knutsford, Cheshire. (*Japanese Garden*)

POOL

The words pool and pond (q.v.) are virtually synonymous but for the purposes of this book we have believed it useful to attempt to establish a distinction between them. Throughout the text, therefore, a pool is formal and of a regular, usually geometrical, shape.

Blenheim Palace, Woodstock, Oxfordshire.
Crathes Castle, Banchory, Grampian.
Easton Neston, Northants. (*Bow-shaped*)
Great Dixter, Northiam, East Sussex. (*Octagonal*)
Heale House Gardens,

Woodford, Salisbury, Wilts.
Hidcote Manor Gardens, Hidcote Bartrim, Nr. Chipping Campden, Glos.(*Raised circular pool*)
Knightshayes Court, Tiverton, Devon.
Sezincote, Moreton-in-Marsh, Glos.

There are bath house pools at:—
Packwood House, Hockley Heath, Warwicks.
Rousham House, Steeple Aston, Oxfordshire.
Wrest Park Gardens, Silsoe, Beds.

PORTICO

A roofed space supported by columns, open or partially enclosed, often forming the entrance and focal point of the façade of a temple or similar building.

Sezincote, Moreton-in-Marsh, Glos. (*The Kiosk*)
Shrubland Hall, Ipswich, Suffolk. (*The Baroque portico at the top of the steps*)

POTAGER

The literal translation of the French 'jardin potager' is kitchen garden. However, during the reign of Louis XIV it became specifically applied to an ornamental, rather than strictly practical, kitchen garden with vegetables planted in patterns between low clipped hedges in the manner of knots (q.v.); and this is how the word is interpreted today.

Barnsley House Garden, Cirencester, Glos.
Upton House, Edge Hill, Warwicks.
West Green House, Hartley Wintney, Hants.

QUINCUNX

A method of planting trees in groups of five within a square or diamond-shaped pattern, the fifth tree being positioned in the centre.

Holkham Hall, Wells, Norfolk.
Sudbury Hall, Sudbury, Nr.
Derby, Derbyshire.
Westbury Court Gardens,
Westbury-on-Severn, Glos.

RILL

A small concrete or stone channel
down which water is led formally
through a garden.

Buscot Park, Faringdon,
Oxfordshire.
Harewood House, Leeds, W.
Yorks. (*In the 'Rock Garden' or
'Dell', fed by a spring rising from
beneath a seat under an attractive
green-tiled canopy*)
Hestercombe House, Cheddon
Fitzpaine, Taunton, Somerset.
Rousham House, Steeple Aston,
Oxfordshire. (*By William Kent*)
Shute House, Dunhead St. Mary,
Shaftesbury, Dorset.

ROCOCO

A form of decoration, fashionable
in Britain during the middle of
the 18th century, which was
developed from late Baroque,
but which was lighter and more
elegant in style while still being
florid and highly ornamental.

RONDEL

A formal circle, usually either of
hedging or treillage, with four
paths leading off at 90° to each
other.

Abbot's Ripton Hall,
Huntingdon, Cambs. (*Gothic style
treillage*)
Levens Hall, Kendal, Cumbria.
(*Hedges*)
Sissinghurst Castle,
Sissinghurst, Kent. (*Hedges*)

ROND-POINT

A circular clearing from which a
number of alleys or avenues
radiate. A rond-point is often
embellished with a dramatic
centrepiece such as a fountain or
piece of statuary as at Versailles.
Most British examples were
swept away by the landscape
gardening movement.

ROOT HOUSE

A rustic retreat formed from the
roots of trees and particularly
popular, as with the moss house
(q.v.), in Victorian times.

Spetchley Park, Worcester,
Hereford and Worcester.

ROTUNDA

A circular domed and pillared
building, usually a temple.

Hatchlands, East Clandon,
Surrey.
The Royal Botanic Gardens,
Kew, London.
Stowe, Buckingham, Bucks.

SARCOPHAGUS

Derived from the Greek meaning
'flesh-eating', a sarcophagus is a
stone, originally limestone, coffin.
Most of the sarcophagi to be seen
in gardens today are of Roman
origin and decorated with
elaborately sculpted reliefs.

Chatsworth, Bakewell,
Derbyshire.
Cliveden, Maidenhead, Bucks.
Hever Castle, Edenbridge,
Kent.
Iford Manor, Bradford-on-
Avon, Wilts.

SEAT

Whether of turf, wood, stone or
metal, a seat is, quite simply, an
object specifically designed for
sitting upon, with a back to lean
against and, very often, arm rests.

Antony House, Torpoint,
Cornwall. (*Recessed into a curved
hedge with statues to either side rather
in the manner of an exedra (q.v.)*)
Bodnant Garden, Tal-y-Cafn,
Gwynedd.
Felbrigg Hall, Nr. Cromer,
Norfolk. (*Unusual 'wheelbarrow'
seat*)
Jenkyn Place, Bentley, Hants.
(*Stone seat framed by a yew hedge
clipped to resemble a giant armchair*)
Knightshayes Court, Tiverton,
Devon. (*Stone seat by a pool*)
Newby Hall, Ripon, N. Yorks.
(*Curved stone*)

SEAT

The Old Rectory, Farnborough, Berks. (*Curved seat in the rose garden*)
Pyrford Court, Woking, Surrey. (*Italianate*)
Rousham, Steeple Aston, Oxfordshire. (*The 'Green' seats*)
Wilton House, Salisbury, Wilts.

SHADED HOUSE

A summer house (q.v.) sited in a heavily shaded position and designed to be a retreat from the heat of the day.

Bressingham Hall Gardens, Diss, Norfolk. (*Norfolk flint and thatched garden house*)
Killerton, Nr. Exeter, Devon. (*The 'Bear's Hut'*) (See also Summer House.)

STADDLE STONE

A 0.6 m (2 ft) high stone mushroom originally designed for supporting the edges of grain stores to prevent rats from climbing up into them.

Staddle stones are frequently used as decorations in cottage gardens, but are less often seen in the gardens of historic houses. Some rather battered specimens line the road leading from the information centre to the lake at Stourhead, and some of the paths at Hidcote are made of broken pieces of staddle stone, indicating how little importance was attached to them in the relatively recent past. Following a visit to Hidcote, a stroll through the Cotswold village of Broadway will reveal many, however.

Malthouse Farm, Hambledon, Nr. Godalming, Surrey has an 18th century granary which still stands on its staddle stones.

STATUARY

Sculpted or moulded figures, particularly of people and animals, constructed of a wide variety of materials — stone, lead, terracotta and marble being among the most popular. Among the subjects most frequently seen in gardens are Roman statues and copies thereof, mythological subjects, copies from both Italian sculpture and painting, cherubs and animals.

Anglesey Abbey, Nr. Cambridge, Cambs. (*Copy of Bernini's David*)
Cliveden, Maidenhead, Bucks. (*Many Venetian*)
Hatfield House, Hatfield, Herts. (*18th century Italian*)
Jenkyn Place, Bentley, Hants. (*Lions plus a copy of Giambologna's Bacchus*)
Melbourne Hall, Melbourne, Derbyshire. (*Delightful quarrelling cherubs*)
Mount Stewart, Newtownards, Co. Down, Northern Ireland. (*Animals and Ark*)
Powis Castle, Welshpool, Powys. (*Lead by Van Nost and others*)
Pyrford Court, Woking, Surrey. (*Boy riding a snail*)
Reninshaw Hall, Bolsover, Derbyshire. (*Italian*)
St. Paul's, Waldenbury, Whitwell, Nr. Hitchin, Herts. (*Marble*)
Waddesdon Manor, Nr. Aylesbury, Bucks. (*Animals and birds*)

STEPPING STONES

Stones set in a pond, pool or stream by which the obstacle can be crossed with a relative degree of security.

Compton Acres, Poole, Dorset. (*In the Japanese Garden*)
Harewood House, Leeds, W. Yorks. (*Across the stream below the cascade, but only suitable for the more adventurous*)
Preston Park Rockery, Brighton, Sussex. (*Stepping Rocks*)
Sezincote, Moreton-in-Marsh, Glos. (*Beneath the Indian 'Bull' bridge*)

STEPS

The universally used method of gaining or losing height rapidly and safely while following a path. They vary from the simplest wood-edged earth steps leading through woodland, to the most elaborate sweeps of stone steps leading to and from terraces.

Biddulph Grange, Biddulph, Staffs.
Chilham Castle Gardens, Nr. Canterbury, Kent. (*Brick*)
Haddon Hall, Bakewell, Derbyshire. (*Leading onto the rose terrace*)
Hatfield House, Hatfield, Herts.
Luton Hoo, Luton, Beds.
Mount Stewart, Newtownards, Co. Down, Northern Ireland.
Shrubland Hall, Ipswich, Suffolk.
Tresco Abbey Gardens, Isles of Scilly
Upton House, Edge Hill, Warwicks.
Winkworth Arboretum, Nr. Godalming, Surrey.

STOVE HOUSE

A building with heavily glazed walls but a solid roof, heated by coal or coke burning stoves. They were the predecessors of the modern conservatory and glasshouse. Similar in appearance to orangeries (q.v.) they were usually far less ornate and were made obsolete when it was recognized that most plants required the greater light intensities offered by glazed roofs.

STREAM

A relatively small scale flowing body of water of natural appearance, even if man-made. As with lakes and pools, it is difficult to define precisely when a stream becomes a river, this again being a matter of relative size. However, few gardens can boast a full-blown river flowing through them, yet many are bordered by rivers and utilize them as features.

Bicton Park, Bicton, Devon.
Bodnant Garden, Tal-y-Cafn, Gwynedd.
Burford House Gardens, Tenbury Wells, Hereford and Worcester.

Heale House Gardens, Woodford, Salisbury, Wilts.
Hidcote Manor Garden, Hidcote Bartrim, Nr. Chipping Campden, Glos.
Hodnet Hall Gardens, Nr. Market Drayton, Shropshire.
Leonardslee, Horsham, West Sussex.
R.H.S. Gardens, Wisley, Surrey.
Sezincote, Moreton-in-Marsh, Glos.
Wakehurst Place, Ardingly, West Sussex.

STUCCO

A plaster medium used for covering walls and ceilings and for making mouldings and other surface ornamentations.

SUMMER HOUSE

Any building designed as a place in which to sit and enjoy the beauties of the surrounding garden can be called a summer house. However the more ornate are usually endowed with grander names such as pavilion, gazebo, kiosk, and even temple. Within the term summer house are lumped all those buildings of less grand pretentions, ranging from the simplest of roofed seats to the Pin Mill at Bodnant.

Abbot's Ripton Hall, Huntingdon, Cambs. (*Cone-shaped thatched roof with Gothic windows. A folly!*)
Ascott, Wing, Bucks. (*At the end of the 'Madeira Walk'*)
Barnsley House, Barnsley, Cirencester, Glos. (*Gothic*)
Bodnant Garden, Tal-y-Cafn, Gwynedd. (*The 'Pin Mill'*)
Clevedon Court, Clevedon, Avon.
Longstock Park, Stockbridge, Hants. (*Thatched*)
The Old Rectory, Farnborough, Berks. (*Modern*)
Peckover House, Wisbech, Cambs. (*In the rose garden walk*)
Snowshill Manor, Broadway, Glos.

SUNDIAL

An early instrument for determining the time of day. It uses the position of the shadow of an ornamental pointer, known as a gnomon, on a circular dial set at right angles to it and marked with the hours.

Ascott, Wing, Bucks. (*Topiary sundial*)
Barrington Court, Ilminster, Somerset. (*Ten faced*)
Drummond Castle Gardens, Muthill, Tayside. (*Extraordinary multiple dial*)
Erddig, Wrexham, Clwyd. (*Decorated with the coat of arms of John Meller, originator of the garden.*)
Packwood House, Hockley Heath, Warwicks. (*Three in all, each with a separate motto.*)
Penshurst Place, Lamberhurst, Kent. (*Vertical dial*)
Pusey House, Faringdon, Oxfordshire.
Queen's College, Cambridge Cambs. *(Vertical dial)*
St. Paul's, Waldenbury, Whitwell, Nr. Hitchin, Herts. (*Supported by Father Time*)
Snowshill Manor, Broadway, Glos. (*Not a sundial, but a very unusual blue ornamental clock set in a wall and called the 'Nychthemeron'*)

SUNKEN GARDEN

An area of a garden set at a level significantly lower than that of the garden surrounding it and designed both to be viewed from above and to give some degree of protection to tender plants.

Chenies Manor, Chenies, Bucks.
Folly Farm, Sulhampstead, Berks.
Great Dixter, Northiam, East Sussex.
Hampton Court Palace, Hampton Court, London.
Hestercombe Gardens, Cheddon Fitzpaine, Taunton, Somerset.
Mount Stewart, Newtownards, Co. Down, Northern Ireland.
Newby Hall, Ripon, N. Yorks.
Old Hall, Stiffkey, Norfolk.
Packwood House, Hockley Heath, Warwicks.

The Priory, Kemerton, Tewkesbury, Hereford and Worcester.
Ryelands House, Taynton, Glos.

TEA HOUSE

A building, usually Japanese in design, specifically built for the making and partaking of tea. (Note — The characteristics of the traditional Japanese tea house are described in some detail in the main body of this book.)

Compton Acres, Poole, Dorset.
Heale House Gardens, Woodford, Salisbury, Wilts.
Hidcote Manor Gardens, Hidcote Bartrim, Nr. Chipping Campden, Glos. (*One of the twin gazeboes which commands no view but is equipped for making tea*)
Tully, Co. Kildare, Eire. (*By Japanese gardener Eida in 1906*)

TEMPLE

A replica of a place of worship, most frequently based on classical designs from Greek and Roman times, but also sometimes in Far Eastern style. They are usually positioned so they provide eyecatchers or vista stoppers.

Anglesey Abbey, Nr. Cambridge, Cambs. (*Two open Doric-pillared temples, one containing a hanging bell, the other a huge porphyry vase.*)
Barnsley House, Barnsley, Cirencester, Glos. (*Tuscan Doric*).
Blickling Hall, Aylsham, Norfolk. (*18th century Doric*)
Bramham Park, Wetherby, W. Yorks. (*Gothic folly temple*)
Castle Howard, York, N.Yorks. (*The Temple of the Four Winds*)
Farnborough Hall, Nr. Banbury, Oxfordshire. (*Unusual oval shape*)
Hatchlands, East Clandon, Surrey. (*Rotunda*)
Stourhead, Stourton, Nr. Mere, Wilts. (*Temple of Apollo*)
Stowe, Buckingham, Bucks. (*Many*)
Studley Royal, Ripon, N. Yorks. (*Temple of Piety*)

TERRACE

The simplest form of a terrace is a flat, paved or grassed area, usually enclosed by a low wall or balustrade on which the house stands and which leads to the rest of the garden. Where a garden includes a steep slope, a series of terraces interconnected by flights of steps makes an impressive and dramatic solution to the problems such terrain represent. The walls and balustrades of terraces are often embellished with ornaments and statuary.

Bodnant Garden, Tal-y-Cafn, Gwynedd.
Cliveden, Maidenhead, Bucks.
Culzean Castle, Maybole, Ayrshire, Grampian.
Drummond Castle Gardens, Muthill, Tayside.
Haddon Hall, Bakewell, Derbyshire.
Harewood House, Leeds, W. Yorks.
Hestercombe Garden, Cheddon Fitzpaine, Taunton, Somerset.
Knightshayes Court, Nr. Tiverton, Devon.
Powis Castle, Welshpool, Powys.
Shrubland Hall, Ipswich, Suffolk. (*Most spectacular terraces*)
Upton House, Edge Hill, Warwicks.

TOPIARY

The art of clipping and/or training evergreen shrubs and trees into elaborate shapes, most frequently free-standing.

Haseley Court, Little Haseley, Oxfordshire. (*Chess set*)
Hever Castle, Edenbridge, Kent. (*Chessmen*)
Hidcote Manor Gardens, Hidcote Bartrim, Nr. Chipping Campden, Glos.
Knightshayes Court, Nr. Tiverton, Devon. (*Fox hunt*)
Levens Hall, Kendal, Cumbria. (*Started in 1692*)
Mount Ephraim, Hernhill, Nr. Faversham, Kent.
Mount Stewart, Newtownards, Co. Down, Northern Ireland. (*Fox hunt in full cry*)

Nymans, Handcross, West Sussex.
Packwood House, Hockley Heath, Warwicks. (*The Sermon on the Mount*)
Rockingham Castle, Corby, Northants. (*Elephant yew hedge*)
Usk Castle, Gwent. (*Hunting scene*)

TREE HOUSE

Either a platform or small house built within the boughs of a tree, usually designed for the amusement of children; or, as practised by the Dutch, particularly in the 17th and 18th centuries, an arbour (q.v.) formed by trained trees.

Ashridge, Berkhamsted, Herts. (*Two trained arbour tree houses*)
Pitchford Hall, Pitchford, Shropshire. (*Gothic-style, half-timbered in lime tree*)

TRELLIS/TRELLISWORK/ TREILLAGE

A trellis consists of light wood or metal struts arranged to form a square or diamond-shaped pattern, secured at each junction.

Complex structures created from trellis are called trelliswork or, on a grander scale, by the French word treillage. These can be arbours, garden houses, domed columns, rondels, etc.

Abbot's Ripton Hall, Huntingdon, Cambs. (*Gothic style rondel*)
Barnsley House Garden, Cirencester, Glos.
Dropmore House, Bucks.
Hazelby House, North End, Newbury, Berks. (*Trellis gazeboes*)
Heale House Gardens, Woodford, Salisbury, Wilts.
Hodnet Hall, Nr. Market Drayton, Shropshire.
Melbourne Hall, Melbourne, Derbyshire. (*Treillage wrought-iron arbour*)
Shrubland Hall, Ipswich, Suffolk.
Sutton Park, Sutton-on-the-Forest, N. Yorks.

TOPIARY

TROMPE L'OEIL

The literal translation from the French is 'deceive the eye' and any feature which attempts to do so can be described by the phrase. Apart from the ha-ha (q.v.), the effects most frequently used involve tricks of perspective or, in small gardens, the use of mirrors.

Kelvedon Hall, Nr. Colchester, Essex.
Stourhead, Stourton, Nr. Mere, Wilts. (*The tree plantings around the Pantheon*)
Wrest Park Gardens, Silsoe, Beds. (*Treillage*)

TUNNEL

The effect achieved when plants are trained, often by means of pergola frames and wires, to completely overhang a path, or when the branches are allowed to grow together over it naturally. A tunnel can also be formed by boring through a thick hedge or even, if only occasionally in gardens, by boring through, or building up, rocks.
Bateman's, Burwash, East Sussex. (*Pear on curved pergola frame*)
Biddulph Grange, Biddulph, Staffs. (*Rock tunnel*)
Bodnant Garden, Tal-y-Cafn, Gwynedd. (*Laburnum walk*)
Grey's Court, Henley-on-Thames, Oxfordshire. (*Wisteria on curved pergola frame*)
Ham House, Richmond, London.
Melbourne Hall, Melbourne, Derbyshire. (*Yew*)
St. Paul's, Waldenbury, Whitwell, Nr. Hitchin, Herts. (*Lime*)
Tyninghame, Haddington, Firth of Forth, Tayside. (*Apple, now cut back*)
Wrest Park Gardens, Silsoe, Beds. (*Lime*)

UMBRELLO

An umbrello was an ornamental umbrella-like canopy built over a circular seat to provide shade, much in the fashion of the modern sunshade but more permanent in character.

Although several are illustrated in *Garden Ornament* by Gertrude Jekyll, as far as we know none now exists in Britain. One of the last was at Stourhead and it is hoped that the National Trust might choose to reconstruct it.

URN

An urn is a funerary vase with a foot and, very often, a lid, originally designed for storing the ashes of the dead. Those seen in gardens today are frequently highly ornamented and many are virtually indistinguishable from vases, especially those lacking lids; and the words are sometimes used interchangeably.

Bampton Manor, Bampton, Oxfordshire.
Blickling Hall, Aylsham, Norfolk.
Cliveden, Maidenhead, Bucks. (*Queen Anne's 'Vase'*)
Erddig, Wrexham, Clwyd.
Harewood House, Leeds, W. Yorks.
Lanhydrock, Nr. Bodmin, Cornwall. (*Modelled by Louis Ballin, goldsmith to Louis XIV*)
Newby Hall, Ripon, N. Yorks.
Powis Castle, Welshpool, Powys (*Lead*)
Shrubland Hall, Ipswich, Suffolk.
Stourhead, Stourton, Nr. Mere, Wilts.

VASE

A tall, usually circular, vessel used either as an ornament or for displaying flowering plants. Many are highly ornamented and spectacular. (Note — Precisely what differentiates a vase from an urn (q.v.) is impossible to define with any real accuracy, but it is reasonable to insist that vases should not have lids nor, for that matter, any significant foot.)

Anglesey Abbey, Nr. Cambridge, Cambs. (*Large porphyry vase in an open temple*)

URN

Belton House, Nr. Grantham,
Lincs.
Castle Howard, York, N. Yorks.
Holker Hall, Cark-in-Cartmel,
Cumbria.
Killerton, Nr. Exeter, Devon.
Melbourne Hall, Melbourne,
Derbyshire. (*Particularly
decorative*)
Newby Hall, Ripon, N. Yorks.
Wimpole Hall, Nr. Cambridge,
Cambs. (*Decorated with pan pipes
and goats' masks.*)

VISTA

A long narrow view, usually
defined by trees to either side or
along a valley.

Blickling Hall, Aylsham, Norfolk.
(*With Doric temple vista stopper*)
Bramham Park, Wetherby, W.
Yorks.
Castle Howard, York, N. Yorks.
(*Both the approach through the
Pyramid and Carrmire Gates and the
view from the reservoir to the obelisk.*)
Grey's Court, Henley-on-
Thames, Oxfordshire.
Holkham Hall, Wells, Norfolk.
(*With an obelisk vista stopper*)
Kinross House, Kinross, Tayside.
Knightshayes Court, Tiverton,
Devon.
Rousham House, Steeple Aston,
Oxfordshire.

WALL

A continuous narrow upright
structure usually made of stone
or brick, either defining the outer
limits of a garden and offering it
protection from marauders, or
enclosing a specific portion of a
garden affording protection to
the plants within it, or support
for them. Many of the most
extensive garden walls were built
to enclose kitchen gardens.

Blickling Hall, Aylsham, Norfolk.
Cotehele House, Calstock,
Cornwall.
Erddig, Wrexham, Clwyd.
Felbrigg Hall, Nr. Cromer,
Norfolk.
Hever Castle, Edenbridge, Kent.
Kinross House, Kinross,
Tayside.

Polesden Lacey, Nr. Dorking,
Surrey.
Pusey House, Nr. Faringdon,
Oxfordshire.
Sissinghurst Castle,
Sissinghurst, Kent.

WEATHERVANE

A revolving pointer set on the
top of a building designed to
indicate the direction of the wind.
Usually manufactured of
wrought iron, they can be of
varied and imaginative designs,
but by far the most popular is a
cockerel.

Burghley House, Stamford,
Lincs. (*Several on the house with the
family crests in their designs*)
Charlecote Park, Warwick,
Warwicks. (*On the top of the gate
towers*)
Felbrigg Hall, Nr. Cromer,
Norfolk. (*On the dovecote*)
Gunby Hall, Burgh-le-Marsh,
Lincs. (*On the dovecote*)
Knebworth House, Knebworth,
Herts. (*Several on the house turrets*)
Polesden Lacey, Nr. Dorking,
Surrey. (*Above the clock*)
Sissinghurst Castle, Sissinghurst,
Kent. (*Two behind the entrance gate*)
Westbury Court, Westbury-on-
Severn, Glos. (*On the gazebo*)

WELL-HEAD

A structure surrounding a well
which acts both as a support for
the water-raising apparatus and
as a protection to prevent the
unwary from falling in. Most are
relatively plain but some,
especially those originating from
Venice, are highly ornamental.

Castle Ashby House, Nr.
Northampton, Northants.
(*Wrought-iron decorations*)
Chenies Manor, Chenies, Bucks.
(*14th century*)
Great Dixter, Northiam, East
Sussex.
Polesden Lacey, Nr. Dorking,
Surrey. (*Marble*)
Portmeirion, Portmadoc,
Gwynedd. (*Venetian.*)
Snowshill Manor, Nr. Broadway,
Glos.

WELL-HEAD

HISTORIC HOUSES AND GARDENS OPEN TO THE PUBLIC

This glossary contains detailed information, listed county by county, on all those historic houses and gardens that are mentioned in the main body of this book and are open to the public. Wherever possible, the features of gardens that are of particular interest have been set in **bold type**.

While the information is correct at the time of going to press, opening times and facilities do change and readers are advised to check with properties wherever possible before a visit. Most buildings and gardens are closed on Christmas Day, Boxing Day and New Year's Day, and some are closed on Good Friday.

Where further information may be required, we suggest contacting The National Trust, English Heritage or, in the case of private properties, the phone number or address as supplied.

AVON

Clevedon Court (*National Trust*)
Somerset, Clevedon BS21 6QU
tel. Clevedon (0272) 872257

Home of the Elton Family; 14th century manor house, once partly fortified, incorporating a 13th century hall with **terraced** 18th century garden; three **summer houses**; rare shrubs and plants.

Opening times: Easter to end September: Wed, Thur, Sun, also Bank Hol Mon 2.30-5.30.
Wheelchairs: No access.
Dogs: Not allowed.

Refreshments: Tea and biscuits at kitchen door 3.30-5.15.
Location: 1½m E of Clevedon on the Bristol road B3130.

Dyrham Park (*National Trust*)
Dyrham, nr Chippenham
SN14 8ER
tel. Abson (027582) 2501

Late 17th century house set in 263 acres of ancient parkland with herd of fallow deer; **orangery**; at Hind Cottage, adjoining Dyrham Park House, cottage garden of shrubs and trees with small **parterre**.

Opening times: Park: all year, daily 12 to 6 or dusk if earlier. House and garden: Easter to late October: daily except Thur & Fri 2-6. Other times by written arrangement with Administrator.
Wheelchairs: Ground floor and terrace only; parking by house.
Dogs: In deer park only, on leads.
Refreshments: Teas in orangery 2.30-5.15. Picnics welcome in park.
Location: 8 m N of Bath; 12 m E of Bristol.

Goldney Hall
(*University of Bristol*)
Lower Clifton Hill, Bristol

Nine-acre historic garden developed in 1731-68 by Thomas Goldney, a Bristol merchant. It contains many fascinating features including a fine period **grotto**, **terrace**, **orangery** and **parterre**.

Opening times: Only a few days each year. Write for information.
Wheelchairs: Suitable access.

Refreshments: Teas in orangery.
Location: At top of Constitution Hill, Clifton.

BEDFORDSHIRE

Luton Hoo (*Private*)
Luton
tel. Luton (0582) 22955

Said to be the best surviving unspoilt 'Capability' Brown landscape in the country; beautiful **lake** and views. House built by Robert Adam in 1767 and now owned by the Wernher family; magnificent **steps** in a wide sweeping curve lead down from the house onto the upper **terrace** of gardens.

Opening times: House and gardens: Easter, then from mid-April to mid-Oct, daily 2-5.45. Closed Mon except Bank Hols.
Dogs: Not allowed.
Refreshments: Teas.
Location: Entrance at Park Street Gates, Luton; 30m N of London.

Woburn Abbey (*Private*)
Woburn
tel. Woburn (0525) 290666

Home of the Dukes of Bedford for over 300 years overlooking 3,000-acre deer park, landscaped by Humphry Repton. **Grotto** room dated at about 1630 is most extravagantly shell-decorated room anywhere to be seen. The Abbey contains one of the most important private art collections in the world.

Opening times: House and gardens: Jan to mid-March: Sat & Sun only. House 11-4.45: Park

10.30-3.45. End March to end Oct: daily. House: Weekdays 11-5.45; Sun 11-6.15. Park: Weekdays 10-4.45; Sun 10-5.45.
Refreshments: Flying Duchess Pavilion Coffee Shop. Restaurant for pre-booked parties.
Location: In Woburn, 8m NW of Dunstable on A418.

Wrest Park House and Gardens (*English Heritage*)
Silsoe
tel. Silsoe (0525) 60718

Here is a history of English gardening in the grand manner from 1700-1850, which would not, of course, be complete without some designs by 'Capability' Brown. Every whim of fashion is represented, from a Chinese **bridge**, artificial **lake**, classical **temple** to a rustic ruin. There is an **orangery**, built in 1836, set on a high grass bank, a **canal**, examples of **treillage**, even a **bath-house** recently restored. The present house was built about 1839 by the Earl of Grey, whose family had lorded it over the Manor of Wrest for 600 years.

Opening times: Easter to end Sept: weekends and Bank Hols only 10-6.
Location: ¾m east of Silsoe.

BUCKINGHAMSHIRE

Ascott (*National Trust*)
Wing, nr Leighton Buzzard
LU7 0PS
tel. Aylesbury (0296) 688242

Beautiful surroundings and layout. Garden contains **summer house**, Venus **fountain**, **topiary**, **sundial**, as well as unusual trees, flower borders, naturalized bulbs and water-lilies.
Opening times: House and garden: mid-July to mid- September: Tues to Sun 2-6; also Bank Hol Mon. Garden only: April to mid-July: every Thur & last Sun in each month 2-6.
Wheelchairs: Ground floor only; limited access to garden.

Dogs: In car park only.
Location: ½m E of Wing; 2m SW of Leighton Buzzard.

Cliveden (*National Trust*)
Taplow, Maidenhead
tel. Burnham (0628) 605069

Historic grounds with many formal gardens: **temples** by Giacomo Leoni; box **parterre**; Shell **fountain**; **amphitheatre**; **pagoda** and **pond** in Japanese water garden; most remarkable collection of eight **sarchophagi** in **walled garden**; **balustrading** compartmentalizes formal and informal areas of garden: scented lime **avenue**; Queen Anne's **vase**; **folly** in the shape of small fascinating concrete tree trunk in the old stable yard now hosts the NT shop. Views of Thames.

Opening times: Grounds: March to end Dec: daily 11-6 or sunset if earlier. House: early April to late October: Thur & Sun 3-6. Last adm 5.30.
Wheelchairs: Grounds largely accessible. Access to house by special arrangement. Shop in Old Grape House accessible. Car park 200 yds from house but special arrangements available.
Dogs: Dogs in specified woodlands only; not in garden.
Refreshments: Morning coffee, light lunches, teas, Easter to end Oct: Wed to Sun & Bank Hol Mon 11-5 in Orangery restaurant.
Location: 3m upstream from Maidenhead; 2m N of Taplow on B476.

Hall Barn (*Private*)
Beaconsfield HP9 2SG

A unique landscaped garden of great historical interest, laid out in the 1680s. Vast 300-year-old curving yew **hedge**. Very fine collection of trees, including the third largest beech in Buckinghamshire. Formal **lake**. Long **avenues** and surviving example of **plashing**, where trees open out the vista. Each avenue terminates in a **temple**, classical

ornament or **statue**; **obelisk** with fine carvings in memory of Edmund Waller's grandson who completed the garden about 1730.

Opening times: Garden open by written appointment only. Applications to Lady Burnham at Hall Barn.
Location: 300 yards S of Beaconsfield Church.

Stowe (*Stowe School*)
Buckingham

Famous 18th century house, formerly the home of the Duke of Buckingham. Gardens and garden buildings by Bridgeman, Kent, Gibbs, Vanbrugh and 'Capability' Brown. Among its many **temples**: the Temple of Venus, the Temple of Ancient Virtue, the Temple of Concord & Victory, the ruined Temple of Modern Virtues; the Queen's Temple, the Temple of British Worthies. The Gothic Temple is an example of a **folly**. Also worth noting, the twin Boycott **pavilions** designed by James Gibbs, and the Palladian-style **bridge**.

Opening times: Grounds, garden buildings and main state rooms: linked to school holidays. Write for details.
Refreshments: Light refreshments available.
Location: 4m N of Buckingham.

Waddesdon Manor
(*National Trust*)
Waddesdon, nr Aylesbury
HP18 0JH
tel. Aylesbury (0296) 651211 or 651282

Nineteenth century French Renaissance-style château; extensive grounds with 18th century style **aviary** and small herd of Japanese Sika deer; Italian Renaissance-style **statuary** surrounding formal **pool** on S front **terrace**; **ice-house**.

Opening times: Mid-March to end

October: House: Wed to Sun 1-5 (open until 6 on Sat & Sun, May to Sept). Grounds and aviary: Wed to Sat from 1 and from 11.30 on Sun. Good Fri & Bank Hol Mon, house and grounds 11-6. *Wheelchairs*: All ground floor rooms and tea-room easily accessible. Most of garden and grounds easy; some gravel. Special car park for disabled visitors at house. *Dogs*: Grounds only, excluding aviary and children's play area. *Refreshments*: Light lunches and teas in Old Kitchen and Servants' Hall. *Location*: 6m NW of Aylesbury on A41.

West Wycombe Park
(*National Trust*)
West Wycombe HP14 3AJ
tel. High Wycombe (0494) 24411

Palladian house fashioned for Sir Francis Dashwood in the mid-18th century; landscaped garden with **lake** laid out at the same time and various classical **temples**, including the newly reconstructed Temple of Venus; lake enhanced by small island and **pavilion**.

Opening times: Grounds only: April & May: Mon to Thur 2-6; and Easter, May & Spring Bank Hol Sun & Mon 2-6. Closed Good Friday. House and grounds: June, July & Aug: Sun to Thur 2-6. *Wheelchairs*: Grounds only; special parking. *Dogs*: In car park only. *Location*: At W end of West Wycombe, S of the Oxford road.

Wotton House   (*Private*)
Nr Aylesbury

Built in 1704 and modelled on the same plan as Buckingham House. Wrought iron by Tijou and Thomas Robinson. 'Capability' Brown landscaped garden.

Opening times: August to end September. Wed only.

Location: 2m S of A41, midway between Aylesbury and Bicester.

CAMBRIDGESHIRE

Anglesey Abbey
(*National Trust*)
Lode, Cambridge CB5 9EJ
tel. Cambridge (0223) 811200

Outstanding 100-acre garden laid out this century; house built around 1600, has associations with the Augustinian order. Garden boasts **avenues** of beautiful chestnut trees; groups of **statuary**, including copy by Fossi of Bernini's David; **hedges** enclosing small intimate gardens; large porphyry **vase** within Doric pillared **temple** with roof of green copper slates. Spectacular hyacinth display in spring.

Opening times: House: Easter to mid-October: Wed to Sun & Bank Hol Mon 1.30-5.30. Closed Good Friday. Garden: Easter to early July: Wed to Sun & Bank Hol Mon 12-5.30: July to mid-October: daily 12-5.30. Lode Mill: Easter to mid-October: Sat, Sun & Bank Hol Mon, 1.30-5.30. *Wheelchairs*: Special entrance arrangements. Garden level; house difficult. *Refreshments*: Lunches and teas in tea-room, by car park (closed Mon & Tues but open Bank Hol Mon), 12-5 same days as house. Picnic area. *Location*: In village of Lode; 6m NE of Cambridge on B1102.

Wimpole Hall   (*National Trust*)
Arrington, Royston SG8 0BW
tel. Cambridge (0223) 207257

The most spectacular mansion in Cambridgeshire in a restrained 18th century style, set in a 350-acre park landscaped by Bridgeman, Brown and Repton: includes a grand **folly** and Chinese **bridge**; walks through park; restored Victorian stable block with heavy horses.

Opening times: Easter to end October: daily except Mon & Fri

1-5 (but open Bank Hol Mon 11-5). Closed Good Friday. Shop: open 1-5 on open days. *Wheelchairs*: Staff may be available to lift wheelchairs up steps to ground floor of house, which is then level and fully accessible. *Dogs*: In park only, on leads. *Refreshments*: Light lunches and teas 12-5 in Great Dining Room on open days. Light refreshments 10.30-5 at the stables. Picnic area. *Location*: 8m SW of Cambridge; 6m N of Royston (A14).

CHESHIRE

Dunham Massey
(*National Trust*)
Altrincham WA14 4SJ
tel. 061 941 1025

Impressive 18th century mansion in 250-acre wooded deer park; Until 1976 home of the 10th and last Earl of Stamford. Over 30 rooms open with collections of furniture, paintings and silver. Extensive gardens recently restored. Woodlands, park with **mount**, formal **avenues**, and fallow deer.

Opening times: Easter to end Oct, daily except Fri. Closed Good Fri. Garden: 11-5.30 (Sun and Bank Hol Mon 11-5.30. House: 1-5 (Sun and Bank Hol Mon 12-5.) Park: always open. *Wheelchairs*: Access available but some steps to ground floor of house. *Dogs*: In park only, on leads. *Refreshments*: Licensed self-service restaurant on first floor of stable block. *Location*: 3m SW of Altrincham off A56.

Tatton Park   (*National Trust*)
Knutsford WA16 6QN
tel. Knutsford (0565) 54822/3

Magnificently varied 60-acre garden; showhouse; **fernery**; Japanese garden with **bridge**; waterfowl; 1,000-acre deer park; restored Italian garden;

orangery; rose garden and arboretum.

Opening times: Park and Gardens: All year (except Christmas Day). Mansion open daily — Easter to Oct 31. House (Sun & Public Hols in brackets): Easter to mid-May and Sept/Oct: Park 11-6 (10-6); Garden 11.30-5 (10.30-5.30); Mansion 1-4 (1-5); Old Hall 12-4 (12-5); Farm 12-4 (12-4). Mid-May to Aug: Park 10.30-7 (10-7); Garden 11-5.30 (10.30-6); Mansion 1-4 (1-5); July/Aug: 1-5 (12-5); Old Hall 12-4 (12-5); Farm 11-4 (11-4). Nov to Apr 1: Park 11-dusk (11-dusk); Garden 1-4 (12-4).
Dogs: In garden on leads and in park under close control.
Refreshments: All meals catered for; restaurant in stable-yard.
Location: 3m N of Knutsford; 4m S of Altrincham.

CORNWALL

Antony House (*National Trust*)
Torpoint PL11 2QA
tel. Plymouth (0752) 812191

One of Cornwall's finest early 18th century houses set in landscaped woodland garden of about 50 acres based on a Humphry Repton design; 200 year-old yew **arbour**, clipped into the shape of a cone; 18th century **dovecote**; 1789 **bath pond house**.

Opening times: Easter to end Oct: Tues, Wed, Thur & Bank Hol Mon 2-6; also Sun in June, July & Aug 2-6.
Wheelchairs: No access available.
Dogs: Not allowed.
Location: 5m W of Plymouth via Torpoint car ferry, 2m NW of Torpoint, N of A374, 16m SE of Liskeard, 15m E of Looe.

Glendurgan Garden
(*National Trust*)
Helford River, Mawnan Smith, Nr Falmouth TR11 5JZ
tel. Bodmin (0208) 74281

Valley garden of great beauty; fine trees and shrubs; **walled** and **water gardens**, laurel **maze** on wooded slope running down to tiny village of Durgan on the river.

Opening times: March to end Oct: Mon, Wed & Fri 10.30-5.30. Closed Good Fri.
Wheelchairs: In parts of garden, but many steep slopes.
Dogs: Not allowed.
Location: 4m SW of Falmouth; ½m SW of Mawnan Smith.

Lanhydrock (*National Trust*)
Bodmin PL30 5AD
tel. Bodmin (0208) 73320

The great house of Cornwall set in formal garden with clipped yews, and **parterre**, laid out in 1857 and of interest and beauty all year round. Rhododendrons, magnolias, rare trees and shrubs; woodland garden and parkland setting.

Opening times: Good Fri, Easter to end Oct: daily except Mon, but open Bank Hol Mon 11-6 (Oct 11-5). Nov to end March: Garden only, open daily during daylight hours.
Wheelchairs: Access to house via some loose gravel and shallow steps, then most ground floor rooms easily accessible. Garden has gravel path; some steps.
Dogs: In park only on leads.
Refreshments: Coffee, lunches and teas in restaurant in house; snacks in stable block.
Location: 2m SE of Bodmin, overlooking valley of River Fowey.

CUMBRIA

Levens Hall (*Private*)
Kendal
tel. Sedgwick (05395) 60321

Ten acres including world famous **topiary** garden laid out in 1692 and first **ha-ha** laid out by M. Beaumont. Magnificent beech circle; formal bedding; herbaceous borders. Elizabethan mansion added to 13th century pele tower, containing superb panelling, plasterwork and furniture.

Opening times: Easter to end Sept: Sun to Thur 11-5.
Wheelchairs: House not suitable.
Refreshments: Home-made light lunches and teas.
Location: 5m S of Kendal, on the Milnethorpe road (A6).

DERBYSHIRE

Chatsworth (*Private*)
Bakewell
tel. Baslow (024688) 2204

Built by Talman for first Duke of Devonshire between 1687 and 1707. Garden with elaborate waterworks surrounded by great park; **fountains**; **canal**; **cascade**, on top of which stands a **temple**, behind which another **cascade** runs over a bridge; classical **bridge** decorated by **balustrades** and **statues** on its piers; unusual beech hedge **allée**; **ice-house**; **sarcophagus**.

Opening times: House and garden: Easter to end Oct: daily 11.30-4.30.
Wheelchairs: Not possible in house but welcome in garden.
Refreshments: Home-made; coach-drivers' rest room.
Location: E of village of Edensor on A623.

Haddon Hall (*Private*)
Bakewell DE4 1LA
tel. Bakewell (062981) 2855

Beautiful **terraced** gardens dating from the Middle Ages; noted for wall and bed roses and many old fashioned flowers. Particularly pleasant stone **steps** lead down from **terrace** to the rose garden, decorated with ball-capped **balustrades**. House is fine example of medieval and manorial home.

Opening times: Easter to early Oct: Tues to Sun 11-6. Closed Mon except Bank Hols; also closed Sun in July & Aug except Bank Hol weekends.
Refreshments: Available at Stables Restaurant.
Location: 2m SE Bakewell; 6m N of Matlock on A6.

Hardwick Hall   (*National Trust*)
Doe Lea, Chesterfield S44 5QJ
tel. Chesterfield (0246) 850430

Finest example of Elizabethan house in the country, designed by Robert Smythson for 'Bess of Hardwick'. Walled courtyards enclose fine gardens, orchards and outstanding **herb garden**; grass walks between yew and hornbeam **hedges**; herbaceous borders; country park contains Whiteface Woodland sheep and Longhorn cattle.

Opening times: Easter to mid-September: Hall: Wed, Thur, Sat, Sun & Bank Hol Mon 1-5.30, or dusk if earlier. Closed Good Friday. Garden: Easter to end Oct: daily 12-5.30. Park: daily throughout year, dawn to dusk.
Wheelchairs: Garden and some parts of park accessible.
Dogs: In country park only, on leads; not in garden.
Refreshments: Lunches: 12-2 and teas 2.30-5 in restaurant in Great Kitchen on days when hall is open.
Location: 6½m W of Mansfield; 9m SE of Chesterfield.

Sudbury Hall   (*National Trust*)
Sudbury DE6 5HT
tel. Sudbury (028 378) 305

Richly decorated Charles 11 house, former seat of the Lords Vernon. Garden with small-scale reproduction of **quincunx**.

Opening times: Easter to end Oct: Wed to Sun & Bank Hol Mon 1-5.30 or dusk if earlier. Closed Good Friday & Tues following Bank Hol.
Wheelchairs: Hall difficult: museum, grounds and tea-room accessible.
Dogs: In grounds only.
Refreshments: Light lunches and teas in Coach House tea-rooms.
Location: 6m E of Uttoxeter.

DEVON

Bicton Park   (*Private*)
Colaton Raleigh, Budleigh

Salterton EX9 7DP
tel. Colaton Raleigh (0395) 68465

Over 50 acres of beautiful gardens with famous monkey puzzle **avenue** giving fine views of parkland and trees; arboretum; **walled** garden and **glasshouses**; rich variety of plants in beds and borders, laid out for teaching and effect.

Opening times: Garden: Easter to October, 10-6.
Wheelchairs: Suitable access.
Dogs: On lead only.
Refreshments: Lunches and teas in cafeteria.
Location: On the A376 midway between Newton Poppleford and Budleigh Salterton.

Castle Drogo   (*National Trust*)
Drewsteignton EX6 6PB
tel. Chagford (06473) 3306

The granite castle, built between 1910 and 1930, is one of the most remarkable works of Sir Edwin Lutyens. It stands at over 274 m (900 ft), overlooking the wooded gorge of the River Teign with beautiful views of Dartmoor. **Terraced** garden, unusual circular **hedge** and miles of splendid walks.

Opening times: Easter to end Oct, daily 11-6 (Oct 11- 5).
Wheelchairs: reasonable access to house and most of garden.
Dogs: Not allowed.
Refreshments: Coffees, light lunches and teas available at castle.
Location: 4m off A30 Exeter to Okehampton road.

Killerton   (*National Trust*)
Broadclyst, Exeter EX5 3LE
tel. Exeter (0392) 881345

Late 18th century house set in 15 acres of beautiful hillside garden containing rare trees and shrubs; **ice-house**; walks in Ashclyst Forest; **Bear's hut**; 19th century chapel; estate exhibition.

Opening times: Good Fri, Easter to end Oct: Wed to Mon 11-6 (Oct:

11-5). Park open all year during daylight hours. Shop: daily 11-4.
Wheelchairs: 3 steps to house, accessible ground floor. Lower levels of garden accessible, but gravel paths and grass. Motorized buggy with driver available for tour of higher levels.
Dogs: In park only.
Refreshments: Licensed restaurant at house. Light refreshments at Coach House 11-5.30.
Location: On W side of Exeter-Cullompton road, entrance off B3185.

Knightshayes Court
(*National Trust*)
Bolham, Tiverton EX16 7RQ
tel. Tiverton (0884) 254665

One of the finest gardens in Devon with specimen trees, rare shrubs, spring bulbs, summer flowering borders of interest all year round; simple but exceptionally attractive garden **pool** surrounded by castellated yew **hedges**; **topiary**. House by William Burges, begun in 1869.

Opening times: Good Fri, Easter to end Oct: Garden: daily 11-6 (Oct: 11-5); House: daily except Fri (but open Good Fri) 1.30-6 (Oct: 1.30-5).
Wheelchairs: House and garden accessible.
Dogs: In park only, on leads.
Refreshments: Licensed restaurant for coffee, lunches and teas daily 11-6 (Oct: 11-5). Picnic area.
Location: 2m N of Tiverton.

Saltram   (*National Trust*)
Plympton, Plymouth PL7 3UH
tel. Plymouth (0752) 336546

A remarkable survival of a George II mansion and its original contents, in a landscaped park. Beautiful garden with unusual wooden **orangery**; octagonal **summer house**; rare shrubs and trees.

Opening times: Easter to end Oct: Sun to Thur, inc. Sat of Bank Hol weekends, house only 12.30-6 (Oct 12.30-5). Art Gallery,

garden and great kitchen 11-6 (Oct 11-5).
Wheelchairs: House and garden accessible but house not suitable for powered chairs.
Dogs: Grounds only.
Refreshments: Licensed restaurant in house; light refreshments at Coach House near car park.
Location: 2m W of Plympton; 3½m E of Plymouth city centre.

DORSET

Athelhampton   (*Private*)
nr Puddletown, Dorset
tel. Puddletown (0305) 848363

One the finest medieval houses in England built in 1485 and set in 10 acres of formal and landscaped gardens: rare plants and trees; **water features**; large 15th century **dovecote** with 1,000 nesting holes.

Opening times: Easter to mid-Oct: Wed, Thur & Sun 2-6; also Good Fri & Bank Hols; also Mon & Tues in Aug.
Dogs: Only in shaded car park.
Refreshments: Tea at House.
Location: ½m E of Puddletown; 5m NE of Dorchester.

Compton Acres   (*Private*)
Poole, Dorset
tel. (0202) 700778

Reputed to be the finest gardens in Europe, overlooking Poole harbour. Includes Japanese, Italian, rock and water gardens; heather-dell; views over sub-tropical glen and viewpoint overlooking Brownsea island; bronze and marble **statuary**; bridge-spanned **water feature**, **tea-house**, **stepping-stones**, and small granite **pagoda** all situated in Japanese garden.

Opening times: April to end Oct: daily 10.30-6.30 or dusk if earlier.
Refreshments: Teas available.
Location: Few yards from Canford Cliffs village, nr Sandbanks.

Cranborne Manor Gardens
(*Private*)
Cranborne

tel. Cranborne (072 54) 248

Beautiful and historic gardens laid out in 17th century by John Tradescant and enlarged in 20th century; several gardens surrounded by walls and yew **hedges**; white garden, **herb**, **mount** and **knot garden** with Elizabethan flowers; many interesting plants, with fine trees and **avenues**; twin lozenge-shaped lodges with pyramid roofs support **gate** leading into walled forecourt.

Opening times: Gardens only: April to Sept, Wed 9-5; Garden Centre, Tues to Sat 9-5, Sun 2-5 (not Jan & Feb).
Location: 18m N of Bournemouth; 16m S of Salisbury.

ESSEX

Audley End House and Park
(*English Heritage*)
Audley End
tel. (0799) 22399

A very substantial mansion built by Sir Thomas Howard, Lord Treasurer to James 1; magnificent brick **ha-ha** set in park.

Opening times: Easter to end Sept, daily 1-6. Park and garden open 12 noon.
Location: ¾m W of Saffron Walden off B1383.

St. Osyth Priory   (*Private*)
St. Osyth
tel. St. Osyth (0255) 820492

Great **gatehouse** *c.* 1475 'unexcelled in any monastic remains in the country', *Country Life*. A unique group of buildings dating from the 13th, 15th, 16th, 18th and 19th centuries, surrounding a wide quadrangle like an Oxford or Cambridge college. Gardens include rose garden, **topiary** garden, **water garden**.

Opening times: Gardens and ancient monuments: Easter, then May to Sept 10-5.
Wheelchairs: Access to gardens.

Refreshments: In village 100 yards from entrance.
Location: 12m from Colchester; 8m from Frinton.

GLOUCESTERSHIRE

Barnsley House Garden
(*Private*)
Barnsley, nr Cirencester
tel. Bibury (028 574) 281

Garden laid out 1770, altered since 1960. Interesting collection of shrubs and trees; laburnum **avenue**; **knot** and **herb gardens**; **potager**; waterlily **pool** backed by Doric **temple**; Gothic **summer house**. House 1697 (not open).

Opening times: Garden only: All year Mon-Sat 10-6 (or dusk if earlier).
Refreshments: In village.
Location: 4m NE of Cirencester on A433.

Frampton Court   (*Private*)
Frampton-on-Severn

Charming **water garden with canal**; **orangery** in Strawberry Hill Gothic style built in 1760 reflected at one end.

Opening times: By written appointment only to Estate Office.

Hidcote Manor Garden
(*National Trust*)
Hidcote Bartrim, nr Chipping Campden GL55 6LR
tel. Mickleton (0386) 438 333

One of the most delightful gardens in England, created by Major Lawrence Johnston; a series of small gardens within the whole, separated by **walls** and **hedges** of different species; pair of **gazeboes** at end of **pleached hornbeam allée**; westernized version of Japanese **tea-house**; circular swimming pool raised to waist height to bring reflection of sky and surrounding hedges closer to eye level; smaller cottage garden-style **topiary**; rare shrubs, trees, herbaceous borders, 'old' roses and interesting plant species.

Opening times: Easter to end Oct: daily except Tues & Fri 11-8 (no entry after 7, or one hour before dusk if earlier).
Wheelchairs: Access to part of garden only.
Dogs: Not allowed.
Refreshments: Coffee, licensed lunches, cream teas in tea-room 11-5. No picnicking. .
Location: 4m NE of Chipping Campden.

Rodmarton Manor Garden
(*Private*)
Cirencester
tel. Cirencester (028584) 219

Terrace and leisure garden; Herbaceous borders; hornbeam **avenue**; beech, holly and yew **hedges**; **topiary**; many small gardens enclosed with hedges; one such garden is dominated by **troughs**.

Opening times: March to end Aug: Every Thur 2-5. Other days by arrangement.
Wheelchairs: Easy access to gardens.
Refreshments: Teas can be provided if booked in advance.
Location: 6m from Cirencester, 4m from Tetbury.

Sezincote (*Private*)
Moreton-in-Marsh

Oriental water garden by Repton and Daniell with trees of unusual size. Includes perfect modern reconstructed **kiosk** in Indian style. House also in Indian style inspiration of Royal Pavilion, Brighton.

Opening times: Garden: Thur, Fri & Bank Hol Mon 2-6 (or dusk if earlier), throughout year except Dec. House: May, June, July & Sept: Thur & Fri 2.30-6.
Refreshments: In nearby Moreton-in-Marsh.
Location: 1m W of Moreton-in-Marsh on A44.

Westbury Court Garden
(*National Trust*)
Westbury-on-Severn GL14 1PD
tel. Westbury-on-Severn (045 276) 461

A formal **water garden** with **canals** and yew **hedges**, laid out between 1698 and 1705; the earliest of its kind remaining in England; restored in 1971 and planted with species dating from pre 1700, including apple, pear and plum trees. Small scale reproduction of **quincunx**.

Opening times: Easter to end Oct: Wed to Sun & Bank Hol Mon 11-6. Closed Good Friday. Other months by appointment only.
Wheelchairs: All parts of garden accessible.
Dogs: Not allowed.
Location: 9m SW of Gloucester on A48.

HAMPSHIRE

Burford House Gardens
(*Private*)
Tenbury Wells
tel. (0584) 81077

The gardens at Burford were created by John Treasure over a period of 35 years and are filled with a wealth of rare and interesting plants; **stream** garden draws water from nearby River Tame.

Opening times: Mid-March to end Oct, Mon to Sat 11-5; Sun 2-5.
Wheelchairs: No access.
Refreshments: Tea rooms situated near entrance.
Location: 1m W of Tenbury Wells.

West Green House
(*National Trust*)
Hartley Wintney, Basingstoke RG27 8JB

Small early 18th century house of great charm in a delightful garden; small **potager**; spectacular modern interpretation of **moon window**.

Opening times: Easter to end Sept: Wed, Thur & Sun 2-6. House by written appointment only, Wed

2-6. Apply to Lord McAlpine of West Green, 40 Bernard Street, London WC1N 1LG (tel. 01-837 3377).
Wheelchairs: House difficult.
Dogs: Not allowed.
Location: 1m W of Hartley Wintney, 10m NE of Basingstoke.

HERTFORDSHIRE

The Gardens of the Rose
(*Royal National Rose Society*)
Chiswell Green, St.Albans
tel. St Albans (0727) 50461

The showground of the RNRS, containing some 30,000 roses of over 1,650 different varieties. Garden also features semi-circular stone **pergola**.

Opening times: Mid-June to Oct: Mon to Sat 9-5. Sun & Bank Hol Mon 10-6. British Rose Festival: 2 days in July.
Wheelchairs: Suitable access.
Refreshments: Licensed cafeteria.
Location: 2m S of St Albans.

Hatfield House   (*Private*)
Hatfield
tel. Hatfield (07072) 62055

Noble Jacobean house and Tudor palace, childhood home of Queen Elizabeth I. House built by Robert Cecil, first Earl of Salisbury in 1611, stands in its own great park. Among the features: a delightful low box **maze** set into gravel, taking the form of a **knot** maze.

Opening times: House: not open on Monday, except on Bank Hol Mondays open from 11-5. From Tues to Sat open from 12 (with guided tours on the hour and half hour with last tour 4.30). Open Sun 1.30-5 (with a guide in every room). West Gardens are open from Easter until early Oct. Daily: 11-6. East Gardens open on Monday only from 2-5. Park open every day 10.30-8.
Dogs: Park only.
Refreshments: Available in adjacent restaurant/cafeteria.

Elizabethan banqueting in the Old Palace throughout the year.
Location: In Hatfield, 21m N of London.

St Paul's Waldenbury
(*Private*)
Whitwell, nr Hitchin
tel. Whitwell (043 887) 229

Formal woodland garden with **temples**, **statues**, **lake**, **ponds**, splendid beech **hedge avenue** and **patte d'oie**, **pleached** lime tree tunnel, **sundial**. Laid out about 1730, covering about 40 acres.
Opening times: Gardens only. Telephone Whitwell 229 or 218 for information on dates.
Refreshments: Tea at the garden on open days.
Location: 5m S of Hitchin; ½m N of Whitwell.

KENT

Chartwell   (*National Trust*)
Westerham TN16 1PS
tel. Edenbridge (0732) 866368

Home of Sir Winston Churchill from 1924; **terraced** gardens and **lake** with the famous black swans; vine **pergola**.

Opening times: House only; first three weeks in March & Nov: Sat, Sun & Wed only 11-4. House, garden & studio: Easter to end Oct: Tues, Wed & Thur 12-5; Sat, Sun & Bank Hol Mon 11- 5. Closed Good Fri and Tues following Bank Hol. Owing to large number of visitors, entry to house is by timed, numbered ticket: waiting time can be spent in garden.
Wheelchairs: Tel. Administrator for special parking; ground floor of house accessible; small lift to first floor; garden difficult.
Dogs: In grounds only, on leads.
Refreshments: Coffee, lunches and teas; licensed self-service restaurant.
Location: 2m S of Westerham.

Chilham Castle Gardens
(*Private*)

nr Canterbury
tel. Canterbury (0227) 730319

25-acre garden with formal **terraces** first made by Tradescant when the Jacobean house was built by the side of the old Norman Castle keep. Informal **lake** garden. Magnificent **vistas** and many fine trees. Park reputedly laid out by 'Capability' Brown; unusual and attractive brick **steps**; **topiary**.

Opening times: April to mid-Oct: daily (inc. Bank Hols) from 11.
Refreshments: Jacobean tea-room.
Location: In Chilham village, 6m W of Canterbury; 8m NE of Ashford.

Crittenden House   (*Private*)
Matfield

Garden completely planned and planted since 1956 on labour-saving lines; old cattle **pond** has been transformed into central feature of the garden. Of interest from the early spring bulbs to autumn colour.

Opening times: Occasional. Please write before visiting.
Refreshments: In nearby Matfield Green.
Location: 5m SE of Tonbridge off B2160.

Hever Castle & Gardens
(*Private*)
nr Edenbridge, Kent
tel: Edenbridge (0732) 865224

Enchanting 13th century **double-moated** castle, childhood home of Queen Anne Boleyn, set in magnificent gardens of 30 acres. The gardens feature fine **topiary** including a **maze**, the magnificent Italian garden with **statuary** dating back 2000 years; terracotta **flowerpot**; **sarcophagi**; an Italianate **loggia** designed by Frank Pearson in the early 20th century and from which one can absorb the tranquillity of the lake; **topiary** chessmen; **potager**; **knot**. The

Castle was restored and filled with treasures by William Waldorf Astor in 1903.

Opening times: Castle and gardens: daily: Easter to early Nov. Gardens: 11-6; Castle: opens 12 noon.
Wheelchairs: Access to Castle and gardens.
Dogs: Gardens only, on leads.
Refreshments: Self-service cafeteria. Picnics welcome.
Location: 4m E of Maidstone.

Ightham Mote   (*National Trust*)
Ivy Hatch, Sevenoaks
TN15 0NT
tel. Plaxtol (0732) 810378

One of the most complete surviving examples of a medieval **moated** manor house; beautiful 14th century half timbering and stone.

Opening times: Good Fri, Easter to end Oct: daily except Tues & Sat, weekdays 12-5.30; Sun & Bank Hol Mon 11-5.30.
Wheelchairs: Garden, courtyard. great Hall and part of shop only.
Dogs: Not allowed.
Refreshments: Tea-bar open from 11.30 weekdays; from 10.30 Sun & Bank Hol Mon until closing.
Location: 6m E of Sevenoaks; 2m S of Ightham.

Penshurst Place   (*Private*)
Tunbridge Wells
tel. Penshurst (0892) 870307

The early house, including the Great Hall, dates from 1340. There were later additions but the whole house conforms to the English Gothic style in which it was begun. 10-acre walled garden with **hedged** enclosures; **pool** set in the centre of the **parterre** — an essential part of a reconstruction of the 17th century garden design. Garden also features unusual vertical **sundial**.

Opening times: April to Oct: every afternoon, except Mon. Open Bank Hol Mon & Easter Bank

Hols. Grounds: 12.30-6. House: 1-5.30.
Dogs: Not allowed.
Refreshments: Light luncheons and teas available in Endeavour Restaurant.
Location: In Penshurst village; W of Tonbridge and Tunbridge Wells.

Scotney Castle Garden
(*National Trust*)
Lamberhurst, Tunbridge Wells TN3 8JN
tel. Lamberhurst (0892) 890651

One of England's most romantic garden landscapes; surrounding the ruins of a 14th century **moated** castle, old castle open during summer months; **ice-house**; **herb garden**.

Opening times: Garden only: Easter to mid-Nov: Wed to Fri 11-6 (closed Good Fri); Sat, Sun & Bank Hol Mon 2-6, or dusk if earlier. Old Castle open May to end Aug: same times.
Wheelchairs: Garden partly accessible, but strong companion necessary; path very steep in places.
Dogs: Not allowed.
Refreshments: Picnicking in car park area.
Location: 1m S of Lamberhurst on A21.

Sissinghurst Castle Garden
(*National Trust*)
Sissinghurst, nr Cranbrook TN17 2AB
tel. Cranbrook (0580) 712850

The famous garden created by the late Vita Sackville-West and her husband, Sir Harold Nicolson, between the surviving parts of an Elizabethan mansion; beautiful herbaceous borders with roses and other climbers clambering up walls behind them; **herb garden**; **sunken garden**; **pleached lime allée** not to be missed in spring; **hedged rondel**.

Opening times: Good Fri, Easter to

mid-Oct: Tues to Fri 1-6.30; Sat, Sun & Good Fri 10-6.30.
Best to avoid weekends and holidays.
Wheelchairs: Admission restricted to two chairs at any one time because of uneven paths. Plan of route available.
Dogs: Not allowed.
Refreshments: Coffee, lunches, teas in Granary restaurant.
Picnicking in car park area and in grass field in front of castle.
Location: 2m NE of Cranbrook; 1m E of Sissinghurst village.

LINCOLNSHIRE

Belton House   (*National Trust*)
Grantham NG32 2LS
tel. Grantham (0476) 66116

The crowning achievement of Restoration country house architecture, built 1684-88 by Sir John Brownlow; formal gardens; **orangery** by Jeffrey Wyattville; stone **exedra** supporting marble busts; famous **vase**: landscaped park with Bellmount Tower; Lion Lodge **gates**.

Opening times: Easter to end Oct; Wed to Sun & Bank Hol Mon 1-5.30. Closed Good Fri. Garden and Park 11-5.30.
Wheelchairs: House difficult; please arrange with Administrator. Park, garden, restaurant and shop accessible.
Dogs: In parkland only, on leads.
Refreshments: Lunches and teas in licensed restaurant 12-5.30.
Location: 3m NE of Grantham on A607.

The Old Hall   (*Lincolnshire County Council and English Heritage*)
Gainsborough
tel: Gainsborough (0427) 2669

An unspoilt 15th century timber-framed manor house, built between 1460 and 1480 by Thomas Burgh. Henry VIII held court here in 1541. Manor house sold to William Hickman in 1597, who allowed the early dissenters to worship here. They were later the core of the Mayflower

Pilgrims. Grounds feature a very fine example of a **well-head**.
Opening times: All the year: Mon to Sat 10-5; Sun (Easter to Oct) 2-5.
Refreshments: Tea-room open daily.
Location: In centre of Gainsborough.

LONDON

Chiswick House
(*English Heritage*)
Chiswick
tel. 01-995 0508

Gardens landscaped by William Kent; **exedra** with **statues** of Roman Emperors. House built as Italian-style villa.

Opening times: Easter to end Sept, daily 10-6; Oct to Easter 10-4.
Wheelchairs: Suitable access for grounds only.
Location: 1m W of A 406, Chiswick roundabout.

Hampton Court Palace
Hampton Court, Middx
tel. 01-977 8441

The splendour of Cardinal Wolsey's country house, begun in 1514, surpassed that of many a royal palace, so that Henry VIII at first coveted and then obtained it prior to Wolsey's fall from power. The surrounding gardens are splendid and contain: Great vine; King's Privy Garden; Great **Fountains** gardens; Tudor and Elizabethan **knot gardens**; grand lion **gates**; a surviving **banqueting house**, set in an angle to the walls of the **sunken garden**; **moat**, filled in during the reign of Charles 11; the **mount** built for Henry VIII in 1533; the **maze**, laid out during the latter half of the 17th century by London and Wise; **patte d'oie** laid out on a massive scale in the later 17th century, although many of the trees have since been destroyed.

Opening times: State Apartments open April to Sept: Mon to Sat 9.30-6; Sun 11-6; Oct to March:

Mon to Sat 9.30-5; Sun 2-5. Gardens open daily until dusk; maze open daily, Mar to Oct 10-5.
Refreshments: Available in the grounds.
Locations: N side of Thames by Hampton Court Bridge.

Kew Gardens
(*Royal Botanic Gardens*)
Kew

300 acres in extent, containing living collection of over 50,000 different plant species. Among the more notable garden features: a 10-storey high **pagoda** designed by William Chambers; 'rotunda' style **temple**; **orangery** by Sir William Vanbrugh, now used as a museum; Princess of Wales **conservatory**; a pleached lime **allée**.

Opening times: All the year: daily, from 9.30. Closing times vary according to season but not later than 4.30 Mon to Sat & 5.30 Sun.
Wheelchairs: Suitable access.
Refreshments: At Pavilion (Mar to Nov); at tea bar (all year).
Location: On south bank of Thames at Kew.

Osterley Park   (*National Trust*)
Isleworth TW7 4RB
tel. 01-560 3918

Elizabethan mansion transformed by Robert Adam 1760-80; 140 acres of parkland; **ice-house**; **orangery**; **garden houses**.

Opening times: House: all year: Tues to Sun & Bank Hol Mon 11-5; closed Good Fri. Park open all year 10-8 or dusk if earlier.
Wheelchairs: House and park.
Dogs: In park only.
Refreshments: Teas and light lunches in stable block.
Location: N of Osterley station; N side of Great West Road A 4.

Syon Park Gardens   (*Private*)
Brentford
tel. 01-560 0881/3

Includes the great **conservatory** by Dr Fowler and Adam's **gate** screen. Within the estate is the London Butterfly House, the British Heritage Motor Museum and an extensive garden centre.

Opening times: All the year: March to Oct: daily 10-6. Oct to Feb: daily 10- dusk.
Refreshments: Light refreshments and meals in bars and restaurant.
Location: On N bank of Thames.

NORFOLK

Blickling Hall   (*National Trust*)
Blickling, Norwich NR11 6NF
tel. Aylsham (0263) 733084

Great Jacobean House; notable garden with early 19th century **orangery**; parkland with good walks; crescent **lake**; azaleas, rhododendrons, herbaceous borders; Joseph Bonomi's unusual pyramidal **mausoleum**; squat stone **vase**; **parterre**.

Opening times: House: Easter to end Oct: daily except Mon & Thur but open Bank Hol Mon 1-5; closed Good Fri. Garden, shop and restaurant same days as house (daily in July & Aug) 12-5.
Wheelchairs: Ramped entrance to house.
Dogs: In park and picnic area only, on leads.
Refreshments: Lunches and teas. Picnic area in old walled garden.
Location: on N side of B1354; 1½m NW of Aylsham.

Felbrigg Hall   (*National Trust*)
Norwich NR11 8PR
tel. West Runton (026 375) 444

One of the finest 17th century houses in Norfolk, with the original 18th century furniture and pictures, and an outstanding library. Walled garden includes a restored **dovecote**, a traditional layout of herbaceous plants and fruit trees; walks in fine mature woodland and around **lake**.
Opening times: Easter to end

October. Daily, except Tues & Fri: 1.30-5.30. Garden same days: 11-5.30. Closed Good Fri. Woodland walks all year, dawn to dusk.
Wheelchairs: Access to ground floor only.
Dogs: In park only, on leads.
Refreshments: Lunches 12-2 (booking advisable); teas 2.15-5.30.
Location: 2m SW of Cromer off B1436.

Holkham Hall   (*Private*)
Wells
tel. Fakenham (0328) 710227

Formal garden laid out by Nessfield, featuring beech and ilex **quincunx**. Fine Palladian mansion.

Opening times: Daily (except Fri & Sat) from end May to end Sept 1.30-5; also spring and summer Bank Hol Mons 11.30-5.
Refreshments: Served in tea-rooms.
Location: 2m W of Wells.

Oxburgh Hall   (*National Trust*)
Oxborough, Nr King's Lynn PE33 9PS
tel. Gooderstone (036 621) 258

Moated house built in 1482 by the Bedingfeld family, who still live there; magnificent Tudor **gatehouse**; garden with lawns, fine trees and colourful borders; unique French **parterre** laid out *c*.1845; woodland walk and traditional herbaceous garden.

Opening times: House: Easter to end April: Sat & Sun 1.30-5.30; Bank Hol Mon 11-5.30; closed Good Fri. May to end Sept: daily except Thur & Fri 1.30-5.30; Bank Hol Mon 11-5.30. Garden: Easter to end Oct: daily except Thur & Fri 12-5.30.
Wheelchairs: Access to house 183 m (200 yd) shallow ramp.
Dogs: Not allowed.
Refreshments: Light lunches and teas in Old Kitchen 12- 5.
Location: At Oxborough; 7m SW of Swaffham on S side of Stoke Ferry road.

NORTHAMPTONSHIRE

Canons Ashby House
(*National Trust*)
Canons Ashby, Daventry
NN11 6SD
tel. Blakesley (0327) 860044

Home of the Dryden family since the 16th century; a manor house, *c.*1550; formal garden with **terraces**, **walls** and gatepiers of 1710 (featuring tiny **obelisks** as finials to cap gate posts); medieval priory church; 70-acre park.

Opening times: House: Easter to end Oct: Wed to Sun & Bank Hol Mon 1-5.30 or dusk if earlier; closed Good Fri. Park open as house, access through garden.
Wheelchairs: Access to garden via 3 steps. House difficult. Please telephone for special arrangements.
Dogs: On leads, in home paddock only.
Refreshments: Afternoon tea in Brewhouse 1-5.
Location: On B4525 Northampton-Banbury road.

Easton Neston (*Private*)
Towcester

Large formal garden; ornamental bow-shaped **pond**; clipped yew **hedges**, the centre of which is cut out to provide a **vista** across an informal stretch of water; **arboretum**.

Opening times: By appointment only.
Refreshments: Tea.
Location: Entrance at Hulcote turning (third lodge); Easton Neston ¼m.

Rushton Triangular Lodge
(*Private*)
nr Rushton
tel. Rushton (0536) 710761

Three walls with three windows and three gables to each . . . three storeys topped by a three-sided chimney: a **folly** and the brainchild of Sir Thomas Tresham, who built it in 1593 as a symbol of the Holy Trinity and the Mass.

Opening times: Easter to end Sept: daily 10-6.
Location: ¾m W of Rushton; 4m NW of Kettering.

NOTTINGHAMSHIRE

Newstead Abbey (*Nottingham City Council*)
Linby
tel. Mansfield (0623) 793557

300 acres of beautiful parkland with **lakes**, **cascade**, a Japanese **water garden**, rock and rose gardens, a subtropical garden and a Monk's fish **pond**. The medieval Priory of Newstead was converted into the Byron family home in the 16th century and restored in the 1820s. It was where Byron lived during the early 19th century and now contains his possessions, furniture, pictures, letters and first editions.

Opening times: House: Easter to end Sept: daily 11.30-6. Also Oct to Easter by arrangement. Gardens open all year: daily 10-dusk.
Refreshments: Tea-room in the grounds.
Location: 11m N of Nottingham on the A60.

Clumber Park (*National Trust*)
The Estate Office, Clumber Park, Worksop S80 3AZ
tel. Worksop (0909) 476592

3,800 acres of parkland with double lime **avenue**; fine Gothic Revival Chapel (reopened 1989, after four years' repairs), built 1886-89 for Seventh Duke of Newcastle; house demolished 1938. Classical **bridge**, **temples**, lawned Lincoln **terrace** and pleasure grounds; walled **kitchen garden**.

Opening times: Park always open.
Wheelchairs: 13 miles of tarmac roads; most areas accessible; special fishing pier with wheelchair access.
Dogs: Admitted to parkland.
Refreshments: Licensed restaurant and self-service cafeteria.
Location: 4½m SE of Worksop; 6½m SW of Retford.

OXFORDSHIRE

Blenheim Palace (*Private*)
Woodstock
tel. Woodstock (0993) 811325

Masterpiece of Sir John Vanbrugh in the classical style. Gardens and park designed by Vanbrugh and Queen Anne's gardener, Henry Wise. Features include Vanbrugh's Grand **bridge**; water **parterre**, below which are two rectangular **pools** with **obelisk** centrepieces; the massive East **gate**, decorated with stone **urns** by Grinling Gibbons; 'Capability' Brown **lake**; spectacular gilded dolphins **fountain**; **ha-ha**; **balustrading**. Palace includes exhibition of Churchill's possessions.

Opening times: Mid March to end Oct: daily 10.30-5.30.
Refreshments: Licensed restaurant and self service cafeteria.
Location: SW end of Woodstock; 8m N of Oxford on A34.

Buscot Park (*National Trust*)
Faringdon SN7 8BU
tel. Faringdon (0387) 20786, not weekends.

18th century house set in beautiful grounds with many ornamental trees; **lake** and **water gardens**; very unusual **canal walk** devised from a series of square **pools** interconnected by small **cascades**; **fountains**; newly planted walled garden with theme of the four seasons.

Opening times: Easter to end Sept: Wed, Thur, Fri (inc. Good Fri) 2-6, and every 2nd & 4th Sat and each Sun immediately following, also Easter Sat & Sun only, 2-6. Closed Bank Hol Mon.
Refreshments: Tea and light refreshments in tea-room.
Location: 2m SE of Lechlade; 4m NW of Faringdon on A417.

Pusey House Gardens

(*Pusey Garden Trust*)
nr Faringdon
tel. Buckland (036 787) 222

Herbaceous borders; walled garden with particularly pleasant curving south facade with inset **sculptured busts**; water garden featuring lovely Chinoiserie **bridge**; small **lake**; large collection of shrubs and roses; many fine trees; attractive **path** running through Lady Emily's garden.

Opening times: Easter to end Oct: Tues, Wed, Thurs, Sat & Sun; also Bank Hol Mon 2-6.
Wheelchairs: Suitable access.
Refreshments: Teas available.
Location: 5m E of Faringdon; ½m S off A420.

Rousham House (*Private*)

Steeple Aston
tel. Steeple Aston (0869) 47110

17th century house with landscape garden by William Kent. **Bowling green**; covered **seats**; winding **rill** flows through octagonal **pool** and on through woodland walk; immense **dovecote**.

Opening times: April to Sept: Wed, Sun & Bank Hols 2-4.30.
Gardens only: daily 10-4.30. No children under 15.
Dogs: Not allowed.
Location: 12m of Oxford off Banbury Road A423.

SHROPSHIRE

Hodnet Hall Gardens

(*Private*)
nr Market Drayton
tel. Market Drayton (063 084) 202

From the glorious daffodils of spring to the magnificent roses of summer, each season brings fresh delights to these award-winning gardens. Set in the valley, over 60 acres of magnificent forest trees, sweeping lawns and tranquil **lakes**, **cascades**, and **streams**.

Opening times: April to end Sept: weekdays 2-5; Sun & Bank Hols 12-5.30.
Wheelchairs: Suitable access.
Dogs: On lead.
Refreshments: Tea-rooms open daily 2-5.
Location: 12m NE of Shrewsbury; 5m SW of Market Drayton.

Pitchford Hall (*Private*)

nr Shrewsbury

Four-acre garden; half-timbered **tree house** in lime tree built during 17th century; Queen Victoria stayed here in 1832 (aged 13).

Opening times: By arrangement.
Refreshments: Home-made teas.
Location: 6½m S of Shrewsbury.

SOMERSET

Dunster Castle (*National Trust*)

Dunster, nr Minehead TA24 6SL
tel. Dunster (0643) 821314

Fortified home of the Luttrell family for 600 years; castle dating from the 13th century, remodelled by Anthony Salvin in the 19th century; **terraced** garden of rare shrubs; oldest surviving **dovecote** in England, with 540 nesting holes; 28-acre park.

Opening times: Castle and garden; Easter to end Sept: daily except Fri & Sat 11-5. Oct: 2-4. Garden and grounds: open as above; in June, July & Aug garden and grounds only are open on Fri & Sat when castle is closed.
Wheelchairs: Garden and grounds only. Because entire property is high on a steep hill it is not really suitable for wheelchairs.
Dogs: In car park and park only.
Refreshments: Picnics in car park and park only.
Location: In Dunster; 3m SE of Minehead on A396.

Hestercombe House and Gardens (*Somersetshire Fire Brigade*)

Cheddon Fitzpaine, Taunton

tel. Taunton (0823) 87222

Historic multi-level garden laid out at the turn of this century by Sir Edwin Lutyens, with planting by Miss Gertrude Jekyll. Restoration by County Council over last 10 years to portray garden in its original form. Attractive stonework; a long **pergola** supported by stone pillars and a magnificent **orangery** on the east side of the garden. Also features a **rill**. Appearance of present house dates from 1870s.

Opening times: All year: Mon to Fri 12-5; also last Sun in June & July.
Wheelchairs: Parts of garden suitable.
Refreshments: Sun only.
Location: 4m NE of Taunton.

Montacute House

(*National Trust*)
Montacute TA15 6XP
tel: Martock (0935) 823289

Magnificent Elizabethan house set in fine formal garden and landscaped park; sunken **pond** in lawn, with **obelisk** finial decorated **balustrades** matching those which sit atop Elizabethan walls: twin **pavilions**, believed to have been built originally as **banqueting houses** at opposite corners of walled garden; **orangery**, now housing ferns.

Opening times: House: Easter to early Nov: daily (except Tues) 12.30-5.30. Closed Good Fri. Other times by written appointment to Administrator. Garden and park open daily throughout year 12.30-5.30 or dusk if earlier.
Wheelchairs: Garden, restaurant and shop only.
Dogs: In park only, on leads.
Refreshments: Licensed restaurant; light lunches and teas daily 12-5.30.
Location: In Montacute village, 4m W of Yeovil, on S side of A3088; 3m E of A303 near Ilchester.

STAFFORDSHIRE

Alton Towers
Alton ST10 4DB
tel. Alton (0538) 702200

Former estate of the Earls of Shrewsbury set in 500 acres. Gardens developed from 1814. Splendid rock and rose gardens, tree-lined valley slopes, pathways bordered by rhododendrons. Woodland walks. Well preserved ruins of Gothic Talbot family mansion. 19th century garden **follies** including replicas of the To Ho **Pagoda** of Canton and Choragic Monument of Lysicrates. Fine **conservatory**.

Opening times: Grounds and gardens open all year. Main season with rides and attractions; Easter to early Nov.
Wheelchairs: Special facilities available.
Dogs: On leads only.
Refreshments: Wide choice of fast food to à la carte. Catering and banqueting facilities.
Location: 12m from Stoke-on-Trent.

Moseley Old Hall
(*National Trust*)
Moseley Old Hall Lane, Fordhouses, Wolverhampton WV10 7HY
tel. Wolverhampton (0902) 782808

Elizabethan house with later alterations. Charles II hid here after the battle of Worcester; small garden reconstructed in 17th century style with formal box **parterre/knot garden**; 17th century plants only grown; old roses, herbaceous plants, small **herb garden, arbour**.

Opening times: March/April: Sat & Sun 2-6; May-mid-July Wed, Sat & Sun 2-6; mid-July-early Sept: Sat to Wed 2-6; Sept: Wed, Sat & Sun: 2-6; Oct: Sat & Sun 2-6. Bank Hol Mon 2-6. Closed Good Fri.
Wheelchairs: Ground floor and garden only.
Refreshments: Licensed restaurant

in 18th century barn. Teas 2.30-5.30.
Location: 4m N of Wolverhampton; S of M54 between A449 and A460.

Shugborough (*National Trust*)
Milford, nr Stafford ST17 0XB
tel. Little Haywood (0889) 881388

Eighteenth century home of the Earls of Lichfield; enlarged *c.*1750, altered by Samuel Wyatt 1790-1806. Set in extensive parkland with neo-classical **monuments**; Victorian **terraces** and rose gardens; garden and woodland walks; attractive iron **bridge** backed by elegant Chinese **summer house**.

Opening times: House, museum, farm and grounds: Good Fri, Easter to end Sept: daily incl. Bank Hol Mon 11-5. Oct to 24 Dec: daily 11-4.
Wheelchairs: Ground floor of house, museum and farm; ramp is being installed at house.
Dogs: In grounds only, on leads.
Refreshments: Lunches, high teas and snacks in tea-room. Picnic sites by main, and farm, car parks.
Location: 6m E of Stafford on A513.

SUFFOLK

Helmingham Hall Gardens
(*Private*)
Ipswich

The house was completed in 1510 by the Tollemache family and is surrounded by a wide **moat** with drawbridges which are raised every night. Smaller but much earlier moat surrounded the walled garden. The large park contains herds of red and fallow deer and Highland cattle and the gardens, which date with the house, are renowned for their herbaceous borders and old fashioned roses. English Heritage Grade 1 Garden.

Opening times: Gardens only: end April to early Oct: Sun only 2-6.

House not open to the public.
Refreshments: Cream teas.
Location: 9m N of Ipswich.

Melford Hall (*National Trust*)
Long Melford, Sudbury CO10 9AH
tel. Sudbury (0787) 880286

Interesting garden and **gazebo** set around turreted brick Tudor mansion, with the original panelled banqueting hall.

Opening times: Easter to end April: Sat, Sun & Bank Hol Mon 2-6. Closed Good Fri. May to end Sept: Wed, Thur, Sat, Sun & Bank Hol Mon 2-6. Oct: Sat & Sun 2-6.
Wheelchairs: Ground floor rooms easily accessible; lift available to first floor. Some steps in garden.
Dogs: Not allowed.
Refreshments: In Long Melford.
Location: In Long Melford on E side of A134.

SURREY

Claremont Landscape Garden
(*National Trust*)
Portsmouth Road, Esher

The earliest surviving English landscape garden, recently restored; begun by Sir John Vanbrugh and Charles Bridgeman before 1720, extended and naturalized by William Kent; 'Capability' Brown also made improvements; **lake**, island with **pavilion**; outstanding example of **belvedere** stands atop the **mount**; turf **amphitheatre**, viewpoints and **avenues; ha-ha; kiosk; bowling green** which sweeps down from the belvedere.

Opening times: All year: daily. May to end Sept 9-7. Oct to end April 9-5 or dusk if earlier.
Wheelchairs: Level pathway around lake; and level grassland.
Dogs: On leads only.
Refreshments: Available in tea-room.
Location: On S edge of Esher; E side of A307.

Ham House (*National Trust*)
Ham, Richmond TW10 7RS
tel. 01-940 1950

Outstanding Stuart house, built around 1610; restored 17th century garden; **orangery**, now used as a tea-room.

Opening times: All year: Tues to Sun & most Bank Hol Mon 11-5. Closed Good Fri.
Wheelchairs: House and garden.
Dogs: Not allowed.
Refreshments: Teas and light lunches in garden restaurant.
Location: On S bank of Thames, W of A307, at Petersham

Painshill Park
(*Painshill Park Trust*)
Portsmouth Road, Cobham
tel. Cobham (0932) 68113

Painshill, contemporary of Stourhead and Stowe, is one of Europe's finest 18th century landscape gardens. It was created by The Hon Charles Hamilton, plantsman, painter and gifted designer, between 1738 and 1773. He created ornamental pleasure grounds dominated by a 14-acre **lake.** Garden buildings and features adorn the park, including a magnificent **grotto, temple,** ruined abbey, Chinese **bridge** castellated tower, and a **mausoleum.**

Opening times: Mid-April to mid-Oct: Sat 1-6.
Wheelchairs: Much of park accessible.
Dogs: Not allowed.
Refreshments: Light refreshments available.
Location: W of Cobham on A245.

Polesden Lacey
(*National Trust*)
nr Dorking RH5 6BD
tel. Bookham (0372) 58203 or 52048.

Originally an 1820s Regency villa, remodelled in Edwardian period. Extensive grounds; walled rose garden; lawns; views;

Venetian marble **well-head** in centre of rose garden; excellent examples of **moon windows** looking into walled garden; **statuary; astrolabe.**

Opening times: House: March & Nov: Sat & Sun and Good Fri 1.30-4.30; Easter Sun & Mon 11-4.30. April to end Oct: Wed to Sun 1.30-5.30; also open Bank Hol Mon & preceding Sun 11-5.30. Grounds open daily all year 11-sunset.
Wheelchairs: All showrooms and parts of garden; some fairly firm gravel paths.
Dogs: In grounds only, on leads.
Refreshments: Lunches, teas and snacks in licensed restaurant.
Location: 3m W of Dorking, 1½m S of Great Bookham, off A246.

Pyrford Court (*Private*)
nr Woking
tel. Woking (048 62) 65880

20 acres of wild and formal gardens; azaleas, Japanese/wisteria **pergola**; rhododendrons; pink marble **fountain**; Venetian **bridge**; Italian stone **seat** backed by curved yew **hedge.**

Opening times: Write for details.
Refreshments: Tea and cakes.
Location: 2m E of Woking.

Wisley Garden
(*Royal Horticultural Society*)
Wisley
tel. Wisley (0483 224) 234

250 acres of glorious garden. Wooded slopes with massed rhododendrons and azaleas; the alpine meadow; the panorama of the rock garden; the new alpine house and a small **lake.**

Opening times: All year. Daily, except Sun (members only): 10-7 or sunset, if earlier.
Wheelchairs: Suitable access.
Dogs: Guide dogs only.
Refreshments: Licensed restaurant and cafeteria.
Location: Just off junction 10 of M25. Guildford 7 m.

SUSSEX

Borde Hill Garden (*Private*)
Balcombe Road
tel. Haywards Heath (0444 412) 151

Large informal garden of great botanical interest and beauty; estrade; rare trees and shrubs; extensive **vistas**; woodland walks; rhododendrons, azaleas, camellias and magnolias.

Opening times: Good Friday to end October. Daily: 10-6.
Wheelchairs: Suitable access.
Dogs: On lead only.
Refreshments: Licensed restaurant for lunch, snacks and tea.
Location: 1½m N of Haywards Heath.

Great Dixter (*Private*)
Northiam
tel. Northiam (07974) 3160

Fifteenth century half-timbered manor house set in a striking **sunken garden** designed by Nathaniel Lloyd, the owner of the house, who employed Lutyens as his architect; central lily **pond**; interesting curving brick **path** running through long grass.

Opening times: Easter to mid-Oct: daily except Mon (but open all Bank Hol Mons); also weekends until end Oct 2-5; Sun in July & Aug.
Dogs: Not allowed.
Refreshments: Available locally.
Location: ½m N of Northiam; 8m NW of Rye; 12m N of Hastings.

Petworth Park (*National Trust*)
Petworth GU28 0AE
tel. Petworth (0798) 42207

Beautiful 700-acre deer park, with **lake**, landscaped by 'Capability' Brown and immortalized in Turner's paintings. Unfortunately many of the fine trees were lost in the storm of October 1987.

Opening times: All year: daily 9-dusk.
Wheelchairs: Car park and part of

park accessible with care; some uneven paths.
Dogs: Must be kept under control.
Refreshments: Available at Petworth House.
Location: In centre of Petworth.

Royal Pavilion
Brighton
tel. Brighton (0273) 603005

Spectacular seaside palace of the Prince Regent, transformed by John Nash (1815-1822) into one of the most dazzlingly exotic buildings in the British Isles. An extraordinary example of a **pavilion.**
Opening times: Daily 10-5; June to Sept 10-6.
Wheelchairs: Ground floor accessible.
Refreshments: Tea-room.
Location: In centre of Brighton (Old Steine).

Sheffield Park Garden
Uckfield TN22 3QX
tel. Danehill (0825) 790655

100-acre garden and four **lakes** laid out in 18th century by 'Capability' Brown and Repton, interconnected by **cascades** and weirs; mature trees, rare shrubs and water lilies; beautiful at all times of year.

Opening times: Easter to early Nov: Tues to Sat 11-6 or sunset if earlier, Sun & Bank Hol Mon 2-6 or sunset is earlier; closed Tues following Bank Hol Mon.
Wheelchairs: Most parts of garden accessible.
Dogs: Not allowed.
Location: Midway between East Grinstead and Lewes; 5m NW of Uckfield, on E side of A275.

Wakehurst Place Garden
(*National Trust*)
Ardingly, Haywards Heath
RH17 6TN
tel. Ardingly (0444) 892701

An important collection of exotic trees, shrubs and other plants; picturesque watercourse linking

several **lakes** and **ponds**; heath garden and rock walk.
Wakehurst Place is leased to the Ministry of Agriculture and is administered and maintained by the Royal Botanic Gardens, Kew.

Opening times: All year: daily. Nov to end Jan: 10-4; Feb & Oct 10-5; March: 10-6; April to end Sept: 10-7.
Wheelchairs: Accessible, but uneven ground.
Dogs: Not allowed.
Refreshments: Easter to mid-Oct: self-service tea-room; other times light refreshments from bookshop.
Location: 1½m NW of Ardingly on B2028.

Nymans Garden
(*National Trust*)
Handcross, nr Haywards Heath
RH17 6EB
tel. Handcross (0444) 400321 or 400002

One of the great gardens of the Sussex Weald; rare and beautiful plants, shrubs and trees from all over the world; walled garden; hidden **sunken garden**; laurel walk, romantic ruins; wisteria **pergola**; **dovecote**.
Opening times: Good Fri, Easter to early Nov: daily except Mon & Fri (but open Bank Hol Mon) 11-7 or dusk if earlier.
Wheelchairs: Garden accessible; special wheelchair route indicated.
Dogs: In car park only.
Refreshments: Available in tea-house near car park.
Location: On B2114 at Handcross; 4½m S of Crawley.

WARWICKSHIRE

Charlecote Park
(*National Trust*)
Wellesbourne, Warwick
CV35 9ER
tel. Stratford-upon-Avon (0789) 840277 (Tues, Wed & Fri 9.15-1.30).

Home of Lucy family since 1247;

present house built in 1550s. Park landscaped by 'Capability' Brown, supports herd of red and fallow deer; brick-built **ha-ha**, with **path** running along the top; scented line **avenue; gatehouse** from Tudor period features central two-storey structure topped by a pierced **balustrade** and supported by twin octagonal three-storey towers; **orangery.**

Opening times: Easter to end Oct: daily except Mon & Thur but open Bank Hol Mon & closed Good Fri 11-6.
Wheelchairs: Access to all open rooms, except the Gatehouse Museum.
Dogs: Not allowed.
Refreshments: Morning coffee, light lunches, afternoon teas in the orangery. Picnicking in deer park only.
Location: 1m W of Wellesbourne, 5m E of Stratford-upon-Avon, 6m S of Warwick on N side of B4086.

WARWICKSHIRE

Hagley Hall (*Private*)
nr Stourbridge
tel. Hagley (0562) 882408

The last of the great Palladian Houses, designed by Sanderson Millar and completed in 1760. Nearby is a **sham castle** built in 1740 from stones from Halesowen Abbey.

Opening times: Jan & Feb: daily except Sat; also Bank Hols 2-5. Telephone for further details.
Refreshments: Tea in the house.
Location: 12m from Birmingham.

New Place/Nash's House
(*Shakespeare Birthplace Trust*)
Stratford-upon-Avon
tel. Stratford-upon-Avon (0789) 204016

Foundations of Shakespeare's last home, preserved in an Elizabethan garden setting that includes a colourful cruciform group of four **knots**; adjoins Nash's House which is furnished in period style.

Opening times: April to Oct:
Weekdays 9-6 (9-5 Oct); Sun
10-6 (10-5 Oct); Nov to March:
Weekdays only 9-4.30.
Wheelchairs: Suitable access.
Location: Chapel Lane.

Packwood House
(*National Trust*)
Lapworth, Solihull B94 6AT
tel. Lapworth (056 43) 2024

Gardens include a Carolean
formal garden and a notable yew
garden topiary of *c.*1650,
representing the Sermon on the
Mount. Other interesting
features include a wrought-iron
entrance gate with series of **bee-
boles** to either side; internally
heated walls with **furnace
houses** in opposite corners of
walled garden; no less than four
gazeboes set in **terraced** walls;
three **sundials**, each with a
separate motto; and fine **topiary**
decorating John Fetherson's yew
garden. Timber-framed Tudor
house contains tapestry and fine
furniture.

Opening times: Easter to end Sept:
Wed to Sun & Bank Hol Mon
2-6. Closed Good Fri. Oct: Wed
to Sun 12.30-4.
Wheelchairs: Access to part of
garden and ground floor of house.
Dogs: Not allowed.
Refreshments: Available at
Baddesley Clinton.
Location: 2m E of Hockley Heath;
11m SE of central Birmingham.

WILTSHIRE

Bowood House and Gardens
(*Private*)
Calne
tel. Calne (0249) 812102

100-acre garden containing many
exotic trees; 40-acre **lake** created
by 'Capability' Brown; informal
cascade; cave and Doric **temple**;
arboretum; pinetum; rose and
Italian gardens; 60 acres of
rhododendrons. Interesting
rooms in the house include
Robert Adam's library, Dr
Joseph Priestley's laboratory and

a series of Exhibition Rooms.
Important collection of drawings
and water colours by English
Masters.

Opening times: House, gardens
and grounds: end March to mid-
Oct, daily, incl. Bank Hols 11-6.
Rhododendron walks mid-May
to mid-June.
Dogs: Not allowed.
Refreshments: Licensed restaurant
and Garden Tearoom.
Location: 2½m W of Calne; 5m
SE of Chippenham.

Heale Gardens   (*Private*)
Woodford, Salisbury
tel. Middle Woodford (072 273)
504

Early Carolean manor house
where King Charles II hid
during his escape. The garden
provides an interesting and
varied collection of plants,
shrubs, musk and other roses,
growing in the formal setting of
clipped **hedges** and mellow
stonework. Particularly attractive
in spring and autumn is the
water garden, planted with
magnolia and acers, surrounding
an authentic Japanese **tea house**
and Nikko **bridge.**

Opening times: Garden: Mon to
Sat and now every Sunday
and Bank Hols from Easter to
autumn 10-5. Plant centre and
shop open throughout the year.
Refreshments: Lunches and teas in
the house.
Location: 4m N of Salisbury.

Iford Manor   (*Private*)
Bradford-on-Avon
tel. Bradford-on-Avon (02216)
3146 or 2840

Tudor house with an 18th
century facade surrounded by a
peaceful **terraced** garden of
unique character. Designed in
the Italian style, it was the home
of Harold Peto, the Edwardian
landscape architect. There are
pools, statues, a colonnade,
antique carvings, and fine
examples of both Roman and

Greek **sarcophagi**, as well as
plants of botanical interest.

Opening times: Gardens only: Wed
and Sun in May, June, July &
Aug 2-5; also summer Bank Hols.
Dogs: On lead.
Refreshments: Sun only.
Location: 7m SE of Bath on A36.

Lacock Abbey   (*National Trust*)
nr Chippenham SN15 2LG
tel. Lacock (024973) 227

Abbey founded in 1232 and
converted into a country house
after 1539. Grounds contain one
of the finest examples of a stone
ha-ha.

Opening times: House and
grounds: Easter to early Nov:
daily (except Tues) 2-6. Grounds
only: open March to early Nov:
daily 2-6.
Wheelchairs: Grounds and
cloisters only; house less
accessible.
Dogs: Not allowed.
Refreshments: In Lacock.
Location: In the village of Lacock;
3m N of Melksham; 3m S of
Chippenham.

Stourhead   (*National Trust*)
Stourton, Warminster
BA12 6QH
tel. Bourton (0747) 840348

Landscape garden laid out 1741-
80, with **lakes** and **temples**, rare
trees and plants; King Alfred's
Tower, a red-brick **folly** built in
1772 by Flitcroft at the edge of
the estate is 160 ft high, giving
wonderful views over
Somerset, Dorset and Wiltshire.
Fine example of **trompe l'oeil** in
tree planting between the **grotto**
and **Pantheon. Temple** of
Apollo set high on hill above the
lake to create a focal point.

Opening times: Garden all year:
daily 8-7 or dusk if earlier.
House: Easter to end April and
Oct: Sat to Wed 2-6 or dusk if
earlier. May to end Sept: daily
except Fri 2-6 or dusk if earlier.
Other times by written
appointment. King Alfred's

Tower: March to early Nov: Wed, Thur, Sat, Sun & Bank Hol Mon 2-5.30.
Wheelchairs: Garden accessible, but 13 steps up to house. Path round lake is recommended.
Dogs: In garden, Nov to end Feb only; in woods throughout year.
Refreshments: Spread Eagle Inn (NT) at garden entrance. Picnicking in car park and garden.
Location: At Stourton; 3m NW of Mere off A303.

Wilton House   (*Private*)
Salisbury

Notable fine cedar trees and Palladian **bridge** built by Henry Herbert before 1735, with small classical **temples** at either end. Italianate **loggia** by William Chambers overlooks formal 19th century garden. House contains superb 17th century state rooms by Inigo Jones (*c.*1650) and later James Wyatt (1810). World famous collection of paintings and other treasures.

Opening times: House and grounds: Easter to mid-Oct: Tues to Sat & Bank Hol Mon 11-6; Sun 1-6.
Refreshments: Licensed self-service restaurant.
Location: In town of Wilton 3m W of Salisbury.

WORCESTERSHIRE

Spetchley Park   (*Private*)
Worcester

This garden, extending nearly 30 acres, is a plantsman's delight, and it contains many fine trees and rare shrubs and plants. Particularly beautiful in April, May and June. Garden features include a very rare **root-house.**

Opening times: Gardens and garden centre: Easter to end Sept; daily (except Sat) 11-5; Sun 2-5. Bank Hol Mon 11-5.
Dogs: Not allowed.
Refreshments: Tea in the garden (Sun & Bank Hol).
Location: 3m E of Worcester.

YORKSHIRE

Bramham Park   (*Private*)
Wetherby LS23 6ND
tel. Boston Spa (0937) 844265

Magnificent grounds with ornamental **ponds, cascades,** beech-lined **allées** and **loggias** of various shapes; unique in the British Isles for its grand **vista** design stretching out into woodlands of cedar, copper beech, lime and Spanish chestnut. Queen Anne mansion built during first half of 18th century.

Opening times: Gardens only Easter & Bank Hols. House and Gardens: Early June to end Aug: Sun, Tues, Wed & Thur; also Bank Hol Mon 1.15-5.30.
Wheelchairs: Suitable access.
Location: 5m S of Wetherby.

Castle Howard   (*Private*)
York
tel. Coneysthorpe (065 384) 333

Designed by Vanbrugh 1699-1726 for the third Earl of Carlisle, assisted by Hawksmoor, who designed the **mausoleum.** Beautiful park and grounds; fanciful Carrmire **Gate** by Hawksmoor; Pyramid **Gate** by Vanbrugh in centre of castellated wall; Atlas **Fountain** set in centre of South **Parterre; obelisks**; Palladian-style **Temple** of the Four Winds, which was Vanbrugh's last work.

Opening times: End March to end Oct: daily. House and costume galleries: 11-4.30. Gardens 10-4.30.
Wheelchairs: Suitable access.
Refreshments: Cafeteria and licensed restaurant.
Location: 15m NE of York; 6m W of Malton.

Duncombe Park   (*Private*)
Helmsley

Two 18th century **temples**. Landscaped gardens with ready-made **folly** in the form of the ruin of Rievaulx Abbey. **Ha-ha** by Vanbrugh.

Opening times: Gardens only: May to Aug, Wed 10-4. Apply to Tourist Information Centre, Helmsley Market Place.
Location: 1m W of Helmsley.

Fountains Abbey and Studley Royal   (*National Trust*)
Fountains, Ripon HG4 3DZ
tel. Sawley (076 586) 333

Fountains Abbey on the banks of the River Skell, founded by Cistercian monks in 1132 and the largest monastic ruin in Britain; the Abbey ruins, now viewed as a **folly**, provide the dramatic focal point of the 18th century landscape garden at Studley Royal; **water-garden, temples, vistas, lake,** deer park, small museum; St Mary's Church, built by William Burges 1871-8.

Opening times: Deer park all year during daylight hours. Abbey and garden all year daily (except Fri in Nov, Dec & Jan). Jan to end March, and Nov to end Dec: 10-5 or dusk if earlier; April to end June & Sept: 10-7; July & Aug: 10-8. Oct: 10-6 or dusk if earlier. Fountains Hall all year: daily, April to end Sept: 11-6; Oct to end March: 11-4.
Wheelchairs: Abbey precincts and Studley Royal garden.
Dogs: On leads only.
Refreshments: Light lunches and tea available. Picnic areas with tables and chairs at lakeside and Abbey tea-room.
Location: 4m W of Ripon.

Rievaulx Abbey   (*Private*)
Helmsley
tel. Bilsdale (043 96) 228

The fluctuating fortunes of the abbey may be read from the **ruins**. Within two decades of its foundation in 1131, Rievaulx – the first Cistercian monastery in the north – was vast, with 140 monks and 500 lay brothers. A costly building programme followed, and by the 13th century the monastery was heavily in debt. By the Dissolution in the

16th century, there were only 22 monks. The church is a beautiful example of early English Gothic. Nearby Rievaulx Terrace (National Trust) has long grass terrace and two 18th century **temples.**

Opening times: Easter to end Sept: daily 10-6. Oct to Easter: daily 10-4. Closed Mon.
Wheelchairs: Suitable on terrace only.
Location: 3m NW of Helmsley.

Ripley Castle   (*Private*)
Ripley
tel. Harrogate (0423) 770152

Home of the Ingilby family since the early 14th century, this beautiful castle contains many historic artefacts; Civil War armour, priest's hiding place. Impressive **gates**, extensive gardens.

Opening times: Castle: April, May & Oct; Sat & Sun: 11.30-4.30. Jun to Oct; daily, except Mon & Fri: 11.30-4.30. Closed Good Friday and all Bank Hols. Garden: Daily: early April to end Oct.
Refreshments: Licensed restaurant in village. Tea-room in castle courtyard.
Location: In Ripley, 3½m N of Harrogate.

WALES

Bodnant Garden
(*National Trust*)
Tal-y-Cafn, Colwyn Bay, Clwyd LL28 5RE
tel. Tyn-y-Groes (0492) 650460

Among the finest gardens in the country, extending for 80 acres and giving spectacular views of the Snowdonia range; Pin Mill **summer house**, built in 1740, and stream feature in **water garden**; modern **terraced** garden, begun in 1875, with **balustrading**; laburnum walk; **seat**, with backing of perfectly clipped yew **hedges**, and highlighted to either side with **statuary**.

Opening times: Mid-March to end Oct: daily 10-5.
Wheelchairs: Garden is steep in places and has many steps.
Dogs: Not allowed.
Refreshments: Tea and light refreshments from car park kiosk. Picnicking in car park area.
Location: 8m S of Llandudno and Colwyn Bay on A470.

Portmeirion   (*Private*)
Gwynedd, North Wales

The ultimate **conceit**. Built in the 1920s, Portmeirion is a dream-like creation of the flamboyant Sir Clough Williams-Ellis, representing his idea of an Italian village positioned on a Welsh estuary. Full of things to see, it includes a **gatehouse**, surmounted by elegant stone **vases**, a fine Italian **well-head, moon window** and Victorian cast-iron **seats.**

Opening times: Easter to end Oct: daily: 9.30-5.30.
Wheelchairs: Access limited because of steps. Some parts of village suitable.
Dogs: Not allowed.
Refreshments: Self-service restaurant.
Location: 2m SW of Penrhyndeudraeth.

Powis Castle   (*National Trust*)
Welshpool, Powys SY21 8RF
tel. Welshpool (0938) 4336

Medieval castle containing the finest country collection in Wales; built *c*.1200 by Welsh princes. The Powis gardens are of the highest horticultural and historical importance: Includes outstanding example of **terracing**(**statuary** and **urns**) leading from house to valley below, with **balustrades** playing host to **lead statues**, and the lowest level being an unusual **orangery**. Also worth seeing is the beautiful Victorian basket design **flowerpot.**

Opening times: Easter to end June: Wed to Sun & Bank Hol Mon

12-5. July & Aug: daily except Mon, but open Bank Hol Mon 11-6. Sept to early Nov: Wed to Sun 12-5. 6 Nov to 8 April 1990* Garden, Clive Museum and tea-room Sun only 2-4.30.
Wheelchairs: Castle not possible for wheelchair users; access to tea-room, shop and parts of garden only.
Dogs: Not allowed.
Refreshments: Light lunches and teas in courtyard tea-rooms.
Location: 1m S of Welshpool on A483.

IRELAND

Castletown House   (*Private*)
Celbridge, Co. Kildare

Built in 1722, the finest Georgian country house in Ireland. Grounds feature 42.6m (140ft) high **obelisk** built 1739-40.

Opening times: Daily: Mon to Fri 10-5; Suns and Bank Hols 2-6.
Refreshments: At the house at weekends.
Location: W of Castlerea town.

NORTHERN IRELAND

Mount Stewart House and Garden   (*National Trust*)
Newtownards, Co. Down BT22 2AD
tel. Greyabbey (024 774) 387

Fascinating 18th century house with 19th century additions, where Lord Castlereagh grew up. Gardens largely created by Edith, seventh Marchioness of Londonderry. Charming modern **conceit** in the form of garden shaped as a shamrock leaf, enclosed by high yew **hedge**; on top, outstanding **topiary** work, including fox hunt in full cry. Unrivalled collection of plants, colourful **parterres** and magnificent vistas; the **Temple** of the Winds, Janes 'Athenian' Stuart's banqueting hall of 1785, overlooks Strangford Lough.

Opening times: House and Temple: Easter: daily 2-6. April: Sat & Sun 12-6. May: Wed to Sun 12-6. June to end Aug: daily except

Tues 12-6. Sept: Sat & Sun 12-6.
Garden: Easter: 12-6. April: Sat
& Sun 12-6. May: Wed to Sun
12-6. June to end Aug: daily
except Tues 12-6. Sept & Oct:
daily except Tues 12-6.
Wheelchairs: Suitable access.
Dogs: In garden only, on leads.
Refreshments: Tea-room open at
house.
Location: On E shore of
Strangford Lough; 5m SE of
Newtownards; 15m E of Belfast.

SCOTLAND

Drummond Castle Gardens
(*Private*)
Muthill
tel. Muthill (076481) 257

Gardens only are open. Features
particularly impressive **terraced**
garden giving views of the great
St Andrew's Cross **parterre;
balustrading**. Also contains
extraordinary **sundial** *c.*1630.

Opening times: May to Aug: daily
2-6; Sept: Wed & Sun 2-6.
Location: 3m S of Crieff.

Edzell Castle and Gardens
(*Historic Scotland*)
Edzell

16th century castle set in unique
renaissance garden with deep
rose-coloured sandstone walls
surrounding beautifully restored
'pleasance'; series of relatively
intricate box-edged **knots.**

Opening times: April to Sept:
Weekdays 9.30-7, Sun 2-7; Oct
to March: Weekdays (except
Tues & Thur morning) 9.30-4;
Sun 2-4.
Location: 1m W of Edzell; 6m N
of Brechin.

Mellerstain   (*Private*)
Gordon
tel. Gordon (057381) 225

Scotland's famous mansion house
is a unique example of the work
of the Adam family. The two
wings were built by William
Adam in 1725 and the main block
by Robert Adam about 40 years
later. The house has beautifully
decorated and furnished

interiors. **Terraced** gardens and
lake.

Opening times: Easter weekend.
Then from early May to end
Sept. Daily: except Sats: 12.30-5.
Refreshments: Tea rooms.
Location: 9m NE of Melrose; 7m
NW of Kelso; 37m SE of
Edinburgh.

Pitmedden
(*National Trust for Scotland*)
Oldmeldrum, Grampian
tel. Udny (065 13) 2445

Reconstructed 17th century
garden with floral designs,
fountains and **sundials**;
colourful **parterre** on a grand
scale. Display on the evolution of
the formal garden.

Opening times: Garden and
Grounds open all year: daily
9.30-dusk.
Wheelchairs: Access to garden.
Dogs: Not allowed.
Location: 14m N of Aberdeen.

BIBLIOGRAPHY

The following three guides, published annually, give details, including dates and times of opening, and directions, of the great majority of gardens open to the public.

Gardens of England & Wales, The National Gardens Scheme Charitable Trust.

Historic Houses, Castles and Gardens Open to the Public, British Leisure Publications.

The National Trust Handbook for Members and Visitors, The National Trust.

The following books are recommended for further reading:—

The Country House Garden, Gervase Jackson-Stops & James Pipkin, Pavilion/Michael Joseph, 1987.

English Garden Design, History and Styles since 1650, Tom Turner, The Antique Collectors' Club, 1986/1987.

The English Garden, Laurence Fleming & Alan Gore, Michael Joseph, 1979.

The English Garden in our Time from Gertrude Jekyll to Geoffrey Jellicoe, Jane Brown, The Antique Collectors' Club, 1986.

Follies and Grottoes, Barbara Jones, Constable, 1974.

Formal Gardens in England and Scotland, H. Inigo Triggs, Reprint by The Antique Collectors' Club, 1988.

Garden Ornament, Gertrude Jekyll, Reprint by the Antique Collectors' Club, 1982.

Gardens in Edwardian England, Country Life, Reprint by the Antique Collectors' Club, 1985.

Gardens of the National Trust, Graham Stuart Thomas, The National Trust/Weidenfeld and Nicolson, 1979.

Gardens of Paradise (The History and Design of the Great Islamic Gardens), John Brooks, Weidenfeld & Nicolson, 1987.

Gardens to Visit in Britain, Arthur Hellyer, Paul Hamlyn, 1970.

Great Gardens of Britain, Peter Coats, Treasure Press, 1977.

The Historic Gardens of Oxford and Cambridge, Mavis Batey, Antler Books, 1989.

A History of British Gardening, Miles Hadfield, Hutchinson, 1960. (Penguin Books 1985)

Houses and Gardens by E. L. Lutyens, Laurence Weaver, Country Life, Reprint by The Antique Collectors' Club, 1985.

Italian Gardens, Georgina Masson, Thames & Hudson, Reprint by The Antique Collectors' Club, 1987.

The National Trust Guide (Revised Edition), Robin Felden & Rosemary Joekes, The National Trust/Jonathan Cape, 1979.

Private Gardens of England, Penelope Hobhouse, Weidenfeld & Nicolson, 1986.

Private Gardens of Scotland, James Truscott, Weidenfeld & Nicolson, 1988.

The Quest for Paradise, Ronald King, Whittet/Windward, 1979.

The Shell Gardens Book, Edited by Peter Hunt, Phoenix House, 1964. (New Edition 1989)

Sir John Vanbrugh (A Biography), Kerry Downs, Sidgwick & Jackson, 1987

Topiary, A. M. Clevelly, Collins, 1988.

A Tour of Italian Gardens, Judith Chatfield, Ward Lock, 1988.

Traditional English Gardens, Arabella Lennox-Boyd, Clay Perry & Graham Stuart Thomas, The National Trust/Weidenfeld Paperbacks, 1987.

Versailles, Gérald Van der Kemp, Sotheby Parke Bernet, 1978.

Victorian Gardens, Brent Elliott, Batsford, 1986.

Water Gardens, Roddy Llewellyn, Ward Lock, 1987.

INDEX

ACKNOWLEDGEMENTS

The publishers gratefully acknowledge the following agencies and photographers for granting permission to reproduce the following colour and black and white photographs: John Bethell Photography pp 12/13, 31T, 32/33, 41, 44/45, 56, 70L, 72, 73, 76L, 90/91, 104B, 116/7, 121, 136/7, 156/7, 159; Country Life pp 55, 57L, 64, 93, 103, 111, 113, 119, 127, 145; Department of the Environment p 35; Derbyshire Countryside Limited pp 71, 143; The Design Centre p 84; Mary Evans Picture Library pp 11, 16, 28, 31BR, 37R, 89T, 107B; The Garden Picture Library pp 74R (ph David Secombe), 75 (ph Marianne Majerus), 107T (ph Brian Carter), 128L (ph David Secombe), 148 (ph Brian Carter), 150/151 (ph Nigel Temple), 158/159 (ph Perdereau Thomas); Jerry Harpur pp 15, 26/27, 29, 36L, 36/37, 86/87, 92T, 106, 123, 128R, 144; Nigel Hughes p 50; Jarrold Colour Publications p 160 (ph Neil Jinkerson); Andrew Lawson pp 31BL, 34, 40, 47R, 49, 89B, 95, 104T; David Masters pp 25, 54, 132; Tania Midgley pp 22/23, 57R, 97, 140/141; National Trust pp 1 (ph Nigel Forster), 30 (ph R. Westlake), 38/39 (ph Nigel Forster), 43B (ph Mike Williams), 52/53 (ph Nick Meers Agency), 60 (ph John Bethell), 68/69 (ph Vera Collingwood Agency), 74L (ph Eric Crichton), 76/77 (ph Rob Hatheson), 78/79, 82T (ph Nick Meers Agency), 82B (ph Richard Hawken), 92B (ph Nigel Forster), 98/99 (ph Nick Meers Agency), 101 (ph Vera Collingwood Agency), 112 (ph R. Symonds), 131 (ph Tymn Lintell), 154/155 (ph Eric Crichton); Hugh Palmer pp 124/125, 133, 146 (courtesy Roy Alderson); Photos Horticultural Picture Library pp 2/3, 7, 9, 17, 62/63, 96, 100, 102, 108/109, 122, 129, 135, 152/153; The Royal Collection pp 80/81; Sotheby's p 83; Ward Lock 18/19, 58/59 (ph Bob Challinor), 114.

The photograph on page 35 is Crown Copyright and is reproduced with the permission of the Controller of Her Majesty's Stationery Office.

The photograph on pages 80/81 is reproduced by Gracious Permission of Her Majesty The Queen.

The publishers would also like to thank the owners of the following historic houses for kind permission to reproduce their photographs: Blickling Hall p 21; by kind permission of Lord Aberconway and The National Trust Bodnant Garden pp 138, 144; Castle Howard p 148; Chatsworth pp 66/67; Hever Castle p 43T; Tatton Park p 67; Wrest Park p 94. Also thanks to Haddonstone for the photograph on pp 46/47.

The publishers would like to express special thanks to The National Trust, The National Gardens Scheme and Historic Houses, Castles and Gardens for information on properties in the glossary.

The publishers are grateful to the following for kind permission to reproduce extracts from: *Follies and Grottoes*, Barbara Jones, Constable Publishers (1974); and *The Shell Garden Handbook*, edited by Peter Hunt, J. M. Dent & Son (1964).